MANAGEMENT IN A RAPIDLY CHANGING ECONOMY

MANAGEMENT IN A RAPIDLY CHANGING ECONOMY

Edited by

DAN H. FENN, JR.
Assistant Editor of the Harvard Business Review *and Member of the Faculty of the Harvard Graduate School of Business Administration*

McGRAW-HILL BOOK COMPANY, INC.
New York Toronto London 1958

MANAGEMENT IN A RAPIDLY CHANGING ECONOMY

PREFACE

IN THE MONTHS that have passed since the 27th Annual National
Business Conference of the Harvard Business School Association,
which generated the ideas in this book, the people of the United
States have been shocked repeatedly by the evidence of great changes
in the world. The launching of the Russian sputniks and subsequent
revelations of Soviet science and technology were piled on top of
a steadily growing mountain of evidence that our American
monopoly of superiority had long since been broken—if, in fact,
it ever existed at all.

Our main attention has been focused on the military implications
of the Communists' achievements. We have learned a great deal
about missiles, anti-missile missiles, guidance, and rocketry, and the
headlines have reminded us repeatedly about our relative position in
the race for armed might. Conflicting reports about just where we
do stand have left us confused, but one hard fact stands out clearly
through the smog of claims, alarms, and educated or semieducated
guesses: we have some catching up to do.

But the beep-beeps of the sputniks send us another warning which is even more important than the message they relay about our military muscle. At a time when the eyes of most of the world's people are watching us, measuring us against our competition, dramatic and important achievements like the conquest of space carry overtones about the worth of our free system vis-à-vis that of the Russians. "Look what Communism has accomplished," say the Soviets. "In forty short years we have outstripped the vaunted Democracies at their own game. They have always claimed to be the masters of science and productive know-how; and we have beaten them."

Those who know the whole story realize that this boast rests on only a corner of the truth. But, unfortunately, most of the world does not see the entire picture. They wonder if the future does not lie in the hands of the Communists, even while they agree that the past is in ours.

The responsibility for grasping—and holding—the future in the hands of freedom falls primarily on the United States. We are being challenged not just to tell about our accomplishments, but to keep making them—and at a rapidly accelerating rate. We cannot count on continued leadership; we must truly lead in order to insure it.

Though the business leaders and astute observers of our society who wrote this book had no knowledge of the events which were so nearly upon them as they spoke, the urgency they express in these pages seems especially appropriate now. For they outline some of the characteristics of the years ahead, point to some of the pitfalls, and laid out some of the tools. They assume no easy solutions to the problems, but they do assume that they must—and can —be solved.

Faced with the two-pronged Soviet challenge—the military and the ideological—it becomes even more important now that American management redouble its efforts to strengthen the workings of our system. Development and production of military hardware and continued progress toward a more satisfying life for the people of this nation and of the rest of the world are our two main objectives. Reaching them has become a matter of survival.

Those who planned and arranged the Conference on which this book is based, working under the effective guidance of Chairman (Lt. Gen.) Charles B. Stone, III, those who participated in it as speakers and as audience, and those who edited the material which they produced hope that the ideas and information contained in these pages will be of use in meeting the challenge.

Many hands and brains are required to complete an undertaking of this kind. I want to express my thanks to the various members of the staff of the *Harvard Business Review* who helped in the preparation of this book, and especially to Mrs. Janet Bertoni, Miss Joan Foster, and Mrs. Abigail Sugarman whose care and skill have contributed so much to the final product.

Dan H. Fenn, Jr.

CONTENTS

INTRODUCTION OF THE THEME

Stanley F. Teele

DURING THE LAST HALF-CENTURY, the period of growth and development of business education and the "professional" approach to management, change after change has crowded the lives of business managers: Changes in technology have created whole new industries and drastically affected whole established companies. Changes in transportation and communication have diminished time and space. Changes in social and political circumstances have placed each business enterprise in a new environment. Changes in management techniques have confronted the businessman with new complexities and new opportunities.

But perhaps the most important change of all has been in the manager himself. Surely one of the most significant developments of this past half-century, though little noted and publicized, has been the separation of ownership from management in a very high proportion of our productive resources. By this process the professional manager has come to the fore, and a system of selection has been established which provides for more assurance than does heredity that the direction of affairs will be in the hands of the competent.

A new educational philosophy was worked out to meet this

Note: Mr. Teele is dean of the Harvard Business School.

development—one in which the Harvard Business School has played a leading role. We are proud that it has proved remarkably well suited to the preparation of business managers for a world of change.

The foundation of this educational philosophy and pattern is the conviction that certain fundamental habits of mind and attitudes of spirit are all important in coping with change.

Far more important for the prospective manager than the current facts of business are the capacity to work through an analysis to a wise conclusion and the courage to translate that logical conclusion into an active decision; a mind accustomed and ready to face new problems, to gather pertinent facts, to order and weigh these facts, and to draw conclusions; and a heart capable of translating these conclusions into decisions. As long as there is no prospect of any deceleration in the rate of change—and if anything, acceleration seems more likely—the broadest possible understanding, the sharpest possible capacity to make wise decisions, and the greatest possible acceptance of basic responsibilities to the community and society, as well as to the particular enterprise, will continue to characterize this approach.

This continuing concern with fundamentals does not mean that we should fail to take a lively interest in all newly developing areas of management. Rather, it forces us to take such an interest. Who can ignore, for instance, the concurrent rise of new concepts in mathematical statistics and of devices for the very rapid processing of all kinds of data, or research in several of the social sciences which is turning up ideas and concepts which may prove important to business management over the years to come? We must interest ourselves vigorously in these findings.

But those of us responsible for the education of business executives must not let these intriguing new developments lure us too far from our central task: helping potential business managers develop the art of management.

While we seek to make progress in the science of management, we must never forget that management remains primarily an art and that the development of managers for a changing economy, and for a changing world, rests on a balanced emphasis on new concepts and methods, and on the everlasting fundamentals.

Part One

FORCES THAT ARE SHAPING THE FUTURE

SOCIAL CHANGES—WHAT THEY MEAN TO MANAGEMENT

Peter F. Drucker

IT IS NO LONGER NEWS that social developments and changes directly and profoundly affect business and management—as directly and as profoundly as do changes in the economy. Nor is it news that businessmen and managers play a major role in shaping social development and have, accordingly, high social responsibility. Indeed, if there is one development in American business during the last 10 years that stands out above all others, it is the eagerness with which business has embraced social responsibilities—from responsibility for the survival of higher education to responsibility for the support of charities and for the furtherance of the Boy Scouts. As a matter of fact, this tendency has advanced to the point where I often

Note: Mr. Drucker is a consultant on business policy and management organization. He is also Professor of Management at the Graduate School of Business at New York University and author of many well-known books and articles on American society and business management.

3

find myself asking the good old question, "And who is left to tend the store?"

I do not therefore think it necessary to stress the importance of social development to us in management or to re-emphasize our social responsibility, for I think today we can take both for granted. Instead I shall try to look ahead and to concentrate on the major social developments that can already be recognized as being directly important to American management over the next decade. And I shall try to outline, at least roughly, what they mean to a business-man and manager, what new decisions they demand of him, what new opportunities they open up for him.

There are three major new social developments, external to busi-ness itself, which have an impact on a manager's professional think-ing and actions, on his planning, his policies, and his practices:

1. The clear emergence of "big government" as a permanent neces-sity independent of party politics or political preferences.
2. The emergence of public spending as the major investment area in the United States and in other countries.
3. The emergence of an educated society.

Let me say a few words about each.

"BIG GOVERNMENT"

If there is one fact that has become quite apparent these last few months in particular, one fact that only the blindest can now refuse to see, it is that "big government" and a permanently high level of public spending are here to stay, no matter what party gains political power or even which wing of a party is in control.

Indeed what has become clear is that this necessity—for it is un-fortunately nothing less—is completely independent even of interna-tional relations. In other words even if, by some miracle, interna-tional tensions should disappear, even if the threat of international communism were to evaporate overnight, the level of government spending—including, above all, the level of military spending—would not be appreciably affected.

Military Spending

There are two permanent reasons for a very high level of government expenditure. The first of these is the state of military technology. Until we assume that we can disarm completely, to the point where all we need are forces for police functions—that is, a kind of internal National Guard—military spending will not only not go down; it will in all likelihood show a permanent tendency to increase.

In fact, it is becoming obvious that the present level of military expenditures, which in every absolute sense is so exceedingly high— to the point of being almost unbearably high—is barely adequate. If we measure our defense expenditures not by absolute dollars but by comparing the peacetime military figure at any given period with the costs of war at that same period, we discover that we are spending less today for defense than ever before in our history, with the single exception of the decades before the Civil War.

This explains why defense costs are such a crucial problem in the world today and why economic progress and political freedom everywhere are threatened by the high level of such expenditures—which at the same time are grossly inadequate. We saw in 1956 that Great Britain and France, who spend as much of their national income for defense as we do, found themselves all but incapable of rapidly mobilizing very small forces against an almost defenseless enemy. Although there may have been considerable bungling in this instance, the fact that English and French military budgets—even though so large as almost to smother the economies of these two rich countries—are grossly inadequate and deficient in terms of modern military technology must also have been largely responsible.

Community Needs

The second major reason for the permanent emergence of "big government" is the transformation of this country—and all other countries as well—into "metropolitan" nations. Population growth and the distribution of that population has created the need for major government activities and major government expenditures.

Whether the federal budget during these last 10 years has grown faster than population and national income or slower (figures will prove either, bearing out the recent statement by the president of one of our large oil companies that the United States has become a country of "countervailing statistics"), we cannot, I am afraid, assume that over the next 10 years government expenditures will become significantly smaller in terms of population or national income. We must assume that they will tend to grow, at the very least, parallel with these two factors.

Economic Pressures

The consequences for management are quite clear, though they are by no means pleasant. First, we have to manage on the assumption that taxes will not go down but will, if anything, tend to go up. Secondly, we have to assume that our economy—and that of the entire world—will continue to carry a very heavy and permanent inflationary load. That burden will force us forever to face the dilemma between government policies that, if effective, will be very painful to major segments of the economy and runaway inflation that will threaten to bring on major depression and widespread economic and social destruction. Personally I have no difficulty in deciding which of these alternatives to take; I have seen far too much of the destructive effect of inflation not to consider even very painful remedies preferable. But it will take a great deal of patriotism, courage, and, above all, responsible business leadership to make this point stick and to resist the temptation to do things the easy, and apparently "painless," inflationary way.

Certainly we will have to expect that the dollar will continue to lose purchasing power even if we control inflation, and that therefore all investment in fixed money will either depreciate over the years or will have to be replenished from time to time. This is particularly relevant in view of the number of pension contracts in industry today. These contracts, by the letter of the agreement, provide for a fixed payment in dollars, but by the spirit guarantee a certain standard of living or purchasing power. I am not very happy about this—in fact I am scared stiff. And I am certainly convinced that it is dangerous, if not utter folly, for a businessman, in view of the social situation today, to be satisfied with a pension trust or a pension insurance which promises only a dollar-for-dollar return and does not contain some hedge against the erosion of dollar purchasing power through inflation.

"SUPER CITIES"

Within this over-all picture of big government and high public expenditures we are particularly concerned with the impact of the population pattern which is responsible for both.

I am not primarily talking here about numbers of people but rather about their geographic distribution, and especially about the rapid development of a metropolitan population. Actually, within the next 10 or 15 years our country will go beyond the "metropolitan stage" and will tend to become one in which the majority of our people live in as few as two dozen "super cities" or "metropolitan areas" such as the one that stretches, almost unbroken, from north of Boston to south of Washington, D. C., along the eastern seaboard.

Incidentally, though our rate of "urbanization" is fast, it is by no means the fastest in the world today. In this hemisphere, Peru, Mexico, and Brazil, to mention the three outstanding examples, are "urbanizing" even more rapidly than we are, and therefore face the same problem to an even more marked degree. Except in the most primitive parts of Africa or central Asia, the trend is world-wide and has the same impact on the economy everywhere.

Community Capital

It is an undeniable fact of life that the more urban a population is, the larger are its demands proportionately for the basic community services like education and sanitation, transportation and housing, power and water, and hospitals. And it is also a fact of life that since the end of World War II we have fallen behind in the supply of basic community capital to our population, even though we have had a tremendous housing, power, and telephone boom. To be specific:

> Despite all the furious housing activity, which has some very dangerous speculative features by the way, we have built just enough dwellings during the last 10 or 12 years to take care of the new families that have been formed since 1945—at a period when, according to birth-rate expectations, the rate of family formation ought to have been very low. Certainly it was under the level we can expect in the 1960's. We have not—and this is a very important fact—built one single home to replace any of the old housing that dates back before the depression—housing that is now rapidly reaching the age at which it should be replaced, the state at which it requires very heavy maintenance and modernization expenditures if it is not to become blighted area and slum.

What conclusion can we draw? First, there is not going to be any "withering away of the state" during these 10 years—the same conclusion in other words to which an analysis of defense expenditure leads me. Secondly—and this is of direct importance to all of us and can be measured—there is going to be real competition for capital and a serious capital shortage. Private business will have to perform very well indeed to get the money it needs for its own expansion and for new ventures: the rate of profitability on which business now operates is too low to attract the capital it needs. This is simply another way of saying, not on the basis of economics but on the basis of social analysis, that the present "shortage" of capital is a long-range condition which, for purposes of business planning today, must be assumed to be permanent.

But this "superurbanization" also has direct economic impact on markets, prices, and the business cycle altogether. We can anticipate a shift in the distribution of consumer expenditures, that is, of shares in the consumer income, under which a larger part will have to go

to the satisfaction of basic community demands and less to the satisfaction of individual consumer needs and wants. Here we can see
new marketing opportunities * and, quite clearly, new problems.

Shifting Terms of Trade

Finally, this "superurbanization" has already created a basic long-
range shift in the terms of trade and with it a basic change in the
pattern of vulnerability to a depression.

The last depression was characterized by an extraordinary vulnerability of all raw materials in their relationship to the prices of
manufactured goods. By and large all raw material, whether
mineral, metal, or foodstuffs, dropped in price four or five times as
fast and as far as did manufactured goods. This of course meant
that the raw material producers bore the brunt of the depression and
that a country which (like Great Britain) was exclusively a producer of manufactured goods on the whole benefited from the depression and had a fairly easy time of it from an economic point of
view. But this has changed. Though agricultural products still seem
to be very vulnerable, industrial raw materials—especially those
that can be considered structural raw material such as the metals—
may very well enjoy a long-range, if not a permanent, advantage
in that they stand to gain proportionately more from good business
and to lose proportionately less, if not very little, in a setback.

This stability would mean a great deal to some of our neighbors
in this hemisphere, such as Canada, Mexico, and the west coast
countries of South America. It would also have a pronounced impact on the direction of investment capital within our own economy—though not right away—and, if maintained over any length of
time, would drastically change our ideas as to what was a "speculative" and what was a "conservative" investment. It would, for instance, completely change the investment character of the steel
industry—indeed it may well have done so already. It might also—

* For a fuller discussion of marketing implications see the chapter by Norman H. Strouse, p. 40.

a very much less pleasant development—be one of the major reasons for the long-range weakness of Europe and especially of the British economy, a major reason why the British economy has proved itself to be as vulnerable as it was in the fall of 1956, despite very great efforts, tremendous patriotism, and very heavy investments and foreign aid.

HIGHER EDUCATION

The third social development that impinges directly on business-men and managers is probably the most important of all. It is the emergence of an educated society, a society in which the great bulk of the people have been educated to work with their minds and to apply knowledge and concepts rather than skill and experience to their jobs.

Let me give you a few simple figures:

❡ In 1927 when I started out, having just graduated from high school, about 20% of the people who entered the labor market with me had finished high school. Fewer than 5% had ever been to college.

❡ Around 1950, less than 25 years later, about 80% in an equivalent situation had gone to high school.

❡ Today almost one-third have been to college, though not necessarily for four years.

❡ By 1975, another 25 years hence, the number of high school graduates among the new recruits to the labor market will not be very much higher—80% is almost saturation of any market—but 55% or more of the young men and women first looking for jobs will have been to college, and the great majority of them will have finished four years. And this is no longer "future." On the east coast and on the west coast almost 50% of the young people are already actually going to college.

This is a radical innovation, unprecedented in the history of the world. It is perhaps the biggest event that we shall witness in our lifetime.

Let me hasten to say that I do not know whether or not the youngsters who come out with all this education will have learned anything. They certainly will not acquire wisdom by having sat on school benches for 16 years or so. But they will have been exposed to a great deal. Furthermore, while one does not acquire learning or wisdom through the seat—which, incidentally, is a very important tool of education—one does gain expectations when one sits on it in classrooms for a long time. The basic personality of these people may not be changed, but their expectations, images, and responses certainly will be. This is most important.

By way of example, I shall discuss only three very concrete and specific, almost measurable, effects of this change:

Automation. The real engine of automation, the force that pushes and drives us into it, is not technical—that is, machines. It is not conceptual—that is, theories, though they are probably a good deal more important than the machines. The real engine is the fact that in our society there will be fewer and fewer people to do nonautomated work. The assembly line of the automobile industry will not be tenable, no matter how sound it may be technically or economically, for the simple reason that tomorrow's worker will not be available to work on it.

The newly educated man or woman undoubtedly will expect to be put to work where he can use knowledge, concepts, and systems, rather than where he will have to acquire manual skills and experience. Thus we will be forced into automation at a very much faster clip than any of us yet anticipate or are prepared for, because whatever automation may mean, it certainly stands for the substitution of work by knowledge, concept, and theory for work by skill and experience.

Personnel policy. We will find our personnel programs increasingly inadequate, if not quite misdirected. They all date back to the time, at the very best, when no more than one-fifth of our work force had any education to speak of; they all date back to our experiences in the 1920's, if not World War I. Our present-day personnel management, which has evolved from our experience with semiskilled machine operators alone, will be found to be grossly inadequate to the job of managing tomorrow's highly educated worker. This is both one of our greatest challenges and one of our really important opportunities.

The professional. Finally we will increasingly have to come to grips with the slippery and tough problem of fitting the "individual contributor," the man with professional and technical training and professional and technical expectations, into an organization. All of the literature these last few years on the "management of engineers" and the "organization of a research department" has been a forecast of a general and chronic concern in the days ahead. If our society is an educated one, then it is the integration of the professional into the business organization that emerges as the central social problem of twentieth-century America.

That the "social issues" which still dominate our public and political oratory, the social issues of the 1860's, are dead and meaningless, we all know—even the people who still mouth them. The new issue, this problem of the professional in industry, is, however, the real social issue. Incidentally, it will decide whether the labor union is going to survive the next 25 years as a major force in our society, or whether, confined to a rapidly dwindling rank-and-file, manual labor group, it will become less and less important if also, I am afraid, more and more reactionary as a result.

BUSINESS LEADERSHIP

So far I have been talking basically about management *reactions* to social change. But this is not the whole story: tomorrow's businessmen are going to find themselves leading and even initiating social change in many areas.

Human Relations

First of these is the whole relationship of business enterprise to individuals.

The term "organizational revolution" has been batted around a good deal lately by the social scientists in the universities. They mean by it something everyone knows and has known for quite some time, though they have not attached quite such a highfalutin term to it: increasingly the business enterprise has become a major institution; increasingly it is the place in which the individual, especially the highly educated, highly qualified, and highly motivated man, finds his opportunities, his career, and his satisfaction.

Now that this has become a commonplace, we will increasingly come face to face with the question of what this means for the power and authority of the manager in his relationship to the individual.

Over the last 10 years all of us have seen a great shift in this field, a new view that is best described by the term "human relations." We have seen a change from an emphasis on a formal relationship of power and submission to one of teamwork, participation, acceptance, and leadership.

But this is not enough, valuable and important though it has been. The emerging concern with the "organizational revolution" —and there have been by last count something like 25 books and articles on it published in recent months—means that we will have to do a great deal more work and more thinking. Are we really justified in using adjustment, teamwork, and psychology as means of manipulating the individual? Are we at all entitled to try to "change" the personality of a man who is tied to the company only by an employment contract? Or are we really entitled to demand performance alone? And is all this emphasis on "persuasion" morally permissible—is this kind of persuasion not perhaps a good deal more corrupt and much more insidious than straight and brutal "command"? Where, in other words, does the individual end and the enterprise begin? Where does human relations become manipulation and "adjustment" become tyranny?

These are very large and difficult questions. During the next decade they will probably cease to be academic and will demand answers from more and more managers. Certainly the human relations phase is over—the very fact that we have not learned anything new in this whole field since the Harvard Business School group, 30 years ago, did its basic research is, I submit, adequate evidence that this is no longer "frontier," no longer fertile land. Yet we must not go back to what we had before human relations—even though some of us occasionally wonder whether these were really, as one wit once called them, "inhuman relations." We must push forward.

International Scale

And finally a major area of social change and of social opportunity opens up as an international society emerges which is built around managing and in which the manager is the center.

During these last 10 years industrialization has become a worldwide movement. In fact, never before has the whole globe been unified in one goal and one vision as it is now in the drive to industrialization. Indeed, the great conflict today is primarily over the *means* by which this goal of industrialization should be reached—the means of freedom or the means of tyranny.

We have learned during this decade that the essential resource of industrialization—and an exceedingly scarce resource it is—is not capital, or land, or labor, or technology, but managers and entrepreneurs. We know that it is the American manager who is the symbol, throughout the world, for this great international society which has in it the seeds of becoming the unifying force for a better world.

We are faced with a very great opportunity, a very great challenge, and a very great commitment to live up to the best in our own vision, in our own beliefs, in our own values. There is little doubt that the next decade is going to be a decisive one—it is the decade in which country after country will be expecting the first fruits of this great movement.

Perhaps the basic human relations problem and the symbolic leadership position of the American manager in the world are not capable of being translated into dollars-and-cents measurements, the kind of yardstick we like to use. But do not make the mistake of calling them "intangibles" simply because you and I do not know enough to be able to measure them. They may not be "tangibles" in accounting terms, but they are very tangible indeed in terms of peace preserved, lives saved, and freedom won. In respect to big government, superurbanization, and educated society, we in management will have to learn to adapt to social developments that have already happened for better or worse. But in the areas of essential, basic human relations in a business enterprise and the leadership position of the American manager in an international industrial society, we have an opportunity to initiate social change, to determine social direction, and to make the future.

RECENT ECONOMIC CHANGES AND THEIR IMPLICATIONS

Martin R. Gainsbrugh

- In the third quarter of 1955 consumer purchases of durables reached a peak of $37 billion which they have not yet surpassed.
- In the same quarter, outlays for residential nonfarm construction reached their all-time high of $16.7 billion and fell steadily thereafter.
- Today, with gross national product up $32 billion, expenditures for consumer durables including homes are fully $5 billion less than they had been earlier.

UPS AND DOWNS

THE IMPLICATIONS of these economic changes, which took place over the past two years, have been difficult to analyze. To some, the

Note: Mr. Gainsbrugh is Chief Economist, National Industrial Conference Board.

prospect of such declines in two of our major industries spelled recession in early 1956. To many more it meant at best a saucering out in that year. The short cycle of recovery, we were told, had about run its traditional course—the bloom was off the postwar boom. The consumer credit spree of 1955 had eaten away consumer backlogs for cars and homes. And, capping all this, the widely respected sensitive indicators were tilted downward, as were the newly developed diffusion indexes.

Yet in retrospect 1956, in the face of these adverse changes, will be entered in business annals as a year of prosperity and expansion. Real gross national product rose by nearly 3%, as did the Federal Reserve Board's index of industrial production. Unemployment for the year was a bit lower than in 1955. Personal income after taxes had grown by $17 billion and was some 4½% higher in terms of constant purchasing power than in the previous year. Obviously, a series of equally rapid and beneficial economic changes had more than offset the adverse combination of changes, which—separately viewed—had foreshadowed downturn. Not until after the summer doldrums of 1956, however, was it clear that the combined forces of upward changes had postponed recession for the present.

At the close of the first half of 1957 an impressive list of factors again suggested that a downward pull was appearing:

- Housing starts were some 15% lower than in the opening months of 1956.
- Heavy construction awards were also sharply lower.
- New car sales were no better than in 1956, and the total physical output of consumer durables was about 10% lower than at the end of 1956.

To these indicators we must add such sweeping changes as the development of productive capacity which can more than meet existing market demand in most consumer and capital goods industries, the switch from inventory accumulation to inventory liquidation, and a sag in the factory workweek, with a modest loss in real as well as current weekly earnings in manufacturing. The postwar boom is one year older, the sensitive indicators have yet to reach their troughs, and the National Industrial Conference Board's diffusion index descended sharply in the opening months of 1957.

UPWARD FORCES

Are there again offsetting upward changes? I believe there are. There were four forces that kept the economy in an expanding phase in 1956. With one possible exception, every one of those forces was still potent in the summer of 1957. They have given us an expanding economy despite the automobile and home-building cutbacks.

More Soft Goods and Services

Rising personal consumption expenditure is one of the reasons economic growth was well maintained throughout 1956 and promises to hold up in 1957. Quarter by quarter, consumers spend more, not less, for soft goods and services:

(True, we are not spending as much as we did for hard goods, but for every dollar that has been withdrawn from the automobile market, more than a dollar has been added to spending for gasoline, food, apparel, and virtually every other type of soft goods.

(We are not only eating more food, but we are eating "higher on the hog." We have upgraded our diets. We spend more per unit for food, for apparel, and for other items; and this upgrading, this "trading up," is still a very active force.

(Durable goods account for only 12% to 13% of total consumer expenditures. Seven of every eight dollars we spend go for the less glamourous types of consumer goods called "soft goods or services." Thus a modest increase in these purchases can offset a substantial decline in hard goods.

What we pay out for services, for culture, for education, for travel of all types already totals over $100 billion. These outlays are going up quarter by quarter, reflecting the higher incomes of our people, population pressures, and primarily the rebudgeting of the dollar. Having acquired a new car or a new home, many people have become better prospects for soft goods and services.

More Exports

The second offset is the growing appetite of western Europe for American goods. Our exports were 25% higher in the first five months of 1957 than they had been a year earlier.

More People

The third force is one businessmen have observed locally. Population pressures are still rampant. At the state and local level, the needs are still intense—not only for schools but also for hospitals, for jails, for every type of public facility—in response to continuing population pressures.

More Investment

The fourth is industry spending for plant and equipment. The NICB's quarterly survey of capital appropriations of the 1,000 largest manufacturing corporations was the first—in November 1956 —to foreshadow the leveling out of capital expenditures. Later returns suggested continued strength in business spending for new plant and equipment in the second half of 1957. This in turn implied that business investment in new plant and equipment would be maintained at a high level throughout the year rather than dip sharply.

In summary, the strength in final product demand has been more than sufficient to offset the loss of demand for inventory purposes. Personal income, employment, and retail trade have more than held their ground. Manufacturing output, particularly of consumer durables, has been cut by nearly 10% below the peak levels of late 1956; and production for inventory purposes is lower than at any time in the past two years. A quick and massive inventory correction has occurred following the large inventory accumulations of the past two years, with prices in general holding firm.

Meanwhile, final demand—that is, dollar outlays by consumers, by government, by foreigners, and by business (excluding inventories) —continued to rise almost as much as they did in the booming fourth quarter of 1956. This helped bring inventories into better balance and implied a rise in factory production in the second half of 1957, closing the gap between current rates of production and consumption. It now appears, too, that business demand for plant and equipment will provide a strong sustaining force rather than dip sharply as had been feared earlier.

An NICB survey of capital appropriations taken at the close of the first quarter of 1957 revealed that business appropriated more money for expansion than it expended in that quarter. This differs markedly from the weak pattern of capital appropriations in the closing months of 1956. In fact, new appropriations in mid-1957 have been at about the same level as in mid-1956. Appropriations have continued to decline in the automotive industry and for non-ferrous metals and steel; but they were up for oil, chemicals, and some other soft goods.

The backlogs of unspent capital appropriations, however, were narrowed for the third successive quarter. Here is another significant change suggesting that capital spending is far more dependent on the rate of current decisions to spend than in many past years. Current trends in profits, and particularly profit margins, have now become a key determinant in near-term planning of plant and equipment outlays.

One basic economic problem that now confronts us is the necessity of bringing total market demand up to the greatly enlarged capacity produced by these record capital outlays. In industry after industry current capacity now seems to be running ahead of demand. In contrast, for much of the past decade, market demand was well in excess of the capacity to produce.

The first postwar decade is always highly stimulative: there are physical shortages to be made up—consumers want more homes, goods, cars; business needs more capacity—plant and equipment; the banks are eager to take on loans of all types. That favorable climate is no longer conditioning our market. We are shifting from an easy environment to the tightly competitive market of the second postwar decade, to the threat which has arisen after every great war —the problem of the secondary postwar readjustment. This is a longer-range economic problem to which all of us will be devoting more and more attention in the course of the years immediately ahead.

Several years ago we coined the phrase "rolling readjustment." It is said that we again had such a rolling readjustment in 1956–1957. I believe that the phrase is no longer adequate. What we have been experiencing can be more accurately described as a restructuring or reallocation of our resources in response to a significantly altered economic environment.

THE MIDDLE YEARS

The outlook for the months immediately ahead still remains good, and there is no need to challenge the glowing outlook for 1965 that so many have assumed for long-range planning purposes.

But what is the outlook for the years between, the "middle years"?

Forces for Expansion

An NICB study published in 1956, "Forty Years of Economic Growth," singled out five long-term factors that have brought us to the promised land of the $400 billion economy. True, the $400 billion figure is in inflated prices, but even corrected figures show that we have more than doubled our nation's output in physical terms since 1939.

The first factor that pushed us up was the reversal of the population curve. That force is still actively at work. The demands of the added population were in turn made effective by the accompanying income and consumption explosion: millions of families have risen from their prewar low-income status to today's new middle-income groups—from which they have a still better chance to rise even higher. The average wage-earning family today is in the $5,000-$7,500 income bracket. Here is a salient distinction between the late 1920's and the mid-1950's. This time we have drastically altered our income distribution. In the late 1920's we had just as many families, proportionately, in the low-income groups as at the start of World War I.

The third growth factor is most frequently cited: the technological revolution and its continuing implications so far as capital investment is concerned.

The fourth is the increasing resort to the debt instrument, first by the Federal Government, then by business, and within recent years by consumers.

The last and final force is the emergence of giant government with all its economic repercussions.

Burning Backlog

These have been the major upward long-term pressures ever since the late 1930's, but some of them are now beginning to wane. We are shifting, for example, from a decade of high liquidity to an extremely tight period as we enter the second postwar decade. As some of these forces lose their potency we may not have the high rates of economic growth which have characterized our system ever since 1940.

The master trend at work during the past decade was the stimulating effect of the war. Wars have historically produced, at least for the victors, huge backlogs of deferred and effective consumer and business demand. These backlogs are highly stimulating for a period of years. Wars, however, not only originate or reinforce the upswing of the business cycle; they may also create imbalances that reinforce or accelerate downswings in the subsequent postwar period.

The true test of greater economic stability and of the firmness of the first decade of postwar expansion will come, therefore, in the second postwar decade.

I have no specific timetable in mind, but for lack of anything more definite, I am inclined to view the period of the late 1950's and the early 1960's as this period of shake-out and reallocation of resources. This is what I mean by the middle-year period. Beyond them undoubtedly lies the golden harvest of 1965, but to alter Edwin G. Nourse's highly descriptive phrase, the middle years come first.*

Problem Areas

In broad strokes, let me paint for you some of the potential problem areas of these middle years:

1. *The threat that wage gains will outstrip the gains in productivity.* Wage increases in excess of productivity have already created pressures for higher prices. As consumer markets become increasingly competitive, producers find it ever more difficult to pass on cost increases through higher prices for their finished products. This, in turn, means narrower profit margins; narrower profit margins could begin to eat away at the base of the models of sustained growth throughout the second postwar decade. Excessive wage increases in the second postwar decade can thus mean less sales and greater unemployment. Here is the problem of wage inflation which we as a people have just begun to face. The way we pay for wage inflation is to price goods out of the market for a significant portion of the population.

In addition, as living standards rise, there will be a further shift to what Colin Clark has labeled the tertiary industries, into culture, education, recreation, health.† And as more people enter the tertiary

* *The 1950's Come First* (New York, Henry Holt and Company, Inc., 1951).

† *The Conditions of Economic Progress,* second edition (London, The Macmillan Company, 1951).

industries, that alteration may very well brake the recent acceleration of national productivity, since output per man-hour in the
service industries is difficult to raise through mechanization.

2. *Debt.* The largest single force working in our economy
throughout the 1940's was the rise in federal debt of $250 billion.
What of the trend in private borrowing, business and individual
combined, during the past decade of virtually full employment?
Private debt in the aggregate increased by nearly $300 billion since
the end of World War II.

Debt should become far less of a stimulant as this second postwar
decade ages than it has been throughout the past decade or more.
Consumer, business, and bank liquidity has been sharply reduced in
recent years.

3. *The rate of private investment in new plant and equipment.* In
industry after industry we are witnessing a "pause for digestion"
since capacity to produce is already in excess of current market demand. Business investment in the past has been subject to extremely
severe contraction, particularly after the catching-up period following great wars.

According to NICB studies, we have about overtaken our stock
and equipment deficiencies of 1930–1945. Our national capital co-
efficients—the relationship of our national wealth to our national
income—are perhaps close, if not back, to their long-term norms.

True, there are several factors, many of them not present to the
same high degree in the 1920's or earlier decades, which may make
capital expenditures less volatile than in the past:

* The ever-rising trend of research expenditures and consequent investment requirements.
* The growing tendency of business managers to longer-range
  thinking, to longer-range planning, and to capital budgeting.
* The continuation of our defense program and the fact that it,
  too, creates demands for capital goods over and above the demands spawned by a peacetime economy.

- The pressures for maximum mechanization to offset higher wage rates and, much more in point, the threat of constantly mounting unit labor costs.
- A more realistic replacement policy. The more generous depreciation schedules provided under recent tax laws should move us in this direction, so that replacement should provide a much larger and steadier demand for equipment than in the past.
- The need of some companies for additional capacity to achieve optimum performance.

In summary on this point, the historic pattern of business investment has been extremely cyclical in character, particularly so after catching-up periods following great wars. Behind the peak rate of such outlays currently there already lies nearly a decade of unprecedented, uninterrupted increases in investment. It is against this background that the outlook for business investment for the second postwar decade must now be weighed. New and strong sustaining, or even expansionary, forces may help to alter the explosive cyclical pattern of the past. Included are two potent primary factors: the technological breakthrough and the wider adoption by industry of planning and capital budgeting. In addition, we have added defense capacity requirements, the heightened pressures to mechanize to beat down rising labor costs, a more realistic replacement policy, and the need for reserve capacities to permit optimum operating economies.

We have made gratifying and possibly giant steps toward building greater stability into the most volatile sector of our highly industrialized economy. It is still too early to tell, however, whether these are sufficient to prevent a repetition of the typical historical pattern.

4. *The rebudgeting of national consumer demand.* Rebudgeted consumer demand in the second postwar decade may not mesh so neatly with existing production capacity as it has in the past. Witness what has already happened in some of the consumer durable industries when the consumers said, "We have enough inventory to satisfy much of our requirements for this year."

Consumer buying grows more optional and dynamic with each passing year. What if consumers should shift their demands sharply toward the service industries? This is the historic pattern of consumption; should it hold true, mortalities in the goods-producing sector might become far more marked in the second postwar decade than they were in the first.

5. *The place of the middle years on the business cycle, particularly on the longer cycle.* We have been in the expansion phase of such a long cycle ever since the end of World War II, if not since its beginning. Combine cyclical periodicity with delayed readjustments to war's imbalances and you have the fifth reason for concern about the middle years.

These are open questions, but mentioning them may militate against complacency or overoptimism about the prospect of automatic economic growth in the second postwar decade. That is what started me down this path; the fact that we may be taking it for granted that because we managed so successfully in the first postwar decade, we are therefore justified in assuming that changes in the second decade will net out as favorably as in the first. The more we explore the product and market implications of the middle years, the more likely it is that we can find our way toward the required structural changes and the proper reallocation of our resources to adapt to them.

TECHNOLOGICAL CHANGE—
WHAT IT WILL MEAN TO MANAGEMENT

C. W. LaPierre

CHANGE CONFRONTS all of us. We are living in a time of accelerating change, in a world of explosive growth, and in an expanding universe. And the technological changes of our age have already outstripped the imaginations of all but the comic strip writers.

Take aviation, for example:

> I flew across the country and back in a commercial DC-3 about 18 years ago. The trip took 24 hours or so each way. Shortly afterwards, I attended a meeting of engineers where we discussed some of my experiences on the trip. One of the experts volunteered the opinion that I had flown in the optimum passenger aircraft: military aircraft would, of course, go faster, he said, but the DC-3 speed was

Note: Mr. LaPierre is Executive Vice President with over-all responsibility for the Electronic, Atomic and Defense Systems Group of General Electric Company.

just right for passengers. Nevertheless, within 10 years the speed of commercial aircraft had doubled to about 300 miles-per-hour. And planes are now on order which, during this decade, will double the speed again to around 600 mph—or very close to the speed of sound.

Several years ago I asked the chief engineer of a leading aircraft company, "When are we going to fly passengers supersonically?" He came out with a flat, "Never," which he then modified a little to, "at least not in my lifetime." A couple of years later I met him again and casually asked him the same question. He said, "You know, that isn't so dumb as it sounds."

Since then the British have announced a project to complete a supersonic transport by 1965 to capture a position in transport aircraft which they narrowly lost by the failure of the initial Comets. Thus, by the end of the coming decade air transport speeds will almost certainly be doubled again, and we will be flying transoceanic and transcontinental planes at 1,200 mph, more or less.

Several military planes are, of course already flying that fast. The 1,200 mph jet engines in existence today are, at full speed, the most efficient engines yet devised by man—yet only a few years ago jet engines were considered so wasteful of fuel as to have no place in commercial transportation.

At 1,200 mph it will be possible to leave New York as the sun is rising and arrive in San Francisco before daybreak, watching the sun set in the east as you make the trip. The dream of outracing the sun has already been fulfilled by some pilots, and passengers will be following suit.

Is that the end? There are experts who think not. We recently delivered the first-stage motors which will project the proposed earth satellite to a velocity of well over 4,000 mph, and many accomplished, practical men, who are at work on the program, believe that manned ships traveling at over 4,000 mph will prove to be the most efficient way to carry people across the oceans two or three decades hence. The ultimate speed of the earth satellite will be over 18,000 mph, and some experts look with real expectation to man's conquest of space at speeds far higher than these. So there is plenty of room to continue doubling the speed of sky travel for many more years.

Although man's conquest of the sky has long been rated as one of his most spectacular achievements, the most amazing advances in aviation are still in the laboratories and shops.

Electricity and Electronics

Nor is aviation so unusual. The electric power output of this country has been doubling every 10 years since the founding of the General Electric Company, and there is as yet no slackening of the trend. On the contrary, in recent years the growth has been accelerated. The impact of such a growth of power output on all business is tremendous. For us at G.E., it means that we must build as much generating, transmission, and user equipment in the next 10 years as we have built in the entire history of the company to date in order to hold our own position in this industry. This is a large order for a company that has been delivering products for over 75 years.

Almost one-eighth of the huge amount of electrical power generated in this country goes to its work through electron tubes the outgrowth of those fragile little tubes which we first saw in our radio sets some years ago. This power is very important to our economy, but the blossoming electronic industry is going to have an impact on all of us that goes far beyond our role as users of kilowatts. Those little radio tubes are assuming new forms ranging from tiny images of their predecessors to huge steel enclosed tubes for the chemical and metallurgical industries. Moreover, transistors are becoming available to do some of the same jobs without the filaments or high voltage long associated with electronics.

The versatility and sensitivity of electronics has never been questioned, but many businessmen and engineers have shunned electron tubes because they questioned their reliability. The electronic engineers flouted this charge in a striking manner recently when they buried innumerable electron tubes in a trans-Atlantic telephone cable. The whole success of this cable depends on the continuous performance of these tubes and circuits. The cost of replacing one of the tubes would run into hundreds of thousands of dollars—and we can be sure the backers are not expecting the need to arise soon. Electronic computers with far greater than human reliability have gradually taken over the job of calculating and writing bills, pay checks, dividend checks, and the like. Some progress has been made in keeping normal business records electronically:

> At least one large banking system has an electronic bookkeeping machine on order which will handle all the bookkeeping details for 50,000 checking accounts every working day. The machine will credit and debit individual checking accounts with the checks and deposits received, remember the details of all these transactions, maintain depositor current balances, and accept stop payments and hold orders. It sorts the checks and deposits into account number, and it turns out a complete, printed statement for the depositors at the end of the month or whenever called upon to do so.

This is a far cry from the electronics that have heretofore performed simple counting and other similar industry functions. The new electronics performs millions of operations per second with at most a few errors in a week, and the computations are so rapid that adequate automatic checking procedures can be set up to detect these few errors.

Not so well known, but perhaps of even greater importance, are the tremendous scientific and engineering jobs being performed by computers or data processors in all major laboratories and technical centers where the designs of complex machines, engines, and weapons are evolved and where their operation is tested in advance of detailed design and construction. For instance:

> Today's military jet engines fight their first battles twisting, turning, climbing, and diving from high in the skies to down on the deck on a jet-engine-simulating computer long before the design is completed or construction started. No longer does the designer wonder if the alternate decision might have been best; he has tried both.

It would take a long time just to list the many ways that these machines may affect business. Suffice it to say that the electronic data processors are the basis of successful automation. It would be a mistake to assume that the automatic factory will come overnight, because, contrary to public opinion, many of the technological problems of automation are still before us. Linking many machines in a continuous, automatic process requires greater accuracy, reliability, and continuity of performance in each one than we have normally attained in production operations. The evolution of machines for the automatic factory is now proceeding on many fronts. As the technology evolves, the benefits of automation will be multiplied by a drastic reduction in the wasted effort and spoiled materials which are inherent in human operation.

Automation has potential uses in other areas. Perhaps electronic data processors will help us break many of the present barriers to man's use of the knowledge stacked away in our libraries:

> The growing storage problems have forced the startling innovation of storing books according to physical size rather than subject matter. This problem could, of course, be taken care of by microfilm, but no one has as yet solved the problem of ready access to the information after it has been stored. Electronics makes all this technically possible.

Electronic data processors will not only keep our business records, operate our machines and direct the flow of goods; they will also give answers to business problems. Just as design engineers can experiment with different possibilities, so managers will be able to set up economic data and marketing information drawn from their own internal statistics and try out various promising solutions to their business problems. They will be able to determine the probability of success in each course of action.

Electronics, however, is not devoted exclusively to handling complex data-processing materials. Rapidly expanding technology in all areas creates new environmental conditions to which normal detection and control cannot be adapted. Electronics can perform their functions in the face of high temperatures, nuclear radiation, deep sea pressures, and many other abnormal conditions, which our rapidly expanding technology is penetrating. Recently, for example, scientists have announced the development of electronic circuits for missiles which operate at red heat.

Materials

The development of these special electronic devices and other products as well is the result of coordinated development of materials in addition to the items themselves. The search for better materials to go into better products and processes has led to:

❰ *Artificial industrial diamonds.* These should make diamond-equipped cutting tools available for wide-scale manufacturing operations, with an assured source of supply. Such gems are now in production.

❰ *Borazon.* As invariably happens, the research that produced the first man-made diamond was able to go even further and came up with an entirely new material called Borazon. Borazon seems to be every bit as hard as diamonds and much superior in that it retains its hardness at temperatures at which diamonds would be consumed. The techniques that produced artificial diamonds and Borazon open up an entire avenue for the exploration of other materials of unexpected characteristics and possibilities.

❰ *Crystals stronger than steel.* In research on iron crystals, some tiny crystal whiskers have been formed with tensile strengths as high as 1.9 million pounds per square inch—more than 150 times that of ordinary iron crystals and many times the strength of the highest grade of steel. Can you imagine what would happen to our products if some of this gain in tensile strengths of metals could be made available in commercial materials? We would have to redesign everything!

❰ *Strong crystalline plastics.* Plastic materials are under detailed, internal study. They normally are not crystalline in structure and as a result are not as strong as metals. The new look points the way toward crystalline plastics, which, while not as strong as the strongest metals, are nevertheless much stronger than the plastics we now use in huge quantities. And, who can say that they will not eventually replace metal for many well-known applications?

Sources and Uses of Power

Nor is all the work being done in inorganic construction materials. Radiation has been applied to oil refining processes and may make these and many other present-day chemical operations obsolete; and algae have been developed in the laboratory in nutrient solutions which can transform light into organic energy two or three times more efficiently than the higher plants. The electric industry would hope, of course, that we can find a practical means for converting solar energy into electricity more directly, as, for instance, through some form of photoelectric cell. Indeed, some practical devices of this kind which depend solely on the sun for their supply of power, have been produced in the last year or so.

Fission reactors born during World War II are now beginning to take their place as sources of power for propulsion and electric power generation.

Nuclear reactions are not exactly new. The discovery of the X-ray, so called because its nature was not fully understood, many years ago disclosed that under certain conditions there was radiation. In the ensuing years, much research and study went into finding out just what was happening inside the atom to produce these radiations and other effects that had been observed. By World War II the basic work had been accomplished. The key concepts and materials were at hand to develop atomic weapons or power.

It has been estimated that the successful utilization of fission alone will provide us an energy reserve roughly 25 times that of fossil fuels such as coal and oil. The coal and oil reserves of this country are still large. Our private enterprise utilities are using this fuel with great efficiency. Abroad, where fuel is already showing signs of depletion since power generation is generally much more wasteful, atomic power is more critical and of greater economic significance. Nevertheless, our electrical industry has gone ahead with tremendous vigor toward the development of atomic power.

The work in the laboratories on fission has already led to fusion for weapons, and extensive research is now under way to develop a practical method of using fusion for power. Several teams of experts are following this exciting possibility, and when they are successful the fuel reserves will be inexhaustible—or at least ample for millions of years at any presently conceivable rate of use.

These and other recent technological gains are tremendous and open up an even more tremendous future. Innovation is certainly a partial answer to the question of excess capacity. There is no excess capacity for the products and services yet to come.

BARRIERS TO PROGRESS

To achieve this, each of us must be alert to the real impediments to technological progress. Some of the greatest of these obstacles are lack of incentives because of governmental policies and limitations in our technical knowledge itself.

Lack of Incentives

In atomic energy, billions of dollars of work has been done by industry with very little, if any, profit to show for the work. Industry is now being invited to make huge private investments on many fronts in the development of atomic power far in advance of any proof of economic feasibility and in the face of other serious risks. This climate is not a favorable one in which to foster the century's most spectacular innovation.

All our experience demonstrates emphatically that the American system of competition and incentives and individual initiative and freedom is the most dynamically effective producer of technological goods and services. There is never a question in our minds as to the over-all superiority of our system in the production of automobiles, refrigerators, and the like.

In our defense and atomic energy work, however, we depart widely from the normal American private enterprise system. Our defense work is carried out with a minimum of incentives and highly centralized governmental control of the detailed plans and operations. And when I speak of government, I am not referring to our officers in uniform, who frequently have as little to say about procurement policies as does business. It seems reasonable to think that the closer we approach the Russian method of operation, the less clear-cut will be the superiority of our results. Unquestioned superiority of American weapons could be assured by finding ways to use the American system fully to evolve and produce them.

The basic problem is simply stated. Advanced weapons necessarily involve all branches of new technology, and the policies under which this work is carried out have an impact on the future of all business. When anyone buys a new technological product or service from industry, two components are involved:

1. A great mass of skills and facilities which have been built up over the years the company and its employees have been in business.
2. A bit of new technology—usually very small—that is needed to add to the very much larger available technology to produce the desired new result.

Every new product or result can be represented, therefore, by a pyramid, with a large base of company experience and ability plus a tiny apex of new work. When a private individual or a company makes a purchase, their real concern is value received, in relation to competitive prices prevailing at the market place. They expect the price to be not only attractive to the customer but also adequate to cover all work performed, including the cost of stimulating the innovations involved in the current product and for ever-better future products—even though the customer may not be an immediate beneficiary—and a profit for the use of the skills and facilities of the enterprise as a whole (including buildings, machines, personnel, patents, know-how, and all other advantages the company may possess to do the job). The physical assets are very frequently one of the least important factors to be considered in allocating profit incentives.

With national budgets running at the present size, government procurement policies are powerful documents. Unfortunately, they are all too frequently directed toward minimizing the incentives necessary to support innovation. Principally, they fail to understand the importance of the base of the pyramid—those basic skills and facilities needed in any organization if important new results are to be achieved.

Private industry has highly developed and acceptable standards for dealing with its various components. The government tends to set up different standards, expecting the same performance, but, in fact, the policies all too often strike at the very base of the system's efficiency, at its human skills, its patents, its proprietary information, its profit incentives, and individual initiative. Profits and incentives of all sorts must in a very real sense be ample to encourage innovation, if the benefits of innovation are to be realized.

Technological Limits

Though it is not commonly recognized, there are still limits to our technology itself, and we have reason to be concerned that our rapid technological advances are depleting our fund of basic research.

Under the incentives of the past, growth industries have maintained large staffs of scientists and engineers and have provided the most modern laboratory facilities for their work. Out of these efforts have come many technological achievements which we now accept as necessary components to our standard of living—as well as many of the principles and techniques we now need in organizing to get the technical work of the nation done.

We have added, today, a new concept—a new way of thinking, or more accurately, a new scale of thinking about innovation. It is simply the belief that once the scientific knowledge is within our grasp, *innovation can be successfully planned,* and with the expenditure of adequate, well-managed effort a needed technological advance can be achieved. The future does not appear devoid of effort. A 1957 McGraw-Hill survey indicates a national expenditure for research and development of $9 billion for 1960 as against $6 billion for 1956.

Thus, it seems likely that more new products will reach the market, and more new processes will be used to produce them in the next 10 years than in any previous decade. The limit will not be in the number of problems that are worth investigating, but in the incentives available to the companies, scientists, and engineers in position and with the requisite training and background to carry out the tasks.

PLANNING FOR CHANGE

The primary role of management throughout these technological changes to come will be one of planning. The task is not an easy one, and the techniques of planning need further development.

Forecasting

The first difficulty is the problem of forecasting. Experience has shown that about the only way to solve the forecasting problem is to use a large factor by which to increase all estimates beyond the immediately foreseeable future. Only one thing is really certain about the uncertain future. Tomorrow's products will *not* be like the products of today; tomorrow's scientific discoveries cannot be predicted on the basis of today's.

Scheduling Innovation

What is new about our economy is not just long-range planning by business—though business is just beginning to learn how to do an effective job of planning, 5 to 10 years ahead. It is not just the expansion of research and development—though industry employs more than two and one-half times as many research scientists and engineers as it employed 15 years ago. What *is* new is the systematic long-range planning for change and the deliberate spending, sometimes of large sums of money, to bring it about on a scheduled basis. Coupled with scientific training in both technology and organization techniques, it is bringing the massive thrust of technology to bear, one by one, on the major problems faced in each specific business.

Such planning assumes success, and there is rarely a place for minor extensions of the present—they almost always become engulfed in the inevitable innovations.

Decentralized Basis

This kind of planning cannot be done effectively by huge centralized planning organizations at the top. State planning, particularly, cannot possibly know enough, cannot possibly visualize enough to take sufficient advantage of all the good things available. It can only be done business by business, industry by industry, community by community, and venturer by venturer—which adds up to, but does not derive from, the national economy and in turn is the source of the nation's progress.

No business plan can be considered adequate which does not provide ample profit to encourage innovation and obsolescence. Innovation has repaid manyfold to the customer as well as everyone else the profit incentive to the innovator.

In its planning functions, management requires a sense of responsibility for what *needs* to be done, for if private business does not make use of the innovations within its grasp, others will feel warranted, if not obligated, to take over the task. Many projects are becoming more complex than any one company can undertake on an isolated basis. Some projects of the future will require teams of companies, or even of industries. We have had a glimpse of the problems involved in the marshaling of thousands of subcontractors toward a defense objective during times of national emergency. The private companies are now teaming up to promote the development of atomic power.

In all activities management cannot help being acutely aware of the business climate in which its operations are conducted. The individual voter must understand business economics well enough to cast his ballot at the polling place to preserve his increasingly valuable ballot in the market place.

THE TECHNOLOGICAL RACE AND THE FUTURE

Business management today is faced with a great challenge. Measured by the *actual results achieved,* American business must be ranked at the top in contribution to the common good. The problem before us, as managers, is to maintain our leadership.

Technology's experts are ready to fly us safely and economically through the skies at unheard-of speeds. They are ready to eliminate detailed mental drudgery, as they have already eliminated physical toil. They are ready to develop power sources of unlimited capacity for an ever-higher standard of living. They are ready to give us more life and more health and accomplish innumerable other tasks as well.

When the record is consulted by the generation which will inherit the results of our decisions—the good along with the bad—the way private enterprise has managed these innovations may very well prove to have been a turning point in the history of the twentieth century.

A LOOK INTO THE FUTURE OF MARKETING

Norman H. Strouse

THE VELOCITY of the economic and sociological changes in this country during the past 10 years has been such that anyone who attempts to look into the future of marketing inevitably finds that much of that future has already come upon him, if it has not actually passed him by.

As evidence of management's difficulty in understanding and keeping up with that change, here are two examples of how otherwise competent and basically optimistic authorities failed even 10 years ago to anticipate what would be happening in our economy by now:

⟨ In 1946, the Census Bureau forecast that there would be 150 million people in the United States by 1955. This proved to be a

Note: Mr. Strouse is President, J. Walter Thompson Company.

forecasting error of 17 million people—a statistical shortage equivalent to the entire population of Canada.

No one had recognized how fundamentally the war years had changed our attitude toward family formation. What had seemed to be a temporary return to earlier marriages and larger families during the war years proved to be a permanent characteristic of the decade following the war.

❡ In 1946, the hard-boiled automotive economists predicted that there would be 36 million passenger cars on the road by 1955. In fact, by 1955 there were 52 million cars registered, a forecasting error of 16 million, or more cars than there are in all of western Europe.

No wonder we have grave misgivings as to our competence to predict the way of growth and change during the next 10 years. It might be disastrous financially to be overoptimistic, and it could be very costly competitively to be too conservative.

NEW DIMENSION

Before World War II, there were many who believed that since our population had surged up against the western boundary of our land and most of our natural resources had been inventoried if not exploited, we were close to the optimum momentum of our economy. There were even those who believed that our growing population would, if anything, tend to dilute our standard of living.

But a new dimension was built into our economy during the war. The numbers of people continued to grow, to be sure—in fact, more rapidly than ever. But, because of an acceleration in technological achievement and a broadened distribution of productive wealth, each individual began to enlarge his ability to produce, to earn, and to consume.

Thus we found ourselves with a vertical economic growth supplementing the horizontal growth we had known before. And this vertical growth is gaining in velocity both in economic and social terms, bringing with it many new factors with which we must learn to deal.

Let us review briefly some of the major changes in the years between 1950 and 1956.

1. *A rapid increase in population*—18,000,000 people added to our total population during the past six years.

2. *A substantial increase in our labor force*—5,638,000 people added to our labor force. And it might be noted here that the annual additions to our labor force will accelerate from 800,000 a year to 1,200,000 a year during the next decade as the huge baby crops of the 1940's come into productive age.

3. *Increased productivity*—Through technological advance, improved skills, and more scientific management, we have increased our production of goods and services by 28% during the past six years—three times the rate of increase of our available labor force.

4. *Increased capacity to consume*—The rewards of our increased productivity have been broadly shared, resulting in an increase in our standard of living of 22% in terms of constant dollars.

5. *Increased mobility*—From a marketing standpoint, perhaps the most significant change is to be found in our increased mobility, a mobility that is displayed in two striking forms: the geographical mobility of people moving restlessly across the land in search of better opportunities and better living conditions, and the economic mobility of people moving rapidly upward in earning capacity. Although these two forms may be studied as separate phenomena, they are interrelated.

   During the past six years, 190,000,000 people moved to new addresses—by all odds the greatest phenomenon of mass migration in recorded history.*

   During the same six-year period, 12,500,000 consumer spending units moved up into the $4,000 a year and above bracket, doubling the number and disposable income of those families.

This is by no means a complete list of the facts which could be used to document the growing velocity of economic and sociological

---

* U.S. Bureau of the Census, *Current Population Reports,* Series P-20, No. 73, "Mobility of the Population of the U.S." (Washington, Government Printing Office, 1957) p. 9, Table 1.

change that surrounds us. It should be a sufficient reminder, however, that there has been enormous growth and change during the past few years with a tremendous impact on marketing, and that this growth and change is likely to continue well into the foreseeable future.

NEW ROLES IN MARKETING

It is not possible, in the space of this chapter, to review many of the broad marketing problems we will be facing during the next few years. Therefore, within this introductory frame of reference, I would like to concentrate first on two problems which have arisen because of changes in marketing channels and are apt to be accentuated by growth and change. Then I want to look at a few ways in which management can recognize and deal with changes in the market itself.

Exit Salesclerk

First, what has happened to the selling "chain of command"—the influence the manufacturer used to be able to exercise over his selling activities from the time his product left the factory until it was passed across the counter to the ultimate consumer? There used to be a certain person-to-person contact in every step of distribution that carried a planned sales program through to the consumer, who may or may not have been conditioned by advertising before encountering the retail clerk or salesman.

A long-term gradual deterioration in this process was hastened by World War II. During the war some consumer products like new cars vanished from the market completely, and a great variety of others moved into short supply. Most good retail salesmen disappeared into the armed services or defense work. Such sales talent as remained was fairly well spoiled by the complacency and false sense of power that result from the assumed right to allocate, and at the end of World War II the personnel demands and rewards of industry were such that many who might have qualified as good retail salesmen were not attracted to a profession which had been characterized by long hours, individual as distinct from group action, and uncertain income.

All of this quickened the growing trend toward self-service which has now taken over vast areas of our retail selling structure. Genuine personal selling at the retail level has rapidly disappeared, and we are at a point where the manufacturer of branded merchandise is almost completely at the mercy of a consumer preference that has already been established before the buyer enters a retail outlet. This is even the case with passenger cars:

> Survey after survey reveals that about 90% of those who enter automobile showrooms to purchase cars have never been reached by a salesman. They may shop several dealers to get the best deal, but in most cases they have already picked out at most two or possibly three makes and have a definite predisposition toward one. The successful automobile salesman—if we may any longer call him that—becomes essentially a specialist in closing deals.

In some ways this development resembles what is going on in the discount house with other types of durable goods. In his brilliant book, *The Organization Man,* William H. Whyte, Jr., describes the manner in which the retailer, who once played a major role in the creation and guidance of human wants, has abdicated that position in more and more fields. Whyte says of the discount house:

> "What has been happening is that the consumer has been taking over part of the selling burden historically allotted to the retailer....
>
> "Manufacturers still give retailers a markup big enough to justify the missionary work retailers once did. With few exceptions, however, retailers no longer do this kind of work; they *service* demand, but they have discarded their former techniques, such as the use of outside sales forces, to create demand. The burden of introducing new products, as a result, now falls upon a combination of advertising and the word of mouth of the consumer group. The real selling job, in short, is done before the customer comes into the store. Guided by the group, the customer already has determined al-

most everything about the purchase—including the fact that he will
make it—except the price and a few minor options." *

The passenger car manufacturers and many of the hard goods
manufacturers can maintain a structure of retail outlets throughout
the country with franchise agreements—outlets which customers
have no difficulty in locating when they wish to make purchases of
such substantial nature. Not so, however, with the packaged goods
manufacturer. He faces a somewhat more difficult problem, one
over which he has little control except through the consumer himself. He must work his major distribution through retail grocery
and drugstores where he has no identification with the owner and
in which his major competitors' products are lined up alongside his
own—that is, if he is fortunate enough to be lined up alongside
his competitors.

And there is the hitch. Retail grocery and drugstore volume has
been rapidly concentrating in the hands of chain stores, corporate
or voluntary, and the supermarkets. Completely self-service as to
packaged goods (they are mass merchandising outlets operating at
thin margins), the chain stores are interested in one thing, and one
thing only—movement. The product that moves fast gets shelf space.
Shelf space is expensive, so unless your product is either first, second,
or third in consumer demand, you are clinging to distribution by
your eyelids. If innovation develops in your line—color in soap or
paper, or variety in mustards or puddings, or size of pack in any
line—the problem is compounded.

A most critical problem today in the marketing of packaged goods
is the dominant position achieved by corporate chains, a position
which promises to be decisive. The 10 largest retail grocery chains
did a total volume of over $12 billion during 1956—nearly 31% of
total grocery store sales.

More specifically, it is the *concentration* of volume that makes
the chain stores and supermarkets of such strategic importance.
Whether you penetrate these areas of retail volume successfully or
not can determine whether you make your sales quotas, and in

* New York, Simon and Schuster, Inc., 1956, p. 315.

many cases whether you reach a volume well beyond your break-even points.

But these are tough segments of the retail market to crack. A recent study of 209 supermarket companies operating 7,241 retail outlets and representing $7.5 billion in sales revealed that 69% now have "a buying committee to decide the fate of practically everything a manufacturer wants to sell through such outlets." Not only do the buyers in chains and supermarkets exercise a decisive power over new products, promotions, and sales plans, but also it is in this area of retail merchandising that we encounter *the private brand.*

The private brand is a serious contender against the national brand:

- A Chicago *Tribune* study revealed that in Kroger stores 85% of the volume of white bread was represented by the chain's own brand.
- A survey by *The New York Times* a few years ago showed that A & P commanded 43% of the coffee market.
- A check of A & P brands in Chicago during 1954 showed that their private brands accounted for 74% of their tea sales, 57% of their canned beans, 38% of margarine, 35% of shortening, and 27% of packaged desserts.

If you are a national marketer of consumer goods, therefore, you must build a strong and persistent consumer demand for your product in order to maintain anything resembling control over your marketing process. You must intercept the consumer well before he goes into the market place and make certain that you have made your sale so complete that the consumer will shop, if necessary, until he finds your product. And if you have pre-empted consumer preferences of this kind sufficiently, you will find yourself in a strong position with the chains, private brand or no.

Enter Advertiser

How do you reach this advantageous position? The answer is advertising.

Because of this revolutionary change in the selling chain of command, advertising has grown enormously to fill the vacuum. It has become a powerful economic weapon, reaching directly the teeming, volatile markets of today to create new wants and to crystallize these into brand loyalties and "brand franchises." The very definition of this word "franchise"—a territory of special privilege or immunity—implies that it must be bulwarked and defended.

It may have been quite natural to think of certain types of business as being "advertising-oriented"—manufacturers of packaged goods, for example. It may have seemed less natural for manufacturers of durable goods, with strong national sales organizations exercising vigorous control or influence down through the channels of distribution to the retail outlet, to be "advertising-oriented."

But today there is *no* exclusiveness of product design, engineering, or manufacturing process that can be retained as more than a temporary advantage. We find ourselves faced normally with approximate technological equality among brands or makes, which operates as a pressure toward the sale of even automobiles or hard goods as "commodities." As the differences between products narrow, these differences must be made to appear significant and decisive in the consumer's mind—and this must be accomplished, if it is to be done at all, before the consumer is confronted with mute alternatives at the point of purchase. There is always the threat that with any evidence of indecisiveness the customer may be vulnerable to a shift to a private brand.

The marketers of the country have come to an extraordinary recognition of this new importance of advertising since the war—witness the fivefold dollar increase since 1940. And because advertising has become such a strategic force in marketing, and no less because such substantial funds are being invested in it, it has moved up to a position of relatively high priority in management considerations. In fact, capable advertising executives often move into broad management responsibilities. The presidents of General Foods Corporation, Procter & Gamble Company, Koppers Company, and American Home Products Corporation are examples of top-ranking executives who came up the advertising route.

It is extremely important that corporate management understand this force as thoroughly as it understands engineering, manufacturing, research, distribution, or cost control. Because management penetrates only the periphery of advertising in many cases, there is unfortunately a constant danger that policy decisions may be based on superficial knowledge or purely personal opinion. How many times we all have heard the opening gun, "I don't know anything about advertising but...," fired by executives who would readily realize the absurdity of saying, "I don't know anything about engineering but..."!

Although sales and advertising must work in complete and intimate partnership, management is increasingly recognizing that both are specialized functions, and that each requires specialized talents not suddenly acquired but produced by years of training, development, and experience. There is a creative technology in advertising, just as there is a steadily growing science of sales and distribution. Although both function dynamically in the profitable movement of goods and services, they involve quite different sets of skills.

For this reason, one of the interesting developments of the next few years will be the repositioning of advertising in the management structure. In my opinion, there will be a growing acceptance of the theory that the principal advertising responsibility in management should be placed at a level comparable to, but separate from, the sales responsibility, and that such an executive should be selected on the basis of proven professional competence in this specialized field.

The advertising manager must often look at advertising in quite a different way from the view of the sales manager. As an editorial in *Tide* said:

> "It is the advertising manager's job to help produce immediate sales, of course. But he has another duty, and perhaps even a bigger one. Call it whatever you wish, he is obligated to maintain and strengthen the company's brand franchise, consumer loyalty, product position, share-of-the-market. Advertising is his principal tool and it is he, more than anyone else, who should determine what

kind of tool and where and how to use it. The less interference he has in that decision, the better result you can expect from his judgment." *

This kind of responsibility, however, requires an executive of considerable stature and sensitive judgment. It demands a man who understands the importance of the creative factor in advertising and who encourages and protects creative work from the attrition of committee or echelon approval. Though the director of advertising may have very few people directly on his staff, he may be drawing on the talents of several score or even several hundred people in the agency servicing the account; and on his ability to understand and bring into effective partnership the rich creative resources of the agency depends the ultimate return on substantial corporate investments.

NEW FACES IN THE MARKET

Management must be prepared to face the problems presented by changes in the marketing process. It must also understand changes in the market itself. As markets are people, the first thing to look at, of course, is the two-dimensional growth of our economy—a growth in numbers and in per capita purchasing power—which I mentioned above.

An "Interurbanite" Market

Numbers are themselves important, of course. Granted a continuation of the present level of reproduction and longevity, there will be 30 million additional people added to our markets during the next 10 years. If this increase were dropped into our population pattern in a neat pro rata fashion, we would all be saved a lot of anxious calculation. But our population is constantly shifting. It is moving to urban areas—but at the same time leaving the core of urban sections for contiguous suburban communities. Simultane-

* *Tide,* January 2, 1954, p. 5.

ously our population is shifting geographically. The center of our population is moving steadily toward the west and south. And on top of all this, our population growth is currently far more rapid among the age brackets of under 20 and over 60—creating strange distortions in our market structure, and at the same time special opportunities.

Meanwhile, huge interurban areas are developing, such as the 600-mile city reaching from Maine to Virginia.* Actually, there are only two stretches in this 600-mile city—one of 2 miles, the other of 17 miles—which are not part of metropolitan areas. And while this 600-mile city covers less than 2% of the nation's land area, it represents 21% of its population and 24% of its retail sales. In all, 14 of these huge interurban areas have come clearly into being, occupying only 4% of the land area of the United States but housing almost half of the country's population. And in this 4% of the land area of the country more than half of the retail sales are generated.

This is an extremely important phenomenon, and one which the marketer must do his best to analyze in relation to his own forward planning. It is most likely that the 30 million population which will be added during the next 10 years will fall largely within these interurban strips. Management decisions on sales organization structure, branch plants, distribution centers, supply depots, and retail outlets will be profoundly influenced by this fact.

A Migratory Market

In addition, we have to consider the new factor of mobility. For the past six years over 30 million people have changed addresses each year, 5 million crossing state lines, and there is no reason to believe that this mobility will not continue during the years just ahead.† Your customer today may well be living 100 to 3,000 miles away next month, and a new customer may move into your com-

---

* For a discussion of interurbia from another point of view, see the chapter by Peter F. Drucker on p. 3.

† U.S. Bureau of the Census, *op. cit.,* p. 1.

munity tomorrow to take his place. With such a migratory market, the building of a national brand "image" can be a great asset—a great competitive asset, particularly against the regional or private brand. The consumer who prefers and buys Lux Soap, Scot Tissue, Shell Gasoline, or Schlitz Beer in New York will carry with him strong preferences for these brands when he moves to California and encounters for the first time such strange names as White King Soap, Zee Paper Products, Union 76 Gasoline, or Olympia Beer. Thus the advantage lies with the national brand, if it is fully exploited. And thus, also, the tendency is for local or regional brands to spread progressively into new territories until they also become national.

A Richer Market

But it is the persistent surge of millions of families upward into higher income brackets that presents the most difficult challenge to the marketer who is planning ahead. We have been witnessing a dramatic inversion of the classic pyramid of income levels. Whereas 77% of the total consumer spending units in 1950 had less than $4,000 in disposable income after federal taxes, it is estimated that by 1960, 60% will have over $4,000.

As he takes each step up the income ladder, the consumer breaks through to a new world of potential wants. New products he could not afford before now become possible—a deepfreeze, a new car or second car, a hi-fi set, or an air-conditioning unit. Quality becomes more important than price. He becomes more conscious of style and more sensitive to the nuances of selling, advertising, and packaging. His instinct is to trade up, to live a richer, more interesting life. Heaven help the manufacturer who rides against this human desire!

MARKET RESEARCH

It is not sufficient for us to determine the location, size, and character of our population at a fixed point in time. We must keep a motion-picture camera focused on people, so that we may watch not only where they are going but also what is happening to them, for, in the course of all this physical movement and economic and psychological change, people are creating new markets for products and services at a very rapid rate, and in many cases superseding old ones.

For this reason research has become an important function in modern management, and we may anticipate that during the next few years the contributions of research will be increasingly significant. To be a constructive guide to product development and the communication of selling ideas, however, research must be creatively designed, rooted in scientific discipline, strongly consumer-oriented, and sensibly interpreted.

In this accelerating economy, it is the consumer-minded producer —the producer who can continually direct his product at answering newly developing needs, or in some cases creating needs—who will enjoy the lion's share of the great potentials. Research can help him anticipate these needs. Here I should underline the word "anticipate," for only to the extent that research can be predictive rather than merely descriptive will it produce the greatest rewards.

Demanding the attention of research today are the enormous surges of development in such fields as psychology, sociology, mathematics, statistics, and economics—fields generating ideas and techniques that can be applied for profit in marketing, if we have the creative market researchers to make the adaptation. There is hardly an area of academic endeavor which cannot be mined for pure gold in marketing by the application of its tested principles within our business framework. But it must be remembered that problem solving in management is a most difficult chore, and the social sciences, attractive as they may seem on first sight, represent no panacea. We will be tempted to give research more head than harness, as the new horizons offered by the social sciences open up. There will be new fads, new substitutes offered for hard thinking, and a growing desire to "domesticate" the elusive creative instinct. These are the dangers we must recognize and meet successfully.

The more conventional research, meanwhile, can single out for us special marketing "targets of opportunity," such as:

1. The abnormally expanding teen-age markets, now handling about $9 billion in cash annually from allowances, gifts, and incomes from jobs.
2. The abnormally expanding over-60, "senior citizen" section of our population with its special dietary, recreational, and psychological needs.
3. The big field of commercial feeding—restaurants, hotels, and so forth—representing $13.2 billion in sales.
4. The multiple ownership of products such as cars and TV and radio sets.
5. The change of public attitudes toward entire industries or professions, such as banking, insurance, medicine, power, railroads, or oil.

FACING NEW CONDITIONS

I cannot help feeling that if we could only stand to one side and observe the velocity of our growth and change, we would recognize that growth itself is the most significant characteristic of our time.

Alfred North Whitehead saw this coming 25 years ago; and I can think of no better way of concluding this "look into the future of marketing" than to quote from an address he delivered at the Harvard Business School in 1932, in which he said:

> Tradition is warped by the vicious assumption that each generation will substantially live amid the conditions governing the lives of its fathers and will transmit those conditions to mould with equal force the lives of its children. We are living in the first period of human history for which this assumption is false. . . .
>
> In the past the time-span of important changes was considerably longer than that of a single human life. . . . Today this time-span is considerably shorter than that of human life, and accordingly our training must prepare individuals to face a novelty of conditions.*

* *Adventures of Ideas* (New York, The Macmillan Company, 1933) p. 99. Used with permission of the publisher.

WHY POPULATION AND INCOME CHANGES WILL BE IMPORTANT IN FUTURE STRATEGY

A. Ross Eckler, Walter E. Hoadley, Jr., and Robert H. Ryan

SIGNIFICANT CHANGES IN POPULATION AND INCOME OVER THE NEXT DECADE *

MOST OF US have become so accustomed to the projections of rapid population growth that we forget how much the prospect has changed in a short 10 years. The comments made by other authors

Note: Mr. Eckler is Deputy Director, Bureau of the Census, U.S. Department of Commerce; Mr. Hoadley is Treasurer, Armstrong Cork Company; Mr. Ryan is Vice President of Cabot, Cabot & Forbes Co. Charles A. Bliss, Professor of Business Administration, Harvard Business School, acted as moderator for the panel session on which this chapter is based.

 * By Mr. Eckler.

in this book about the dangers inherent in forecasting are, therefore, particularly appropriate. The examples cited by Mr. Strouse,* especially, bring us up short.

I believe it is safe to say that demographers are about as well united today on the projections of large population growth as they were 10 and 20 years ago on the projections of declining rates of growth followed by a slow decline in actual numbers. We have certainly learned that demographic trends can have sharp changes in direction, and that it is important, therefore, to allow for the possibility of another change in direction. The widespread knowledge of methods of limiting population is a significant factor to bear in mind as one studies population projections.

The past 10 years have been notable for many changes, but those in the field of demography have been among the most dramatic and most widely discussed. We are now in our eleventh year of high birth rates, and demographers have ceased to interpret the high levels as either a temporary phenomenon to be explained by the effects of the war or a compensation for depression losses. Sets of projections have repeatedly become obsolete because the birth rate has remained so high that the actual population has been appreciably above the highest of the series of projections. The rapid growth of population and the prospects for further substantial increases have received much attention from economists and sociologists, as well as from many business analysts. Confidence in the prospects for increased markets for most kinds of consumer goods has been an important element in the substantial expenditures of business for new plant and equipment in the past few years.

Our Projections for 1965

One of the useful functions of the Bureau of the Census is to prepare projections of the population based on combinations of several different assumptions as to future birth rates, death rates, and net immigration. We call these figures projections rather than fore-

* See the chapter entitled "A Look into the Future of Marketing," p. 40.

casts in order to emphasize the fact that they result mathematically from applying certain assumptions. They do not take into account sharp changes that might result from developments like the outbreak of war or a prolonged period of substantial unemployment.

I shall not describe the particular assumptions which we have used, but will indicate merely that the projections for 1965 range from 186 million to 193 million, increases of 12% and 17% respectively over 1955 (see *Exhibit I*). By far the most important and most uncertain element in these projections is, of course, the birth rate in the next eight years. *Exhibit II* indicates the considerable increase that took place between 1945 and 1947, after which the changes have been relatively small. Most population experts have been chastened by the abrupt change in the 1940's and would hesi-

Exhibit I. High and Low Projections for 1965 and Comparisons with 1955 for Population, Labor Force, and Households for the United States

	Number		Change, 1955 to 1965	
Item	*1955*	*1965*	*Amount*	*Per cent*
Population *				
All ages—high	165,271,000	193,346,000	28,075,000	+17.0
low		186,291,000	21,020,000	+12.7
Under 5 years—high	18,305,000	20,413,000	2,108,000	+11.5
low		16,265,000	—2,040,000	—11.1
5 to 9 years—high	17,151,000	20,252,000	3,101,000	+18.1
low		17,345,000	194,000	+1.1
10 to 14 years	13,342,000	19,152,000	5,810,000	+43.5
15 to 19 years	11,191,000	17,199,000	6,008,000	+53.7
20 to 24 years	10,775,000	13,461,000	2,686,000	+24.9
25 to 29 years	11,752,000	11,355,000	—397,000	—3.4
30 to 34 years	12,400,000	10,900,000	—1,500,000	—12.1
35 to 39 years	11,608,000	11,791,000	183,000	+1.6
40 to 44 years	11,217,000	12,327,000	1,110,000	+9.9
45 to 49 years	10,096,000	11,369,000	1,273,000	+12.6
50 to 54 years	8,815,000	10,714,000	1,899,000	+21.5
55 to 59 years	7,854,000	9,307,000	1,453,000	+18.5
60 to 64 years	6,694,000	7,735,000	1,041,000	+15.6
65 to 69 years	5,349,000	6,354,000	1,005,000	+18.8
70 to 74 years	4,067,000	4,813,000	746,000	+18.3
75 years and over	4,653,000	6,204,000	1,551,000	+33.3

Exhibit I. High and Low Projections for 1965 and Comparisons with 1955 for Population, Labor Force, and Households for the United States

	Number		Change, 1955 to 1965	
Item	1955	1965	Amount	Per cent
Labor Force *				
Both sexes—high	68,899,000	79,442,000	10,543,000	+15.3
low		77,446,000	8,547,000	+12.4
Male	48,040,000	52,536,000	4,496,000	+9.4
		53,554,000	5,514,000	+11.5
Female	20,859,000	26,906,000	6,047,000	+29.0
		23,892,000	3,030,000	+14.5
Households *				
—high	47,788,000	56,145,000	8,357,000	+17.5
low		53,345,000	5,557,000	+11.6

Source: U.S. Bureau of the Census, *Current Population Reports,* Series P-25, Nos. 123, "Revised Projections of the Population of the United States by Age and Sex: 1960 to 1975" (Washington, Government Printing Office, 1955); and 146, "Estimates of the Population of the United States by Age, Color, and Sex: July 1, 1950 to 1956" (Washington, Government Printing Office, 1956); Series P-20, No. 69, "Projections of the Number of Households and Families: 1960 to 1975" (Washington, Government Printing Office, 1956); and Series P-50, No. 69, "Projections of the Labor Force in the United States: 1955 to 1975" (Washington, Government Printing Office, 1956).

* Population and households relate to July 1. Labor force figures are annual averages. See appropriate sources for explanation of series listed.

tate to rule out the possibility of another change greatly affecting the projections. The concentration on birth rates does not imply that there is no possibility of significant changes in death rates and in the amount of net immigration. It is clear, however, that the effect of these variations is likely to be much smaller than the effect of changes in the birth rates.

Comparisons of Growth

The present rate of natural increase (i.e., excess of birth rates over death rates) in this country, although extremely large by comparison with that in the 1930's and early 1940's, is not particularly high when compared with rates of increase in the nineteenth century.

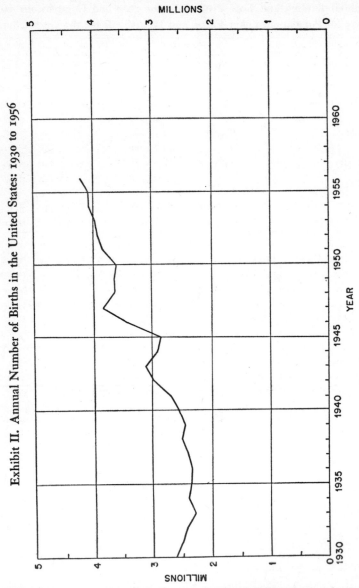

MILLIONS

Exhibit II. Annual Number of Births in the United States: 1930 to 1956

Source: Figures for 1930 to 1939 from National Office of Vital Statistics, "Births and Birth Rates in the Entire United States, 1909–1948," *Vital Statistics —Special Reports,* Vol. 33, No. 8 (September, 1950). Figures for 1940 to 1956 from reports of the National Office of Vital Statistics.

Note: Figures are adjusted for underregistration.

Precise historical comparisons with the nineteenth century are not possible since birth and death figures are not available for analysis of the components of population change in that period. It appears, however, that the present rates of natural increase are about as high as any experienced since 1900.

When we compare our current rates of population growth (including net immigration) with those of other countries for which comparable figures are available, we find that currently we are growing at a more rapid rate than most of the highly industrialized countries of the world, but at a lower rate than most of the countries commonly referred to as "underdeveloped." Our annual growth rate of about $1\frac{2}{3}\%$ in the last six years is much above the rate for most countries in Northern and Western Europe. Our rate also exceeds that for the satellite countries in Eastern Europe, except for Poland and Albania, while, on the basis of available data, it is likely that the rate of increase for the USSR is about the same as our own. In general, the rates of growth are considerably higher than ours in Central and South American countries and in a great many countries in Asia and Africa. Thus, such countries as Brazil, Ceylon, Turkey, and Egypt have growth rates of 2% or more.

Rates of Change for Individual Age Groups

It is important to bear in mind that all the population projections which have been prepared show widely varying rates of change for different age groups of the population. The dependability of the projections, however, varies greatly from one age group to another, according to whether we are projecting the expected number of births in future years, or simply projecting the survivors of a group already born.

Perhaps the easiest way to see the differences in rate of change from one age class to another is to look at *Exhibit III*. The rapid growth for the groups between 10 and 20 years old is, of course, explained by the sharp increase in birth rates that took place after 1945. The considerable variation between the high and low assumptions for births is reflected by two sets of bars presented for the groups 0 to 4 years of age and 5 to 9 years of age. It is obvious that companies concentrating on goods sold largely to particular age groups will be well advised to give careful attention to the prospective changes in the different groups.

On the one hand, there are in prospect extremely sharp increases in the younger school-age groups, which create, of course, the need for large school construction programs in most communities. On the other hand, from 1955 to 1965 there is a decline in numbers for the 25- to 34-year old group. In the older age classes moderate increases are indicated in the next decade. The effects of the higher birth rate will not be reflected in these age groups until the group born in the 1945 to 1954 period reaches these ages. In the age groups above 65, relatively large percentage increases will take place between 1955 and 1965.

Areas

When we turn to population projections for states, the complications increase, since assumptions regarding internal migration are required in addition to those for births, deaths, and net immigration. The Bureau of the Census has recently prepared four new sets of state population projections up to 1965. Reflecting assumptions that the extensive population shifts in recent years will continue, these projections show quite wide differences in rates of change over the decade.

Rapidly growing states like California and Florida show increases of one-fourth to two-fifths above the 1955 level. At the other extreme, the various projections for Oklahoma and Arkansas show a population decline as high as 10% to 15%. As examples of intermediate changes, the projections for New York are between 10% and 16% higher than the 1955 level, and those for Massachusetts from 7% to 9% higher. Clearly, if we are to judge by the record of interstate migration in past years, the population prospects vary greatly from state to state.

Exhibit III. Estimated and Projected Changes in the Population of the
United States by Age Groups: 1945 to 1955, and 1955 to 1965

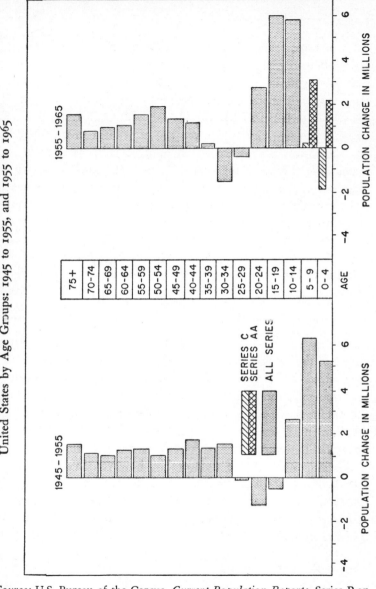

Source: U.S. Bureau of the Census, *Current Population Reports,* Series P-25,
Nos. 98, 123, and 146.

Labor Force

Labor force projections have the added complication of requiring assumptions regarding the rates at which various population groups will participate in the labor force. Most of us are familiar with the long-run tendencies for labor force participation rates to decline in the case of teen-agers and of men near retirement age. On the other hand, for many years the percentage of women in the labor force has been increasing. Recently there have been particularly sharp increases in the percentages of women 35 years and older who are members of the labor force, since high-level employment has furnished attractive opportunities to many who, under other conditions, would remain at home. Low birth rates in the 1930's and high birth rates in the postwar years have limited the supply of younger workers, making it easier for women past 35 to get jobs.

In most of the projections which we have made for 1965, the percentage of males 14 years old and over in the labor force decreases a little and the percentage of females increases, the increase for the latter being particularly sharp for those 35 years old and over. Our projections suggest that in the next decade the number of women added to the labor force will be about as great as the number of men added—roughly 5 million each. This will represent an important change in the composition of the labor force and its suitability for certain kinds of pursuits, but it does not appear likely that the distribution of work will be at all out of line with the new labor force distribution.

The situation may be unfavorable, however, in certain age-sex groups. For example, if males from 25 to 34 years old are a prime source of young executives to be trained for heavier responsibilities in later years, it is worth noting that the number in this class will decrease until about 1965.

Households and Families

Projections of the future numbers of households or families are of particular interest to builders and to others producing goods that are sold to families rather than to individuals. Such projections depend on assumptions regarding total population growth, and attention must also be given to changes in marriage rates and in the average age at first marriage. From 1955 to 1965 the range of increase in number of households, according to our projections, is from 12% to 18%, or about the same as the projected increase in the number of persons over the same period.

Income

We have seen that projections become progressively more complex as we proceed from projections of survivors among people already born to projections of births, then to the projection of the number in the labor force, and finally to marriage rates. When we undertake to make projections of income, we need to make a series of assumptions regarding the level of economic activity, the demand for goods, changes in the price level, changes in productivity, and changes in the length of the workweek, to mention some of the most obvious points.

If the problem is extended to projecting income size distributions, additional assumptions must be made about household formation, tax policy, other government programs, etc. Various people have made projections of income, and, fortunately, the differences among their assumptions are small enough that the conclusions reached, for the present purposes, are largely independent of the set of assumptions used. Obviously, no great assurance is justified in areas such as these, and none is claimed by those who prepare the projections.

I should like to mention the projections of national income made by Dr. Grover Ensley, who plans to leave his position as Staff Director of the Joint Economic Committee, and who has developed a 1965 economic model based on assumptions that are reasonably consistent with others that have been made. In this model the gross national product is projected at 37% above 1955, and personal income is projected at 40% above 1955.

For many purposes, of course, it is interesting to look at projections of the distribution of income in 1965. For this purpose some unpublished estimates prepared by Hyman Kaitz, formerly of the Office of Business Economics, Department of Commerce, are very helpful (*Exhibit IV*). These figures were prepared according to a relatively simple formula. The 1955 data were projected into the future on the general assumption that the annual rate of increase in average real income that prevailed in the postwar period would continue, although slightly dampened. On this basis, the mean income and the income limits for each interval were increased at a compounded annual rate of 1.7%. Over the decade this resulted in a 19% increase in average family personal income after taxes from about $5,000 to about $6,000 (in 1955 dollars).

Exhibit IV. Estimated Distribution of Families and Unrelated Individuals by Family Personal Income after Taxes for the United States: 1955 and 1965

(In 1955 dollars)

Family personal income after taxes *	Number (Thousands)		Per cent	
	1955	*1965*	*1955*	*1965*
Total	52,200	60,500	100.0	100.0
Under $3,000	15,764	14,278	30.2	23.6
$3,000 to $3,999	8,091	7,381	15.5	12.2
$4,000 to $4,999	8,300	8,168	15.9	13.5
$5,000 to $7,499	12,737	17,181	24.4	28.4
$7,500 to $9,999	3,967	7,623	7.6	12.6
$10,000 and over	3,341	5,869	6.4	9.7
Mean income	$ 4,950	$ 5,890	—	—

Source: Unpublished estimates prepared by Hyman Kaitz, formerly of the Office of Business Economics, Department of Commerce.

* Includes money income, as defined by the Bureau of the Census, plus non-money items such as wages in kind, the value of food and fuel produced and consumed on farms, the net imputed rental value of owner-occupied homes, and imputed interest. Moreover, the family personal income estimates, unlike the Bureau of the Census' estimates, are adjusted for consistency with the national income accounts.

It also resulted in a sharp decrease in the proportion of families and individuals with incomes under $3,000 and a marked increase in the proportion at the highest income level. Despite an expected 16% increase in the total number of families over the decade, the number in the lowest income level is expected to decrease slightly. In contrast, the number of families and individuals with incomes of $10,000 or more (in 1955 dollars) is expected nearly to double during the decade.

Summary

I am confident that market analysts as well as many business statisticians will find it desirable to study carefully these various projections of population and its components for the years ahead. The prospective large increases should contribute greatly to our nation's economic development. The marked differences in pattern from area to area and from one population component to another will require particular attention if business enterprise is to take full advantage of the opportunities that lie before it.

WHAT THE FACTS MEAN TO MANAGEMENT*

Although forecasters frequently are more successful when they predict economic developments several years into the future than when they look just a few months ahead, the pace of recent and current economic changes makes it impossible to state what the next decade will offer with any high degree of certainty. But every management is, in fact, making decisions which will influence the course of business over the next 10 years, and these decisions necessarily presuppose some explicit or implicit forecast of what lies ahead. Thus there is simply no escape from forecasting, and all of us, therefore, must try to do a better job of it. Furthermore, apologies do not step up the accuracy of our predictions or strengthen the decisions resting upon them.

In this spirit, most of the larger corporations in the country today are making their long-range plans on the assumption that there will be a substantial population increase, running somewhere between

* By Mr. Hoadley.

15% and 20%, and that the characteristics of this mass of humanity will change as indicated by Mr. Eckler in his section of this chapter.

The Future—in Figures

Specifically, they expect that there will be about 195 to 205 million inhabitants of the United States by 1967. Within this over-all population growth they anticipate pronounced shifts in age distribution; the sharpest population increases are projected among high school and college age groups and older persons, with below-average gains in the 25 to 65 age brackets. Consequently, the outlook is for rapid expansion in the so-called dependent or nonproductive groups at both ends of the age scale with relatively little gain among those comprising the most active work force.

Turning to income prospects, which are evaluated and discussed much less widely than population for the reasons mentioned by Mr. Eckler, we find that an equally lively growth is foreseen. Most economic forecasters agree that over-all income gains of 20% to 30% are in sight by 1967. In other words, total personal income is expected to increase from an annual rate of roughly $340 billion at present to about $425 or $450 billion 10 years hence. Correspondingly, average annual income per family will rise from a level in excess of $4,500 currently to a range of perhaps $5,500 to $6,000 a decade ahead. With continued inflation also widely anticipated (at a rate of at least 1% per year), real income gains will probably be more modest. Changes in income distribution are expected to reflect the broad advance in purchasing power, with most workers and families moving gradually into higher income brackets. A moderate further "bulge" of families in the middle income brackets is also probable.

Hard Climb Ahead

These population and income predictions seem fairly reasonable to me. We can start our 10-year appraisal of population and income trends, therefore, with considerable confidence in substantial *growth* and *change* ahead. To keep our perspective, however, we must recognize that population is now increasing at a rate which, if continued, will double the number of people in this country somewhere between 40 and 45 years from now. General business in dollars now doubles in slightly more than 20 years. So-called "growth companies" are commonly distinguished by their ability to double their sales every 5 to 10 years. One pretty obvious conclusion seems to emerge —if population and income advance at the rates projected here, no company is going to qualify as a "growth" business if it merely keeps pace with these general economic levels.

When we add the almost certain prospect that the increase in general economic activity over the next decade will occur as an irregular—perhaps even bumpy—advance instead of a smooth and steady climb, we have little reason to be complacent about the growth of our own individual businesses, even with important gains ahead in population. Similarly, unless income increases are at least matched by productivity improvements, many prospects for business over the next decade that seem buoyant today will be badly upset by inflation and profit deflation.

These comments may seem a bit pessimistic, especially in the face of my acceptance of some very optimistic expectations of population and income gains for the coming decade. I certainly do not mean to be gloomy, but I do want to put in a small plea that all of us be realistic as we face the future. The general outlook may be very encouraging indeed, but in my judgment growth over the next 10 years is not automatically guaranteed for any business.

Let me now look at some of the specific impacts of these two factors. To start with, the expected changes in population will be important to business managements from at least three standpoints:

1. Impact on markets.
2. Influence on public policies.
3. Internal operations.

Know Your Market

The impact of population growth on future markets has been widely discussed. Suffice it to say here that the greatest market-sales-profit opportunities lie in keeping abreast of the various age-group waves which will be plainly evident over the years ahead. The most spectacular will be those among teen-agers and young adults, on the one hand, and the older folks, on the other.

We have only scratched the surface thus far in our attempt to determine "buying chronology"—to find out more precisely at what ages major and minor decisions are made to purchase goods and services. For example:

> In the home-building industry it is important to know that large numbers of families nowadays buy a new home when their first child reaches 4 to 5 years of age—just before starting school—and add to the house or move into another when that same first child becomes a teen-ager. Furthermore, these same families are almost universally do-it-yourself fans when the man of the house is under 35–40, but tend to lose interest gradually thereafter until he reaches 55 years of age—unless he is a born hobbyist!

It will pay management real dividends to study consumer wants and markets more closely over the next decade to make sure that they have the "right" products available and are pursuing the "right" merchandising policies. In this way, the needs of the changing numbers of people in the various age brackets will be met more fully and the batting average of new products will be improved.

Public Policies

Management should not overlook the fact that the same population waves which will stimulate new market opportunities may well also bring about some far-reaching changes in political thinking affecting the social environment within which business will operate. As an illustration, some changes in legislation pertaining to business could easily result from wide-spread adoption of full voting rights for 18-year-olds.

But we can be more certain of some other developments. For example, the problems in education posed by mounting numbers of junior high, senior high, and college age students point to a further enormous increase in the prestige and power of educators over the next decade. In my judgment, the "gown" is likely to recoup much of its former status in the community which has been pre-empted by the "town" group during the past 20 years.

The aging of our population is also likely to have significant political implications. Can major continuing tax reductions for business or individuals really be in prospect when Social Security and allied health and welfare programs are likely to be progressively liberalized in the face of mounting political pressure by older voters?

These few illustrations are limited, but they do suggest some of the broadest kinds of changes in public policies which are likely to follow from the expected shift in population age distribution.

Impact on Operations

Nor can the internal operations of most businesses escape the effect of future population changes. Take one small item: the demand for summer jobs will be simply terrific. Far more important to management will be the sustained and pressing need for skilled and experienced workers. At a time when early retirement demands may be rising, businesses may be less able to lose valued older workers. Industrial relations problems promise to become more complex. Can management find new ways to strengthen its position around the bargaining table when skilled workers are so scarce and other employees want not only more benefits but more leisure too? What will be management's answer to even more "raiding" by companies desperately short of managerial skills? Will it be necessary to urge former women employees to return to work after their children are well established in school? In short, it seems fairly clear that there will be increasing numbers of people living in or near the business community, but it is nowhere near as certain that the supply of skilled and experienced workers will be adequate to meet the demand. Management incentive to mechanize plant and office operations can only grow.

Income Changes

Rising incomes generally, and more specifically the steady advances in family incomes from bracket to bracket, obviously have had a profound effect on United States markets during the postwar years. It is well recognized that a near revolution has taken place in income distribution over recent decades. Important further income gains are in sight, as noted earlier. It is unlikely, however, that the next 10 years will see quite the same favorable economic impact of relative income gains as marked the earlier postwar movement of millions of families from income-spending levels providing largely for basic necessities to much higher levels affording wide discretionary spending for modern conveniences and luxuries. This is not to imply that increased incomes will have little future effect on business. On the contrary, advancing incomes without inflation are essential to the future growth of the economy.

From a management standpoint, the most important implications of further income gains would seem to involve:

1. Acceleration of consumer and business demands for something "new" and for improved quality.
2. Relentless demands of employees for still higher wages, salaries, and fringe benefits.
3. Shifts in the availability of long-term funds to finance future expansion into the hands of pension trusts and allied institutional investors.

Shopping for Value—and Style

Research studies in recent years have revealed an important change in the attitude of many consumers toward the goods and services which they buy. No longer do shortages dominate consumer thinking; no longer does the average family feel committed to buy through distribution channels just as the manufacturer or wholesaler deems best; rather, the average buyer is becoming more selective in what and where he buys. Almost any consumer product which now looks or performs substantially as it did before World War II—or even just a few years ago—is rapidly on its way out, if indeed it has not already disappeared from the market.

Consumer emphasis is on "newness" in product selection to a degree at least as high as at any previous time, and the outlook is for this attitude to persist and strengthen. Obviously this attitude is based on an increased opportunity to be selective, thanks to higher income.

Equally important to management, however, is the noticeable tendency for higher income families to insist on recognized quality and typically branded merchandise so long as the latter continues to be competitive in style, performance, and value. But this trend does not imply any guarantee for well-known or "big" companies. In short, the odds are very strong that the projected increases in income for the next decade will mean an acceleration of obsolescence in consumer markets—with an obvious carry-back effect on manufacturer and distributor practices and policies. "Trade-up" should become an even stronger keynote in product development and merchandising. Business success will depend increasingly on better knowledge of markets and the introduction of products which have well above average prospects of high consumer acceptance.

Wages and Profits

I recall with mixed emotions that the typical wage and salary earner has received successive increases in income for at least 17 years. It is only human to want more income; it is equally human for management to wonder where the money is going to come from, especially when profits are being squeezed.

When looking forward to the next 10 years, let us not underestimate the power of sheer precedent or "momentum" in wage and salary demands. A company may well have to suffer substantial declines in profits for more than one year before it can expect reduced union demands for higher wages and benefits. Who is to say that labor costs will not become increasingly "fixed" rather than "variable," as they continue to rise over the next decade? Under these circumstances, can management afford not to study its future labor requirements with increasing care to insure that every effort is made to improve productivity?

Management faces an allied problem to the extent that "automatic" pay increases are allowed to become a substitute for "merit" raises, and "across the board" increases are permitted to undermine pay differentials between jobs of varying skills. Thus personal income gains over the next 10 years will involve rising costs at least as much as opportunities for expanding markets.

Enough Capital?

Will current "tight money" conditions persist during the next decade? This is a very debatable subject, but I personally believe that money will be a good deal tighter, though there will be plenty of variation with different times and circumstances. In any event, a great deal of money is going to be needed to keep the general economy expanding at recent rates. In all probability, more funds will be needed than can be generated from within business organizations, especially under present tax laws.

Rising incomes will provide some answers to this problem, but the crucial question of how much of the projected larger incomes will be saved and how the funds will be channeled into business still remains. All that can be said here is that continued institutionalization of savings through pension and allied funds will have a profound and growing impact on business finances. The economic and political overtones of future trust investment policies and the degree of exercise of voting power by professional institutional investors through their mounting stockholdings are not to be dismissed lightly by any management planning its strategy for the next decade. If there ever was a time when attention to longer-range financing was important, it is now. A growing economy with rising incomes will demand much more in the way of new products and services. All this cannot be achieved without adequate financing.

While the key to financial success obviously lies in profitable operations, the businessman's ability to compete for institutionalized savings will be closely allied and highly important.

Conclusion

Let me repeat my plea that we be realistic—rather than pessimistic or optimistic—about the decade ahead. Certainly, the opportunity for profitable growth will be at hand—almost everywhere—and that is all any management can really expect. Moreover, if there were no difficult problems to solve, there would be no real need for most of us. Accordingly, I'm happiest making a forecast of growth *and* problems rather than one which predicts the absence of either factor! Make no mistake, we shall have both over the next 10 years.

THE PROBLEMS BEHIND THE FACTS *

Recently I watched a cartoon which attempted to describe what life would be like for all of us 20 years from now. The presentation was replete with all the outward manifestations of heavenly luxury, including advanced models of equipment now in existence which would roll us out of bed to music, make our breakfast as we shave with electronic razors guided by printed circuits molded to the shape of our faces, and entertain us by self-selecting television plates available in every room of our circular, solar-heated house. All this would happen whether we were in the ultraviolet-lit bathroom, complete with automatic air-dryer, or in the self-operating library electronically indexed to provide the right record or the right page in the right book for the right mood.

Now I would submit that this artist's conception of how we shall live in 1977 in the United States, while most entertaining, may prove to be ill-conceived in that it completely bypasses the problem stage which must be worked through before we can achieve Utopia, U. S. A. This stage, I take it, was the subject of Martin Gainsbrugh's

* By Mr. Ryan.

concern in his mention of "the middle years." * It is this period with which I, too, am concerned.

Brave New Suburbs

We all know that the industrial and residential trends of today point toward sprawling diversification and decentralization, a motorized pattern of living, and a flight from the central city. This exodus is not limited merely to the evening hours when commuters race to suburbia, but rather is a permanent kind of flight which leaves behind a central core city that is in need of a new function and purpose.

Highways...

Part of the reason for this shift lies in the development of limited-access and high-speed highways, which have had a powerful effect on our economic complex. Take the famous Route 128 in Boston, well publicized as an excellent example of a circumferential highway, as an example:

> This road has brought with it the beneficial effects of economic growth, as manifested by modern, one-story industrial facilities located in planned industrial centers. With their setbacks, off-street parking, and landscaping, they look like schools. Presumably, all the employees drive to work in convertibles, being careful not to damage the bluegrass lawn or the boxwood hedge as they park.

...and Byways

But what is the impact of all this industrial and residential expansion on the periphery of metropolitan areas? What problems must we solve before we can reap the benefits of these great changes? Let us look at some of them:

* See the chapter entitled, "Recent Economic Changes and Their Implications," p. 16.

Familiar indeed is the plight of the growing suburban community, faced with capital expenditure programs far beyond its fiscal resources. These communities are being forced to seek some new economic balance in order to finance their local spending needs, since they are rapidly coming to require taxable resources other than residential housing. Local pressures for industrial growth, which come without the requirements for new metropolitan services, will increase, until we achieve a whole new concept of a balanced residential suburbia, replacing the traditional rural bedroom village.

Familiar also is the problem of the old city, or portion of a city, which is left behind as the new industrial and residential pattern emerges. A dying New England textile town, designed and built within the framework of nineteenth century economics, or a depleted coal-mining community of southern Illinois or Pennsylvania, or a neighborhood slum in an otherwise healthy metropolitan area —they are all the residue of change. Thus we are reaching the point where our older industrial and residential areas like Chicago, Philadelphia, or Boston need redeveloping. Redevelopment, of course, is a costly and burdensome task, but it is a necessity if we are not to leave behind abandoned facilities, neighborhoods—even communities—as monuments to a day which has passed, simply because we have been unable to find any economic use for them.

It is relatively easy to convert raw land along a new, limited-access speedway for a prepared industrial site, and then design, build, and finance industrial facilities. By the same token, it is relatively easy to create a modern shopping center, built around two new characteristics of the American way of life: the automobile and the weekly or even daily family shopping excursion. But it is relatively difficult, by comparison, to think through, and then do something about, the problem of the old congested downtown facilities which stand by and depreciate as the new pattern unfolds. The redevelopment of these older areas may mean not only fantastic expenditures of funds to clear out slums and raze dilapidated areas, but also a completely new approach to the need for, and function of, the central city. After all, most of our cities, whether ports, centers of commerce, or hubs of transportation systems, were built around a function, and if that function has changed they will fade out unless we can establish a new role for them.

Maybe that new role will be as centers of commerce, finance, arts and theaters, hospitals and medicine, education, and heavy industry, since none of the outlying communities want large manufacturing installations. But the cost of upkeep will remain—and no single redevelopment can support this new kind of city. Look at Boston, for instance. The incoming Prudential Fund of Boston, Inc., development is alleged to be worth $100 million. Following the practice of assessment in Boston, this may be figured at $70 million, or about $4 on the tax rate. That does not even scratch the surface in terms of the job to be done.

We are still struggling with the problem of rural governments in large, metropolitan areas. The physical extent of the service establishment is limited by arbitrary political boundaries, which causes tremendous waste. Many forms of local government leave much to be desired; city councils, boards of selectmen, and even town meetings begin to look pathetic and helpless in the maze of technical knowledge now necessary to exercise properly even the limited powers with which each of them is endowed.

Needed: Repairs

The question, then, is whether a free society can replace that which it has worn out with something which is new. I am suggesting that where we shall live and work in the years ahead is directly related to what we are able to do with that which we have worn out.

I see no pattern, no answer. I see no profile, except for the obvious: where we shall live and work in the time to come is in large measure going to be determined not by projections of national population, or by complacent reliance on the expanding gross national product, but by grass-roots and local solutions to local problems which deal with specific issues like transportation and congestion and slum clearance and the fiscal abilities of local communities.

QUESTIONS AND ANSWERS*

From the floor: The classical economic theory of population was the Malthusian doctrine that war, pestilence, and famine regulated the number of people on the globe. We are spending $46 billion for war preparations today, and our papers are full of the fall-out danger to man and his genes. In this kind of international climate, what factor are you putting in for the possibility of war?

Mr. Eckler: All these projections assume we will not see any remarkable or sharp change like war or major depression. Certainly if any such catastrophe occurred, projections would all be out of the window at once! Consequently, we simply have to exclude such possibilities from our thinking; they are outside the range of projection.

Mr. Hoadley: Before making any projections, whether for business or government, you have to accept certain basic assumptions. The standard assumption for any economic forecast is that there will be peace. Of course, that doesn't mean no one is thinking about the problem. The Central Intelligence Agency, for example, estimates that Russia will catch up with us at about the end of this present decade, if her present rate of economic growth continues. We may well ponder whether or not, at that time, the Russian rulers—whoever they may be—may not seize the moment to strike. But, in the area which we have been discussing, nothing holds good unless you leave out the possibility of war.

I don't mean, incidentally, that a continued cold war is not considered. For example, in our assumptions we have included a plus factor in population because there will be many young men moving in and out of service over the course of the next ten years. By the same token, heavy military spending figures in the picture. We can —and must—deal with these factors.

*Businessmen present at the panel session on which this chapter is based raised certain questions which brought about the interplay of ideas reported more or less verbatim in this section.

From the floor: But in analyzing the state of a country, as you have been doing, you cannot put fences around "pure" economics. You cannot divorce it from the political situation, the military situation, or the psychological situation.

Mr. Hoadley: True, but the severity of the alternative of war is so great that it is idle to predict it and make plans until there is something more tangible to go on. Economic forecasting always takes noneconomic factors into account. No forecast is worth listening to unless it goes into those points. But you have to stop somewhere, and this is the place, to my mind.

From the floor: What about the future of shopping centers in this pattern of decentralization?

Mr. Ryan: Since the pattern for shopping centers hasn't jelled anywhere as yet, there is certainly going to be some attrition in existing facilities. Many theories about shopping center location and design have developed, but none seem to me to be especially helpful. I can point to one horrible example, for instance, which was built equidistant between two large centers of population and confidently expected to draw from each. It drew from neither. I can point to another which, from a shopping center planner's point of view, was badly located, badly designed, badly laid out, and aimed at the wrong kind of clients. Yet this happens to be one of the most successful enterprises in the country in terms of volume and return on equity. I do think that the pattern is going to stabilize within the next five years, and we will have a clearer picture of the "dos" and "don'ts." In the meantime, we can only make some guesses— such as the need for at least two prime tenants, a good balance, and careful checks on the income distribution and classes of customers in the area to be served.

From the floor: I was in New York recently, and was quite amazed at all the building going on there. I was further amazed at the number of people who live in apartments and are—or at least appear to be—happy with their living conditions. Is it true that some people are a little disillusioned with "suburbia" and are moving back to the inner city? Would the proper kind of reconstruction of the core city attract former residents to return to it? As the children get married and leave the family might there be a tendency for people to go back into the city?

Mr. Ryan: Certainly New York is a place apart and things happen there which do not happen anywhere else! But you are quite correct. There are some people who grow a little bit tired of suburbia after their children are educated, and set up a nice downtown apartment with a week-end retreat in the country for the short week and the long week end. How permanent this pattern is I do not know, nor can I estimate what income is needed before you can afford this kind of luxury. But I can see little possibility at this point that these "returnees" will constitute an important factor.

LABOR SKILLS, EXPECTATIONS, AND ATTITUDES

James J. Healy, John S. McCauley, Elmer E. Walker, and Clarence C. Donovan

IN CONFRONTING THE PROBLEM of today's very rapidly changing economy, it is essential that we accept one premise: what we are talking about is nothing new. We have all seen a changing economy before; as a matter of fact, we have had a great deal of experience with a changing economy for 100 years or more. What *is* new is the word, *rapidly*. Suddenly, we are trying to cram into a very short space of time rapid changes in technology which heretofore would have been spread over a far longer period.

Note: Mr. Healy, who makes the introductory observations, is Associate Professor of Industrial Relations, Harvard Business School; Mr. McCauley is Director of Research, Bureau of Apprenticeship and Training, U.S. Department of Labor; Mr. Walker is Executive Vice President, International Association of Machinists, AFL–CIO; Mr. Donovan is Manager, Labor Relations Services Department, Ford Motor Company.

The topic of "labor skills, expectations, and attitudes" to which this chapter is devoted is one which itself implies an era of rapid change ahead. Further, it suggests that much of this change will be due to the efforts of labor. But I wonder if this will prove to be so.

I once heard Professor Benjamin Selekman of the Harvard Business School say that the real revolutionaries here in the United States are not the union leaders but the management representatives. They are the ones who are constantly shifting things, disrupting things, and embarking on programs of change. Professor Selekman took the position, in this analysis of the key to labor-management relations, that it was much better to classify the labor group as the conservative element, and management as the radical!

I would not mean to suggest that a changing economy is entirely a function of management ingenuity, of course. Labor has been extremely alert and most ingenious in developing patterns of change in the economy. Some years ago I heard someone ask a member of a panel, "Hasn't organized labor dreamed up about everything it can? Where else can it go?" The speaker replied with a story:

> Two wealthy dowagers were discussing their vacation plans. One volunteered the information that she and her husband had gone to South America the preceding year and had had a splendid time wandering through most of the countries in that area. The other answered, "Last year my husband and I took off almost the entire year and made a trip around the world." "Excellent," said the first. "What do you plan to do next year?" "Oh, we are going somewhere else," was the reply.

We must not forget that organized labor takes a rather pragmatic approach. No matter how successfully its leaders may seem to have reached their goal, I have faith enough in their initiative and ability to assume they will find somewhere else to go. And these efforts of theirs contribute very actively to this rapidly changing economy.

In this chapter, we are primarily concerned with the very great technological changes which we have all heard so much about.

Though the growth of automation is merely one facet of this rapidly changing economy, it will clearly bring about marked changes in the whole role of labor—its skill patterns, attitudes, and expectations.

THE DEVELOPMENT OF JOB SKILLS IN INDUSTRY *

My section of this chapter will be based on a few of the studies recently conducted by the U.S. Department of Labor's Bureau of Apprenticeship and Training concerning the implications of technological change for skilled manpower requirements and training needs. After discussing some of our findings, I will comment on some of the solutions we think may be indicated by these studies.

In the Foundry

One of our most interesting surveys was undertaken in cooperation with the American Foundrymen's Society. The industry was anxious to get a closer look at the many technological changes in their operations and to ascertain what these developments would mean to their manpower requirements. We visited 41 of the most highly mechanized foundries in the country during 1956.

The foundries were asked to estimate the numbers of workers required in various occupations in 1960. Data on plans to install new machinery and equipment were also requested. In forecasting 1960 employment in various occupations, the foundries were asked to assume that general business conditions and the international situation would not change significantly, but to take into account any changes that were planned in production techniques. Notwithstanding the fact that the production foundries were already highly mechanized, more than three-fourths of the plants indicated that they would probably install new and improved equipment between now and 1960.

The over-all average increase in production expected between 1956 and 1960 was about 37%, coupled with an increased employ-

* By Mr. McCauley.

ment of 20%. But within this general framework we found a great deal of variation from one occupation to another in the way that this impact would be registered. Electrical maintenance men were expected to increase 31% and metal pattern makers 30%. In addition, we found new occupations being introduced in some foundries. For example, metallurgical assistants and other technicians, who work very closely with the engineers, are expected to increase 35%. The number of engineers employed was expected to expand only slightly more than the estimated increase in over-all employment.

Similar studies were made in aircraft manufacturing, electric power companies, airlines, and ordnance plants. In all of these industries it appears that there will be a continuing and growing need for skilled workers.

Planned Development of Skills

What is being done in these industries to meet the needs imposed by the new technology? We found a close relationship between the preparation of comprehensive plans and the size of the establishment. I do not mean, necessarily, that small business has no grasp of these developments, but the correlation between the size of the plant and the sophistication of the planning was a direct one. Managers of small firms were often too preoccupied with day-to-day problems to give attention to their future manpower needs.

Some of the larger companies had gone so far as to conduct research studies of the key people on their payroll in an effort to discover through which channels they arrived at their present positions. Although the studies revealed a variety of routes, it was usually found that key people had come into the company at a relatively low grade and worked their way up. These who had been upgraded within the organization showed a marked tendency to stay with the company. Real stick-to-itiveness was shown by workers who felt that they had a clear and definite future with the organization. On the other hand, persons brought in from the outside at a relatively high level frequently remained with the company only a year or two. These data guided the foundries in their skill development programs.

For example:

Some of the foundries recently decided to give some of their more promising workers greater opportunities for advancement. Workers already familiar with certain foundry operations were sent to technical courses sponsored by the American Foundrymen's Society to provide instruction in the latest technological developments.

An increasing number of the companies which are becoming automated are sponsoring training programs designed to qualify their employees for higher positions.

The Training Challenge

What implications does this have for the process of selection and initial training of employees? Without going into all the ramifications, our studies indicate that a person who has a rather broad basic training and education is much better able to adjust to technological change than a person who has had only specialized training.

What about the small tool and die shops and the many other small employers who are not able to develop their own training programs? A typical owner of a small shop will say, "Oh, yes, I could train some craftsmen and upgrade my people, but what about my competitor down the street? He doesn't do any training. If I train some men he may bid them away from me in a few years." The small businessman may not be in a position to develop training, but a group that gets together, possibly in cooperation with the union representing their employees, can make real strides toward solving what is essentially a mutual problem.

Some Solutions

The Bureau of Apprenticeship and Training has field representatives, located in 150 cities, to give advice and technical help to assist labor and management in developing training programs. Over 5,000 area-wide apprenticeship programs are jointly sponsored by labor and management in the United States. For example, a community-wide apprenticeship program for machinists is being run by the

International Association of Machinists, District No. 9, and by over 180 employers in St. Louis, Missouri. Approximately 100 apprentices were in training in January 1957.

As the training challenge becomes constantly more demanding, these committees tend to administer their programs on a more formal basis. Instead of meeting about once a month and relying on volunteers to conduct the program, an increasing number are providing for a regular budget to finance the operations. Over 120 of the committees now employ full-time coordinators.

In addition, some communities are attempting to develop training in a wide range of occupations on a community-wide basis. Recently a survey of manpower needs and training requirements was conducted in Waterville, Maine, by the local Chamber of Commerce and other community organizations. Vocational classes and additional programs of training on the job were developed to meet needs revealed by the survey.

If management and labor will join in taking a closer look at the implications of technological change and then take the action which is indicated by their studies, we will be able to develop the skills that are so important not only to the peacetime economy, but also to the national defense.

FROM THE VIEWPOINT OF LABOR *

As the theme of this book indicates, our economy is undergoing vast and far-reaching changes. From all indications, the changes are going to continue for some time to come. Change always raises problems, and we can minimize the problems and capitalize on the advantages only through alertness and teamwork.

All in the Same Boat

No single segment of our society will escape the effects of the stage through which our economy is passing; therefore, no segment can afford to remain aloof from the main stream of society. For

* By Mr. Walker.

example, businessmen cannot escape the fact that the expectations and attitudes of their employees, who are union members second and employees first, will be heavily influenced—negatively or positively—by management's own approach to the new developments which are so characteristic of our age. None of us can afford the kind of social and economic isolation which is exemplified in a story I heard recently:

A gentleman who had made a great financial success of his life applied for membership in a very exclusive community organization. To his chagrin, his application was rejected. Determined to get to the bottom of the trouble, he bedeviled the committee on admissions until he was granted a hearing. The chairman of the committee was frank. He displayed the application for membership and said, "Mr. Dewing, I'll be honest with you. We were favorably impressed by your application until we came to this question which asked how much you had given to charity last year. Here in a bold hand is written, 'Nothing.' Mr. Dewing, do you actually mean that you contributed absolutely nothing to charity last year?"

Dewing's answer was forthright. "That's correct," he said. "I gave nothing to charity last year, or the year before—in fact as far back as I remember." The chairman of the committee was flabbergasted. "Mr. Dewing," he replied, "it is absolutely amazing that in times like these any person should be so callous and untouched by the problems of his fellow man."

"Perhaps it would help you if you knew my circumstances," said Dewing. "My father has been bedridden for 25 years. My mother is crippled with arthritis. I have a widowed sister—the mother of seven children—who has no means of support. And my brother—he has a family, too—has been out of work for five years. I don't give anything to them. Why should I contribute to strangers?"

The plain fact is this: no segment of society can afford to "go it alone." The rewards for success in handling the economic changes which confront us are too great. The price for failure will be too high. Science and technology have placed in our hands the potential for the greatest, most productive economy the world has ever known. If we make the right decisions, we will be able to lift mankind out of the morass of poverty and deprivation which breeds plague, pestilence, and war; we can place mankind on a new plateau of peace and plenty. If we fumble the opportunity, the initial disadvantages of change may overwhelm us and plunge us into economic chaos.

By and large, the techniques of meeting change are already available. We have perfected the basic methods of training, retraining, placement, and the means of tiding workers over periods of temporary unemployment. What we need above all is the alertness to use available methods quickly and effectively and the breadth of vision to work together in the process.

Management Cooperation

Management, by dint of its key position in our industrial economy, will have a leading role to play in meeting the challenges and solving the problems which the future will bring. Under our systems of industrial control, no labor union, however powerful, can force a reluctant management to quick action or a social consciousness. Under our system of free enterprise, no governmental decrees can produce the desired results. We can solve the problems and reap the benefits of economic change best and most surely by voluntary cooperation.

I would be less than honest if I did not express my fear that many segments of management today are spending less time and thought on the challenges of change than they are in taking advantage of what they consider an opportunity to undermine the power and position of labor as a force in economic life. Organized labor is an essential partner of modern management in economic progress, and any considerable diminution of labor's position in that partnership can do nothing but harm. It is our sincere hope that the tide of openly antilabor activity, which is in full flood today, will soon be on the ebb so that labor can resume its role in partnership in every phase of activity designed for the progress and prosperity of the nation and for the triumph of freedom throughout the world.

The specific topics of this chapter are labor skills, expectations, and attitudes. I am going to take them up in reverse order.

High Hopes of Labor

Labor's attitude toward the changes taking place in our industrial economy may best be described as hopeful anticipation. The trade union movement in the United States has never been openly averse to economic or technological change. In fact, in many ways, labor has been primarily responsible for the changes in our economy and the industrial techniques which have made this country great. In contrast to the labor movement in other sections of the world, which has been inclined to be doctrinaire and subject to the gloomy philosophies of Marx and Malthus, American labor has favored and fostered change in the hope of obtaining a greater share of a more plentiful prosperity.

Some unions, it is true, have opposed technological advance, and the penalty for their short-sightedness has been a marked decline in both membership and prestige in the over-all labor movement. But the average union has been cooperative in meeting the problems of change and quick to take advantage of it. My own union, for example, started in the railroad industry, but its alertness has made it the leading labor organization today in both the aircraft and air transportation industries. And the same factors of alertness, flexibility, and progressiveness have marked the history of most American unions. In labor, as in other walks of life, oblivion is the certain end for the stick-in-the-mud.

Labor's Demands

Our favorable attitude toward current trends is conditioned by only one factor—an insistence that immediate steps be taken to ease the burden on those who will feel it most heavily, the workers who are displaced. History, and reason, prove that increased leisure time is an immediate and certain result of improved technology. That leisure can take one of two forms:

(1) If no attention is paid to the problem, increased leisure will create areas of unemployment, which will be an immediate economic drag on society and threaten us with social upheaval.

(2) By careful foresight, this newly found free time can be evenly distributed throughout society, to the benefit of all.

In this framework, labor is willing and anxious to cooperate with management and with government in developing a well-rounded program of action designed to ease or eliminate the social and economic stresses which rapid change is bound to produce, and to make sure that the nation gains the maximum possible benefits.

Because of a forthcoming shortage of people in the employable age bracket, resulting from the low birth rates of the depression years, we expect that the transitory problems of economic and technical change will be less marked than they would be ordinarily. I do not mean to imply that we will completely escape the problems of displacement and technological unemployment. Rather, we shall have less difficulty in restoring displaced workers to profitable employment—if we are ready with the necessary programs of retraining, relocation, and re-employment. The need for action will be no less marked. But we will be striving more for the competent manning of our improved industrial machines than against the social and economic consequences of pools of unemployment. The spur of a short supply of workers will not permit us to quibble or procrastinate in doing what must be done to fit employees and potential employees to the demands of new industrial processes and techniques.

New Levels of Skill

And that brings us face to face with the crucial question of labor skills in our changing economy, a question which is on a par with the methods we use to absorb the shock of transition on workers directly affected.

There is no doubt at all, on anyone's part, that our rapidly improving technology will produce a growing emphasis on skills and will markedly alter the mix of skilled, semiskilled, and unskilled workers in the work force.

I was horrified recently to hear someone remark that few, if any, skills will be needed to tend the modern automatic machines. Maybe the control panels look simple, but I cannot imagine management entrusting the responsibility of a complex and expensive piece of equipment to a totally unskilled worker. I know full well from shop experience that the building and maintenance of such machines demand the highest order of skill, though the actual operation of automated systems may be less demanding.

So we cannot afford to drift into the requirements of the new technology. We must look as far ahead as technological foresight will permit and plan ahead on a threefold basis:

(1) We must devise methods of training which will upgrade semiskilled workers to meet the requirements of an advancing technology.

(2) We must give our present supply of journeymen constant opportunity to acquire new knowledge and new skills as they develop.

(3) We must carefully analyze new skills and new combinations of old skills and just as carefully devise methods of apprentice training to produce a new generation of craftsmen fitted to the needs of changing technology. That means alert and full cooperation by all three of the groups represented in this chapter—industry, government, and labor.

Apprenticeship Programs

Specifically, management must bring into our apprenticeship committees and councils as deep a view into the future as its research and development programs make possible. Labor's cooperation must be wholehearted in the effort to devise realistic programs of training and apprenticeship to produce the levels of skill needed by management. And the federal and state apprenticeship agencies must continue, and where necessary expand and improve, their work in promoting apprenticeship and job training. I would like to mention here that government apprenticeship agencies have an important function to perform; they are not dumping grounds for political hacks. I used to work for the Federal Bureau of Apprenticeship, and I know well the significance of the job of such agencies.

Unfortunately, being involved in such science-fiction stuff as guided missiles, artificial earth satellites, and space ships does not automatically endow management with common sense on down-to-earth problems, like the training of a skilled labor force. The aircraft industry has been notably negligent in the field of apprentice training, as revealed in a survey on "Apprenticeship and Training in the Aircraft Industry" which was released in 1956 by the Federal Bureau of Apprenticeship.

Our organization has agreements with most of the principal airframe manufacturers, and I can testify from my own firsthand knowledge that there is no bona fide training program in the airframe industry, the largest industry in the United States which calls on the force of skilled labor. Furthermore, that industry is now taking full-page advertisements, endeavoring to attract workers out of an area where they are already established in the business and community pattern, in order to evade the responsibility for training its own people.

As the dominant union in the aircraft industry, the International Association of Machinists is taking steps to rectify the situation through direct negotiations with management, as well as by cultivating a better understanding of the situation among higher federal officials.

I want to explain one point right here, so no one will misunderstand what we are seeking through Washington. We are reminding the government of the need for a training program in the guided missile program because of the lack of workers, but we do not believe this problem can be solved through any legislation enacted by Congress. We are not seeking a handout, but rather the establishment of a cooperative labor-management-government operation on a voluntary basis.

Clashes between Unions?

Management may well wonder what effect the development of new skills and the combination of old ones will have on its dealings with organized labor. Will new unions move into the picture, claiming jurisdiction over newly developed skills? Will combinations of old skills result in jurisdictional conflicts among existing groups?

It is my own view that management has little to worry about along these lines. Strict craft jurisdictions persist only in such fields as building and construction, and on the railroads, where crafts are traditional and where various unions have been long accustomed to working side by side in relative peace and harmony. In the general manufacturing field strict craft lines have, in general, fallen victim to vertical unionism. Two decades of the National Labor Relations Board have fairly well stabilized the patterns of representation. In addition, the merger of the American Federation of Labor and the Congress of Industrial Organizations has been a further stabilizing factor.

The current dispute between such organizations as the United Automobile, Aircraft & Agricultural Implement Workers of America and the United Steel Workers of America, and the building and construction trade unions does not mean that new frictions have developed within the labor movement. Rather, it means that merger brought smoldering and long-hidden frictions out into the open where they can be discussed and resolved.

Despite the croakings of the prophets of failure, the merged AFL-CIO has shown remarkable progress in a short space of time. And it is the kind of progress which will bring benefits not only to the labor movement itself, but to management and to the nation as a whole.

Specifically, it is the kind of progress which will help labor contribute more fully and more effectively to the absorption of the shocks and the reaping of the benefits of our changing economy.

With a divided and warring labor movement, management's problems in this period of change might well have been complicated by overlapping jurisdiction. A united labor movement will minimize such conflicts and bring to management's assistance the combined resources and thinking of the many individual and autonomous organizations which make up the AFL-CIO.

In summary, our attitude is one of hopeful anticipation. Our expectations are for cooperative action to reap the fullest benefits of our changing economy. And we plan to work closely with other segments of our national economy in developing the skills essential to the successful operation of our rapidly advancing industrial technology.

FROM THE VIEWPOINT OF MANAGEMENT *

It is not only proper but indeed necessary that management give serious and practical thought to its future manpower problems. In view of some of the statements that have been made about the factory of the future, perhaps I should start by saying that I expect industry in general and the automotive industry in particular to be employing production and maintenance people in very large numbers as far into the future as I can see.

The subject of "manpower" has many aspects, all important, all complex and far-reaching in their implications. In this chapter we are discussing but one facet of this entire subject—the skilled labor force. But though it may be only a part of the whole, it is in itself highly complex and extensive, and its impact on our economy is and will be considerable. My comments are designed to point up some of the major areas of interest concerning the skilled labor force:

(1) What are the influences on our skilled manpower situation?
(2) What can management do?
(3) What will be the important labor issues involved?

* By Mr. Donovan.

Power behind Manpower

Undoubtedly one of the most significant influences on manpower in the future will be our population growth. On January 1, 1957, our population reached 169.7 million people. It is expected that by 1965 the total will rise to 190 million, and by 1975 to 220 million. There is no doubt that this growth in the national population will have a significant impact on the size of our available labor force as well as on the volume of goods and services that will be demanded. This development, in turn, will again involve our manpower needs.

The second most significant factor will be the relative decrease in the size of our working population in the years ahead. While there is no question that our working population will grow along with our total population, it will grow at a very much slower rate.*

These two factors—the fast growing total population, and the relatively smaller work force—mean necessarily that fewer people will have to produce more goods and services for more people.

Manpower Needs

What do these facts mean in terms of our manpower needs, particularly our needs for skilled manpower? At the very least, there will be no labor surplus in the coming years; there may well be a shortage, particularly in the area of skilled manpower, where more time and effort will be required to educate and train personnel.

Secondly, evolving production processes and marketing methods will demand more skilled workers in all fields. The dynamic nature of United States industry is leading us inevitably into a situation in which the professional and the nonprofessional skilled technician are at a premium. For example:

> The automotive industry must offer the customer an ever-widening selection of products, and these products must be changed

* For further discussion of population growth and change, see the chapter entitled, "Why Population and Income Changes Will Be Important in Future Strategy," p. 54.

frequently. Our model change cycle requires at least some change every year and major changes every two or three years.

To fill these requirements we have to maintain a proportionately greater number of product design engineers to conduct the research our competitive position demands. We must also increase the number of manufacturing engineers, the engineers who concern themselves with how a product is to be built. Frequent changes and a wide range of products produces a high obsolescence rate for production equipment and demands constant equipment redesign and modification.

The need for greater volume and increased productivity has inspired the development of more complex multipurpose machines, and it will continue to do so. This technological trend indicates an increasing demand for skilled manpower in the future. While these new machine tools will reduce the need for operators who will physically handle the production parts, proportionately greater numbers of skilled personnel will be required to design, build, and maintain them.

According to our calculations, it is reasonable to believe that the automobile industry will sell a greater number of cars in the future. This, of course, will require a greater number of people in all classifications of manpower.

Management Action

All these factors prove that management should analyze its needs in this area and take effective action. If we recognize that the demand for skilled personnel will be increasing over the next decade and the available work force from which this group must come will be growing at a much slower pace than the entire population, we will be in a better position to evaluate the particular needs of our individual firms in the light of the over-all picture.

Each individual company will be facing a different manpower problem, and each manager who is responsible for his company's manpower requirements will have to consider his firm's product, the nature and design of that product, the methods of production and marketing, the product's market, his firm's place in that market, the make-or-buy decisions, and finally the company's financial position.

All these factors will have important influences on the firm's manpower needs. Undoubtedly, the manpower needs of one company will be materially different from those of another, and from those of the economy as a whole.

Looking into the future, therefore, each individual firm will have to assess its needs and take whatever steps are possible to make sure that they are met. More and more companies will have to provide for themselves by training their employees today for the better jobs of tomorrow, by being selective in their hiring practices, and finally by assuming their appropriate responsibility for the training and education of our youth in schools and colleges.

In the case of the individual company, three steps might be taken:

1. Consider the present skilled force.
2. Consider anticipated needs in terms of projected losses due to death, retirements, promotions, quits, and discharges.
3. Draw up a definitive plan of action for replacement through training, placement, and recruiting.

The Story at Ford

Up to this point I have been speaking rather generally. I would like now to turn specifically to the situation at the Ford Motor Company. To simplify the story, I shall restrict my comments to skilled craftsmen as distinguished from scientists, engineers, and the like.

Ford's needs for skilled manpower will differ from the needs of a company in the textile industry, for example. To a degree, they will even differ from those of our competitors in the automobile industry. As suggested previously, the need will turn on such factors as make-or-buy decisions, the design of cars, production methods, the automobile market in general, Ford's share of that market, and our expansion program.

We intend to meet our projected needs for skilled craftsmen in the future as we have in the past: through proper training of employees, selective recruiting, and sound hiring practices.

Ford has operated an apprentice training program since 1915 and has had an apprenticeship standards agreement with the UAW-CIO since 1942. Since then we have instituted 12 new trade courses for apprentices to meet developments in the various skilled trades. Currently, we are training apprentices in 24 different courses.

In addition, we have undertaken these activities:

- A management development program.
- A supervisory training program.
- Certain specific technical and professional programs, as needed.
- Special courses at a college level in administration and industrial techniques.
- A cooperative training program. We make arrangements with colleges and universities to allow selected students to alternate between college study and work experience.

In selecting professional and technical employees for our future needs, we rely heavily on our college recruiting program. We believe that we must hire at least 1% of our salaried work force each year from the colleges and universities if we are to meet our minimum needs for management.

In the field of higher education, the Ford Motor Company Fund —a separate corporation which receives its primary income from the Ford Motor Company—grants approximately 75 four-year college scholarships annually to children of Ford employees. These awards are made on a competitive basis. The scholarships are unrestricted so far as choice of institution and course of study are concerned, within the limits of proper academic standards.

Realizing the nation's need for pure research and further development of scientific manpower, the company has made additional grants from time to time to technical and scientific institutions to encourage basic research.

Thus by training, selective placement, and assistance to educational institutions, Ford is attempting to make sure that its skilled manpower needs will be met in the years ahead.

In all this planning, we would be foolish if we did not take into consideration the influence of organized labor on the economy in the years ahead.

How Labor Can Help

I believe that organized labor has a very real obligation to eliminate or avoid any and all restrictive practices which cramp the utilization and training of skilled people. The wasteful practices of featherbedding must be stopped if industry is to produce the goods and services so vital for our rapid increasing population. The union custom of imposing restrictions on the admission of new members to the trades does not jibe with the need for more skilled manpower in this country.

One of the most important aspects of management-labor relations in the future will be the strict maintenance of management's right to make work assignments to its skilled employees without being restricted by outdated and outmoded concepts of craft jurisdictions. Past experience indicates that the job content of the various skilled classifications is constantly changing. Jobs, like technological progress, cannot remain static in a progressive society, and conditions are ill-suited to the importation of traditional construction trades concepts. Changes and advances in technology in the years to come will require a greater flexibility of job assignment in the skilled fields than heretofore. If organized labor opposes this need for flexibility and is successful in its opposition, serious inefficiencies will result which our economy can ill afford. For example:

> An abundance of electrical, mechanical, and hydraulic work is involved in maintaining the highly integrated complex in-line machines used in the automotive industry today. In addition, maintenance of this equipment usually demands a knowledge of the specific machine under repair. It is essential that some of the skills for these machines be interchangeable. We believe it is necessary, for instance, that hydraulics men assist electricians when electrical work is being performed, or electricians assist machine repairmen

when mechanical repairs are being performed. A certain amount of job enlargement is necessary if industry is to maintain its plant on an efficient basis to supply the needs of our growing economy.

This problem of job assignment is one that must be solved by both management and labor. Both have the responsibility to see that our economic progress is not impeded in the very important area of the skilled trades. Organized labor must be made to realize that flexibility in the skilled trades must not be limited by age-old craft idealisms, which are as outdated in today's factories as the Model T Ford.

Just as management is in a constant state of flux and must plan ahead and adjust for changes if it is to be successful, so organized labor must accept its responsibilities and adjust to change if it is to play its important role in our industrial society in the years to come.

How well we meet the manpower needs of tomorrow, especially our skilled manpower requirements, will reflect in large measure on how management and organized labor face up to their respective responsibilities today.

QUESTIONS AND ANSWERS*

From the floor: I have heard a great deal recently about the need for apprenticeship programs in the new industries, such as electronics, nuclear fission, and so on. Is anything being done there?

Mr. McCauley: The Hughes Aircraft Company in California has been developing a very interesting apprenticeship program for electronic systems technicians which offers more classroom instruction than apprentices ordinarily get. Instead of going to classes only three or four hours a week, they have at least six hours in class and four hours in an electronics training laboratory every week.

General Electric is another company that is adjusting its training to meet the needs of the new technology. Training and experience

* Businessmen present at the panel session on which this chapter is based raised certain questions which brought about the interplay of ideas reported more or less verbatim in this section.

received by apprentices on the job are supplemented by attendance in college classes.

Mr. Walker: In some of the companies with which we have agreements, like Remington Rand, our machinists are being given additional training in such areas as the electrical field where it relates to basic machinists' repair work. I hope we will have no difficulty with management in going ahead on this kind of training program, because it clearly falls into the category of new skills. But we are disturbed about the reluctance of some firms to tackle the job jointly with us. So long as they can recruit help from other companies to do this work—I could substitute a word for "recruit" that some might not like as well—they think it is not necessary to plan along these lines.

Take the aircraft companies, for example. As I mentioned before, just so long as they can pirate skilled workers from someone else, they will continue to do so.

There are no substitutes for training. Companies can take men from one another only for so long, and then the pool dries up. What we need is an ever-growing reservoir—not simply constant reallocation of the same supply.

From the floor: Human nature plays a part in this matter of training. There is, for instance, such a thing as the "shellback" attitude. When I was a young officer in the Navy during World War II, I remember talking to one of the old shellbacks—a quartermaster, first class—about the wartime training programs that were so successful in teaching civilians how to operate those complex ships. He pointed out that this was a complete reversal of the prewar approach, when each new enlisted man was expected to acquire a skill as best he could, in the face of real opposition from the old-timers. For example, a quartermaster, first class, used to be extremely reluctant to teach a second-class quartermaster what he knew; he would not want anyone on that ship to pick up the know-how that he had. So many of the essential skills aboard ship were kept deep, dark secrets.

Then we are familiar with the kind of attitude shown by coal miners who apparently have resisted the idea of acquiring any new skill. Many of them have summed up their attitudes by saying, "Once a coal miner, always a coal miner"—they just don't want to be anything else.

Thus we are faced with the reluctance on the part of people who have these skills to allow others to learn them, on the one hand, and reluctance on the part of some people to acquire new skills, on the other.

Mr. Walker: You are absolutely correct, and I am referring now to craftsmen as I know them. There are "tricks of the trade" everywhere. I recall an experience I had back in 1926, when we were making some dies for a new type of 10-quart pail:

> We were using a special kind of steel, one with which I had never worked before. In most tool and die shops in those days the tool and die maker did his own heat treating. One union member who had never done any heat treating on this steel before went over to another, who was sitting on a stool at his bench, and asked, "Bill, what temperature do you bring this steel up to before you put it in the oil bath?" The man on the stool replied, "I will tell you. I get it as hot as it is supposed to be, and then I get it a little hotter, and then I stick it in the oil." And just about that time he wasn't sitting on the stool any more; he was sitting on the floor. Then the fellow went over to the boss about it, as he should have in the first place, and the boss graciously told him.

Facetiously, let me observe that this custom is more prevalent in a nonunion shop, and there are not very many of those today! But I do think the problem is more easily overcome where there are collective bargaining relationships. If the employees in a plant realize that their opinions and suggestions and ideas as to how to do a job best are important, a long step toward eliminating this secretiveness has been taken.

Not that this is a sure cure; we have found that a joint management-labor approach to the problem does help in finding a solution, as it will on many other undesirable practices.

Mr. Donovan: I go along on that point of view willingly. In our experience we have had very little of this sort of thing, though I do recall one small shop in the Rouge area where there was some opposition on the part of the molders and core makers when we instituted an apprentice program. But by training, persuasion, and the exercise of a lot of patience on the part of management their opposition was overcome.

Mr. Healy: A couple of observations should be made on the problem of the miners. Regardless of what one says about John L. Lewis, he has always welcomed any and all technological improvement in the mines. He does not mind if his organization drops from 350,000 to 50,000, so long as the 50,000 have a high standard of living. If that ever happens, Lewis says his organization will engage in an active campaign to get the children of the miners off to college so they can get better training and be something other than miners.

After all, if a man has been a miner for 20, 30, or 40 years, he is somewhat loath to undertake a new occupation, and that is very understandable. But training the children of miners in new skills is something else again. Probably it is best undertaken before they become adults.

Mr. McCauley: Just one comment on that: although miners have an attachment to a particular industry, they have an even stronger attachment to particular communities. There may be no employment in the mines, and no other employment opportunities in the area, but people hate to move away just the same.

From the floor: Based on figures issued by the Federal Reserve Board, labor costs have gone up 212% while productivity rose 18%. Does the panel have a comment?

Mr. Walker: I will take the first crack at that because I opened it up before the legislative committee when they investigated us on the steel case, and productivity was very much a part of the discussion in that instance.

I have always tried to avoid getting into percentages of production increase because the figures have rambled all over the field. I am not competent to say just exactly what the right figures would be, but I do believe in measuring the wage cost against over-all operating costs. I have said many times that I don't care what the arithmetic of wages is, just so long as the people in our country—all of us—continue to purchase a little more with an hour of their wages, a week of their wages, or a month of their wages this year than they were able to purchase a year ago.

Incidentally, neither my union nor I subscribe to the theory that we are justified in asking for a percentage increase in purchasing power when there is no appreciable increase in productivity. It is an entirely different story, though, when high profits have resulted from unjustified high prices. In such cases workers are entitled to a share of such profits without regard to the question of increased productivity.

Mr. Donovan: In computing the rate of productivity, it is a mistake to use a short period of time. Yet some union representatives, and maybe some representatives of management do it. They take the year 1955 productivity, say it was higher than the year 1956 and claim there was no increase in production. But if you look at a 20-year span, it averages out. Going back to about 1910, for instance, and running it up to 1956, the productivity increase would be about 2.2%.

Mr. Healy: It is quite true that many wages have outgrown the increase in production in 18 years' time. It would be interesting to examine some of the causes for this as opposed to some of the conclusions that we make, like the one that money wage increases are responsible for inflation. I don't know what the full answer to inflation is—we can suggest that money wages are a contributing factor, but we can also point to the need for holding prices up in order to enable management to make enough money to reinvest in capital improvements.

FINANCING INVESTMENT IN A LARGER ECONOMY

Roy L. Reierson and Donald B. Woodward

CREDIT REQUIREMENTS AND ECONOMIC GROWTH*

ONE OF THE MOST WIDELY ACCEPTED CONVICTIONS of our era is that of sustained economic growth. Indeed, projecting the expanding output of the American economy five or ten years ahead has been a favorite activity not only of the economists but of business managements and government officials as well.

Until fairly recently little attention had been given to the financial implications of economic progress. In the past several years, however,

Note: Mr. Reierson is Vice President and Economist, Bankers' Trust Company; Mr. Woodward is Chairman, Finance Committee, Vick Chemical Company. John Lintner, Professor of Business Administration, Harvard Business School, acted as moderator for the panel session on which this chapter is based.

* By Mr. Reierson.

the high and rising level of capital goods spending has put the question with increasing insistence: Will the volume of new savings be sufficient to finance a sustained advance in production? Finally, in the past 12 months or so, growing pressures on liquidity positions prompted really serious inquiry into the adequacy of the credit supply and the prospective availability of short-term funds.

There is, of course, no clean-cut line between short-term credit and long-term capital. Rather, both the physical assets of the business world and the financial instruments issued against them have lives of varying length, ranging from days to decades. Nor do assets and liabilities in our economy necessarily match up in maturity. Business concerns may finance long-term projects for a time with short-term borrowings, and vice versa. Commercial banks may hold medium-term securities against demand deposit liabilities, while other institutions with relatively fixed liabilities will hold sizable amounts of short-term obligations. Thus, the markets for short-term credit, for medium-term funds, and for long-term capital are rather closely interrelated.

Nevertheless, meeting short term financing requirements involves questions and decisions of the highest importance to the welfare of the economy as a whole. The volume of bank credit is subject to considerable control by Federal Reserve policy and is significantly affected by Treasury financing practices. Thus, the amount of short-term funds available to support business activity, and the terms at which they are supplied, relate closely to problems of economic policy and, consequently, to the prospects for economic growth.

Short-term Needs

Our economy has experienced a surfeit of liquidity for most of the past two decades. Large idle funds accumulated in the depression, when foreign capital sought shelter here and investment opportunities were sparse. The money supply increased further, and substantially, in World War II, when the government financed most of its deficit through an enormous expansion of bank credit. In the postwar era, however, this trend was reversed as the Federal Reserve strove to restrain the expansion of the money supply while the economy continued to advance and the commodity price level rose materially. As a result, liquidity has gradually been reduced to a point where it is no longer excessive in relation to the volume of business.

Pressures on Liquidity

The experience of the past year or more in both the capital and the credit markets has demonstrated the fallacy of the comfortable assumption that the financing requirements of a growing economy will invariably be met without stress and strain, and that borrowers can raise practically unlimited funds at easy terms.

For business began to find its liquidity position under pressure from various sources. Financing requirements for rapidly rising inventories and receivables were compounded by advances in prices. Higher payrolls added to the need for working capital, as did the upsurge in plant and equipment outlays. Corporate working capital was drained by the acceleration of tax payments. Finally, in many instances the amount of internal financing fell short of expectations as profits failed to keep pace with sales at a time when dividend payments were increased.

This deterioration in the liquidity of business made itself felt significantly through 1956, and the trend continued into 1957. Although the ratio of current assets to current liabilities eased only slightly, the ratio of liquid assets (that is, cash and government obligations) to current liabilities dropped sharply to 47½% at the end of 1956, compared with almost 54% a year earlier. It continued its descent in early 1957, hitting an estimated 45½%. Present levels can hardly be described as low by prewar standards, but the decline from the peak of 93½% reached in 1945 is indicative of the sweeping change that has come about with the passage of time. Furthermore, prospects are that business needs for working capital will continue to grow as our economy expands over the long term.

Working Capital

There is an obvious and discernible relationship between general economic conditions and the amount of short-term assets needed by business. Cash requirements for material purchases, payrolls, and other operating expenses vary with production. Inventories and receivables likewise may be expected to fluctuate with the volume of goods sold. Moreover, funds need to be accumulated regularly to cover income tax payments, which in turn depend largely on profits and thus indirectly—and within very broad margins—on the business trend.

Conditions will obviously vary from industry to industry and from company to company, but in general terms we may conclude that working capital requirements are closely affected by the volume of output and sales, by the behavior of wages, other costs, and prices, and by the level of employment. Thus, appraising the outlook for the gross working capital requirements of business in the years ahead necessitates formulating some notions about the major trends in our economy.

A secular rise in economic activity has been under way since the start of our industrial history. In recent years, the physical volume of the gross national product has increased at an average rate of about 3% annually. At present, there are no grounds for doubting that this secular rise will persist over the long term at a rate at least as high as in the past. If allowance is made for the possible effects of the many growth forces at work today, such as the greater emphasis on industrial research and new product development, the growth rate could possibly turn out to be slightly higher.

In addition, despite conspicuous price corrections for a few basic raw materials in recent months, there is no evidence that the forces promoting a rise in costs and prices have been brought under effective control. On the contrary, the record of 1954–1956 demonstrates that, even in a relatively peaceful world and in the face of balanced budgets and credit restraint, good business and full employment generate powerful inflationary pressures. For the present, therefore, we will have to assume that the long-term trend of costs, and consequently of prices, will be upward. The combination of physical growth and rising prices could well increase gross working capital requirements of corporate business at an average rate of perhaps 5% a year over the long term. At current levels, this would imply average annual additions to business inventories of some $4 billion and to cash assets and receivables of possibly $6 billion.

Over the next few years, furthermore, working capital needs will continue to be boosted by the current acceleration of corporate income tax payments. In 1949, enactment of the Mills plan led to a concentration of income tax payments in the first half of the year. Under the provisions of the 1954 Revenue Code, moreover, large corporations were required to pay 110% of their tax liabilities in each taxable year for the following 5 years in order to arrive at a partial pay-as-you-go basis. At current levels of profits, this acceleration of tax payments is siphoning about $1.5 billion annually from corporate working capital—and this drain is scheduled to continue through 1959. It is not beyond the realm of possibility—regardless of the merits of the situation—that a business version of the tax payments plan now applied to individuals might be enacted by a Congress that began to wonder why corporations should be dealt with more generously than individuals. The pressures to take such a step might be generated from several sources, including the fact that business is currently operating on only a partial pay-as-you-go basis. Furthermore, the chances are that the government will continue to have fiscal difficulties and this windfall will look very tempting.

It is true that not all the forces at work are operating uniformly toward higher requirements for short-term assets. Prior to World War II, for instance, the trend seemed to be toward a lower ratio of business inventories to sales, reflecting growing efficiencies in production and transportation. Developments in the postwar period have been too varied to determine whether or not this trend is continuing, but it is reasonable to expect that further economies in inventory keeping will be possible over the years, although perhaps moderated by the need to carry a greater variety of goods in stock to meeting a growing diversity of consumer wants and keener competition. Likewise, improvements in accounting methods from the use of modern recording and communication equipment may help cut back the required holdings of inventories and cash balances significantly over the long term. Finally, receivables today are unusually high relative to the volume of sales, and the pace of their growth may slacken over the next several years.

After taking all these considerations into account, it seems reasonable to estimate that corporate business faces an average secular increase in gross working capital requirements of some $10 billion a year. However, while a rising trend is in prospect for the long run, wide fluctuations are to be expected from year to year.

Internal Financing

Financial practices of business vary so widely that generalization is difficult and may indeed be misleading. Nonetheless, the virtue of aggregate data on the sources and uses of corporate funds is that they help us to appraise the dimensions of the problem that confronts business in financing its future working capital requirements. These statistics suggest that, by and large, business may find it increasingly difficult to finance additions to working capital out of internal funds, namely, noncash expenses—mainly depreciation— and reinvested profits. Much internal financing is being absorbed by large business outlays on plant and equipment, which have risen sharply during the past two years and show no sign of early or protracted weakness. At the same time, it seems that the increase in internal funds may not fully match the expansion in financial needs.

In recent years, depreciation charges have been enhanced materially by a government policy which permits rapid amortization for tax purposes of new facilities certified as essential for defense. This policy was adopted at the time of the Korean War, and certificates of approval have been granted to new projects aggregating more than $38 billion, of which almost $23 billion is subject to rapid amortization. As a consequence of the rapid write-offs, depreciation charges are estimated to be running about $2 billion above normal, with the result that large amounts of cash are being generated currently.

Recently, however, the approval of applications for accelerated amortization has been substantially curtailed. Consequently, despite the record level of business outlays on business plant and equipment and the more liberal depreciation provisions of the 1954 tax code, it seems reasonable to surmise that the increase in depreciation charges will slow down in the course of the next half decade. This will carry with it a corresponding increase in tax payments and a slackening in the provision of cash from internal sources.

Retained profits, the other major source of internal funds, constituted a relatively large share of corporate earnings in the early postwar period. This percentage has tended to decline in recent years because of higher dividends. Furthermore, not only has the proportion of retained earnings declined, but total corporate profits have failed to keep pace with the growth of the economy for years. Thus, reinvested earnings lag significantly behind the expansion in the dollar volume of the nation's business.

There is little to indicate that this situation will improve substantially in the near future. Taxes seem destined to remain heavy, and many industries report that their profit margins are being squeezed by the constantly rising costs of labor and materials. Higher productivity may provide intermittent relief, but the record clearly suggests persistent pressures on profits over the longer term. In addition, dividend payout ratios are still relatively low—55% in 1956—despite their rise, and corporate managements generally feel an obligation to maintain and moderately increase the level of dividend payments if earnings permit. Also, the need to raise additional funds through new stock issues may stimulate more liberal dividend policies. Consequently, reinvested profits are likely to feel the compound effect of less favorable profit margins and a more generous payout ratio.

Borrowing Requirements

The prospect that internal funds may supply a lesser share of total financing needs in the years ahead underscores the forecast of continuing large—and possibly growing—borrowing requirements by American business.

Corporate debt has expanded rapidly since the end of World War II from a total of $85 billion at the start of 1946 to $208 billion at the start of 1957 (exclusive of the banks and the insurance companies). To a large extent, this advance was the obvious corollary to the great rise in business assets, especially plant, equipment, and inventories, as well as to higher activity, prices, and costs. Also, the tax advantage of borrowing as against equity financing provides a powerful incentive to new debt issues. In addition, the postwar environment has been most favorable to new debt financing, since credit through most of the period was easy and interest rates, relative to other periods of active business, were low. Finally, the flow of funds from internal operations, supplemented by a relatively small but recently rising volume of equity issues, enabled corporations to increase their debt without jeopardizing the stability of their capital structures.

Now, however, the financial climate has become less advantageous to debt financing. With total demands for long-term financing by business, real estate, and public bodies high and rising over the years, the flow of savings has proved insufficient to meet all needs for investment funds in years of active business. Long-term interest rates have been climbing for the past 2½ years, and the trend accelerated rapidly after mid-1956. The rise has been particularly sharp for new corporate issues. On top of all these factors, call provisions have become considerably less favorable to issuers of new securities.

When signs of pressure began to develop in the capital markets in 1955 and 1956, some long-term borrowers tried to circumvent the shortage of new savings by shifting their requirements to the commercial banking system. Apparently part of the permanent working capital needs of business were met with the help of bank credit rather than out of savings, and corporate liquidity declined sharply as a result.

Unless cost and price inflation can be restrained more successfully in the future, business is almost certain to require additional large increases in permanent working capital while new savings are likely to fall short of demands for funds, at least in years of economic expansion. Should a long-term growth in demands for bank loans be augmented by persistent inflationary pressures, these requests may advance, on the average, by amounts fully as large as the approximately $6 billion annual increase in business loans in the boom years 1955 and 1956. This suggests that the availability of bank credit on the one hand, and the course of inflation on the other, will be of decisive importance to the problems of business financing.

Availability of Bank Credit

In meeting the financing requirements of our economy, the commercial banking system plays a crucial role. Not all bank loans outstanding, of course, represent the working capital needs of business, nor does business meet its residual requirements for short-term funds exclusively from the banking system. Nevertheless, it is no historical accident that the development of the industrial economy has gone almost hand in hand with the growth of commercial banking. The need of businesses and individuals to hold liquid assets would be unimaginably greater—and the drain on economic resources substantially larger—were it not for the existence of a highly developed financial system, ready and able to provide short-term funds whenever they were required for proper and sound transactions.

The contribution of bank credit to meeting the increasing short-term capital requirements of an expanding economy depends on several major considerations. One is the financial condition of the banking system itself—that is, the degree to which the size of capital funds and the distribution of bank assets encourage or discourage bank managements in their lending operations. Another relates to the supply of monetary reserves on which the expansion of bank credit, and hence of the money supply, is based. In other words, are reserves sufficient to permit credit to grow as required? Finally, but perhaps most critically, there is credit policy, which determines whether money is easy or tight and thus sets the pace at which the money supply may expand.

Banking Conditions

The business boom of the past few years, superimposed on a decade of broad and almost uninterrupted loan expansion, has materially affected the condition of the commercial banking system. Loans have become the largest single class of bank assets in the system— about 44%. Moreover, the banks have become hard pressed to maintain the reserves which they are required to hold against their deposit liabilities. As a result, loan expansion has been accompanied not only by sizable reductions in government security portfolios, especially of the shorter maturities, but also by sustained member bank borrowings from the Federal Reserve banks. In addition, the upsurge in loans in recent years has been far more rapid than the gradual growth in capital funds, so that the ratio of capital funds to risk assets, which had been declining throughout much of the postwar era, has registered a further significant drop.

Pressures of this kind are not only a symptom of but also a prerequisite to an effective policy of credit restraint, and some of these pressures can be relieved by a reversal of credit policy. The strain on reserve positions, for instance, is subject to the operations of the Federal Reserve authorities, who can provide substantial additional reserves to member banks over the years through open-market purchases of government securities, if they choose to do so. As an alternative, the Federal Reserve can reduce the amount of reserves which member banks are currently required to hold against their deposit liabilities, thus allowing each dollar of reserves to support a larger amount of deposits.

Despite cutbacks in 1953 and 1954, reserve requirements are still about two-thirds above the statutory minimum. Moreover, member banks in the United States, and especially in the larger cities, must now keep a considerably greater percentage of reserves against deposits than is either customary or required in Canada, Britain, and other important countries. Thus, further reductions in reserve requirements in the United States appear feasible over the years to meet the secular rise in credit needs without jeopardy to the health of the banking system or the soundness of the credit structure.

Other consequences of loan expansion, however, such as the increased proportion of loans in total assets and the resulting decline in capital ratios, are less readily subject to reversal by way of credit policy. Assuredly, these changes have not been such as to impair the ability of the banking system to continue making its contribution toward financing the requirements of a growing economy, and neither loan ratios nor capital ratios appear out of line in historical perspective. Some banks are still actively seeking loans. However, soaring bank loans in the past few years have made most banks, especially in the larger centers, less eager to expand their lending operations and more interested in rebuilding liquidity by adding to holdings of short- and intermediate-term government securities— a trend under way since the latter part of 1956.

Furthermore, while credit policy can readily help improve bank liquidity if the authorities find such a step appropriate, it would require substantial additions to bank capital out of retained earnings or sale of stock to bolster materially the amount of capital funds relative to the loan portfolio of the commercial banks in the aggregate. The build-up of bank capital is likely to continue, but at the fairly gradual rate of the past decade, and this adds to the likelihood that the commercial banks may be less aggressive in their lending policies for some time to come.

Gold Reserves

Ultimately, of course, the expansion of bank credit and hence of bank deposits—or, in other words, the money supply—is limited by the size of the gold reserve available to the central banking system. However, all indications are that the present gold reserve is more than adequate to support a secular rise of bank credit for many years. Under the statute in effect since 1945, the Federal Reserve banks are required to maintain a gold certificate reserve equivalent to 25% of their Federal Reserve note and deposit liabilities. At the end of May 1957, these reserves, aggregating $22 billion, provided a coverage of 47%. Therefore, at least as far as the arithmetic of the matter is concerned, the present gold reserve could support nearly a 90% increase in Federal Reserve notes and member bank reserve balances.

These calculations bolster the conclusion that existing gold reserves are adequate to provide for an expansion in member bank balances, which recently have averaged around $19 billion, by an additional $18 billion or so—more, if currency in circulation should rise more slowly than bank reserves. This expansion alone, on the basis of present reserve requirements, might serve as the base for an increase in bank deposits of about $125 billion, which would nearly double their present level. Moreover, the discretionary power of the Federal Reserve authorities to reduce reserve requirements within existing legal limits would make it possible to expand bank deposits by a further amount which might approach the $200 billion mark. Thus, present reserves and statutory provisions would seem adequate to allow for an approximate tripling of bank deposits.

These broad estimates, obviously, are presented here simply to illustrate the mathematical dimensions. Credit expansion of the size indicated, unless achieved gradually and over a long period of time, would raise a host of problems in every sector of the economy. Nevertheless, these speculations do indicate that the present reserves of the American banking system, properly managed, are adequate to meet the secular increase in bank credit and the money supply for many decades ahead. Thus, the real problem is not to cope with a shortage of reserves but rather to keep the vast expansive potential of our monetary base under proper control.

Gold reserves may fluctuate, and sound management of our banking and economic affairs is a fundamental prerequisite if reserves are to be kept from declining below the levels adequate to support the expansion of bank deposits in prospect. So far, the progress of inflation has not been a menace to our gold reserves, possibly because inflation is a world-wide phenomenon and is even more pronounced in many leading foreign countries than it is in the United States. However, the continued strength of our monetary situation should not be taken for granted. On the contrary, should the United States dollar continue to lose its purchasing power and should widespread apprehension develop over further inflation or a possible devaluation of the currency—that is, an increase in the price of gold —our monetary reserves might well become exposed to a substantial drain on the part of foreign holders of dollars seeking to withdraw their funds, and possibly also of Americans shifting balances abroad. This is but another instance of the way in which inflationary pressures, if permitted to proceed unchecked, could hinder the long-range growth of the American economy.

Credit Policy and Inflation

These considerations emphasize the strategic importance of credit policy in determining the availability of bank credit as well as in restraining the progress of inflation. Unfortunately, there is no ready touchstone to ascertain the size of the money supply that is appropriate to a given level of business activity or to the general state of the economy, especially since fluctuations in the turnover of money, which are largely beyond the control of the credit authorities, may materially increase or reduce the effective supply of funds at work. However, while the day-to-day decisions of the Federal Reserve obviously must be keyed to developments in business and finance, it is quite evident that if bank credit and the money supply are permitted to expand more rapidly over the years than can be validated by a rising physical volume of goods and services, the inflationary potentials prevalent in our economy will be greatly strengthened and will be readily translated into ever-higher prices. By the same token, naturally, too sparse an expansion of credit over the long run could hold the growth of the economy below its attainable possibilities. Thus, the credit authorities face the delicate task of facilitating an increase in the money supply fully adequate to sustain the long-run physical expansion of the economy but not so great as to countenance the acceleration of price inflation.

Credit Restraint

In the past two years of booming business, soaring loan demands, and acute inflationary pressures, the Federal Reserve has endeavored to restrain credit expansion by doling out bank reserves gingerly and reluctantly. By this action they have curbed the growth in the total amount of bank credit outstanding, and thus in the money supply.

Since there is no effective way to control the velocity, or turnover, of money, the restrictive effects of current credit policy have been moderated by a rapid advance in the rate at which cash balances are being utilized. However, it would probably be misleading to consider this rise in velocity as completely offsetting the effects of credit restraint. The very necessity to use cash resources more economically and efficiently would appear to operate as a restraint on overly ambitious expansion plans; it would tend to check, for instance, the speculative accumulation of idle inventories or the generous expenditure of liquid assets for investment in fixed capital. Moreover, pressures on the supply of cash assets clearly make for greater selectivity in lending and investing decisions. In the current environment, therefore, credit policy, probably for the first time since the depression years, has been able to make itself felt without being frustrated by the presence of excessive liquidity in the business and financial system.

Treasury Problems

While recent declines in the liquidity of business and banking thus appear to have enhanced the efficacy of credit policy, its use as a weapon against inflation now seems about to be blunted by the growing financing requirements of the United States Treasury.

In recent months, a rapid increase in the Treasury's cash requirements has made it necessary to raise unexpectedly large amounts through the commercial banking system. Underlying this sharp deterioration in the Treasury position is the persistent pressure of inflation, which has boosted the cost of government and has recently led to a material increase in expenditures. Moreover, the inroads made by inflation on business and financial liquidity, coupled with the abundance of attractive investment outlets in an inflationary environment, have contributed materially to large cash redemptions of nonmarketable savings bonds as well as of maturing marketable obligations.

At the same time, the Treasury's difficulties have been enhanced by current fiscal and debt management problems. Much of the debt is short term, requiring frequent financing. An additional large portion consists of nonmarketable savings bonds, which are redeemable on demand, and since their yields are fixed at levels substantially lower than prevail today, there is a strong inducement to redeem such holdings and to shift funds into more attractive securities. Finally, but perhaps most importantly, the Treasury budget is showing only a small surplus for the year despite peak employment and output; as a result, budget operations are not producing sufficient cash to permit large debt retirements.

Under these conditions the Treasury finds it expedient and necessary to rely heavily on the commercial banking system to provide a market for its financing, which means, in effect, offering securities of short or, at best, intermediate maturity. The Federal Reserve, in turn, has no real alternative but to supply the banks with additional reserves in support of the Treasury's operations, even though this may lead to a more rapid growth in bank credit and the money supply than the authorities deem appropriate in an economy exposed to inflationary pressures.

These problems of Treasury financing and credit policy may not be of a transitory nature. Rather, they point to a basic and chronic difficulty which may well inhibit credit policy throughout the years ahead. Experience has shown that in periods of business prosperity like the present the competition of other borrowers markedly curtails investment interest in long- or even medium-term Treasury securities, thereby effectively limiting their opportunities to extend the maturity of the debt except at serious risk to the stability of the market place. When business is slack, however, refunding the debt into long-term bonds has appeared equally impractical for fear of absorbing investment funds which might otherwise stimulate a renewed economic upturn. This suggests that only rarely will economic conditions be favorable to funding operations. The consequent prospect of a further rise in the already huge short- and medium-term government debt could well give an upward bias to the money supply for years to come.

Implications for Growth

This review of some of the major factors affecting the supply of bank credit suggests that recent trends have not diminished the ability of the credit system to grow with the economy. The country's gold stock is adequate even for a rapidly growing economy; reserves of the commercial banking system are substantially higher, relative to deposits, than in other countries and could readily support additional credit expansion as required. The strong and sustained rise of bank loans has made commercial banks more reluctant to engage in further large loan expansion and has thus facilitated the task of credit restraint. However, the banking system is neither overloaned nor undercapitalized.

Consequently, if inflationary pressures are successfully curbed, business management should have no difficulty in obtaining the bank credit needed to support the rising short-term capital requirements of an expanding economy. Loan applications for fixed capital purposes and for the acquisition of assets may be received less favorably, but the banks may be expected to continue to give high priority to loans designed to meet the legitimate working capital needs of business as well as to installment loans and, in some cases, to loans for home financing. If, however, the normal secular expansion of working capital requirements continues to be inflated by the wage-cost-price spiral, business managements may find themselves confronted with a growing squeeze on liquidity positions and, possibly, with more serious problems of financing than they have encountered so far in the postwar era. In a very real sense, therefore, continuing inflation could significantly reduce the growth prospects of the economy over the long term.

—for Business

Business in the past few years has come to learn that inflation is not the unmixed blessing superficially indicated by rising dollar figures for sales and, occasionally, for profits. Business has found its requirements for funds enhanced substantially by mounting costs of plant and equipment, larger investment in inventories, and growing receivables. While substantial additional requirements have been met by borrowings from the commercial banks, these borrowings have contributed to a general decline in business liquidity. Unless the sustained rise of costs and prices can be brought under control, the pressures on savings, on credit, and on business liquidity could well become chronic.

There is obviously no easy way to check the wage-cost-price spiral. In its own self-interest, however, business may find itself gradually compelled to become less tolerant of rising costs and prices than in recent years. This would seem to require a firmer stand against large annual wage increases, which have been running well in excess of gains in productivity in many industries. The cost of such a stand is not to be underrated; however, the assumption that rapidly rising production costs can be constantly passed on to the consumer in form of higher prices is not only likely to prove even more expensive to business over the years, but may place serious obstacles in the path of our long-run economic progress as well.

—for Credit Policy

Business probably cannot halt the inflationary spiral through its own efforts alone. In a period of economic expansion, with a shortage of savings and sustained inflationary pressures, a policy of credit restraint is essential to keep the economy on an even keel. Needless to say, such a policy is viewed critically by those borrowers, including business borrowers, who are disturbed at the higher cost and diminished availability of credit at a time when a booming economy makes expansion programs appear particularly rewarding. Frequently such criticism is echoed in political circles, as it is today, thereby further complicating the task of the Federal Reserve.

Much of the current opposition to a restrictive credit policy reflects a reluctance to face up to the financial implications of our great investment boom. These implications are not limited to the United States but are apparent throughout the world; they are reflected in an international shortage of savings in relation to the tremendous demands for investment funds. Under such conditions, rising interest rates are a natural result. Clearly, efforts to prevent interest rates from responding to the forces of demand in the capital and credit markets would require the adoption of an easy credit policy, which would open the floodgates of inflationary credit expansion in the present environment.

—for Fiscal Policy

The financing problems of the Treasury may well become a growing encumbrance on credit restraint. The problems are too huge to be dispatched rapidly, but their impact can be moderated substantially by determined efforts to build a larger budget surplus and by persistently whittling away at the short-term debt.

After some contraction in recent years, federal spending is once again taking an increasing share of the economy's output. Much of the renewed expansion in government outlays is obviously traceable to the unsettled state of world affairs, but outlays for such civilian purposes as public works, price supports, and veterans' benefits are also on the uptrend. At the same time, there are strong demands for tax relief. Achieving a budget surplus of sufficient size to be an effective instrument of countercyclical fiscal policy would thus involve some hard decisions, and the nature of the debate suggests that the decisions will reflect mainly political rather than economic considerations.

Nor is any spectacular solution in sight for the Treasury's debt problems. Clearing the way for more effective use of credit policy will require continuous efforts to extend the debt and to reduce the frequency of Treasury financings. Perhaps the most feasible approach would be to undertake small but regular offerings of long-term Treasury securities, with amounts tailored to market conditions. They could let it be known that these issues will be fairly regular. In addition, they might well work out some partial payment plan for institutional investors. A flexible but constant program of this kind, carried out modestly during a boom and pursued with greater vigor whenever business activity slackens, could be followed without curbing a business upturn. In fact, if investors were assured of a steady outlet for funds, their planning could proceed in orderly fashion with less concern over the possible vagaries of the business cycle. In all likelihood this would enhance the prospects. But I am not optimistic about the chances for such a program in the months immediately ahead.

Appraising Our Prospects

The forces affecting short-term credit conditions in our economy are not only varied but have been operating in diverse directions. During the recent rapid business expansion, those making for tighter liquidity positions have had the upper hand. Credit policy has been restrictive, the increase of the money supply has been moderate, and economic expansion and inflation have made inroads on liquidity. These pressures have undoubtedly helped to prevent a runaway boom and have contributed to a flattening out in the economic trend. The results achieved so far may thus set a precedent for policy during business booms in the future.

However, the menace posed by a persistent inflationary trend is too real to be dismissed out of hand. On the contrary, we seem to be approaching a time—if we have not already passed it—when crucial decisions regarding the future course of our economy can no longer be deferred. If we continue to accept the repeated turns of the inflationary spiral, either out of complacency or concurrence, there is every probability that inflationary pressures will gain cumulative strength. In that event, we shall have exchanged the promise of sustained economic growth in the years ahead for a highly dubious and insecure future.

MOTIVATION TO SAVE IN A GROWING ECONOMY *

The question of financing a larger economy—not to say the present one—seems especially relevant to anyone who has recently done or attempted to do any borrowing or has engaged in underwriting. The anguish accompanying attempts to float new issues or arrange mortgage or other financing has been so acute that it seems unkind to throw the salt of further discussion on so many lacerated backs. Yet, the very distress involved in financing the present level of the economy makes poignant the problem of financing an enlarged volume of activity.

People Won't Save

The lugubrious position of the new issue market recently springs essentially from the fact that this society is unwilling to save an amount equal to that which it wishes to invest in public and private capital improvement even at present incomes and interest rates. This attitude has now become chronic in the United States.

It existed during World War II and brought about an explosive expansion of the banking system to double its prewar size, as bank credit was used to pay for much of our war investment. The consequence was, of course, a sharp reduction in the purchasing power of the dollar. This same tendency has continued since the war, usually producing an expansionary use of bank credit, drafts on the

* By Mr. Woodward.

central bank to maintain a fictitious level of government security prices, and conversion of bank holdings of United States Government securities into private loans and investments.

Official Anxiety

During recent months the monetary authorities have increasingly frowned on this chronic situation, which became still more acute in 1956 and early 1957. Their frowns have even been accompanied by action which has been somewhat more vigorous than mere admonition or knuckle-rapping. Let us take a brief look at the facts which have produced this atmosphere of concern.

The investment demand is unusually high. The 1956 statistics show it to have been greater in proportion to production than in 1936 or 1929, two previous periods of high economic activity. Consumer credit outstanding, total mortgage debt, and gross private domestic investment all formed a larger per cent of gross national production in 1956 than in either of the two preceding peak years. And in all three cases, the volume of activity to be financed and consequently the bidding for funds became still more pronounced in 1957.

This high level of attempted investment arises from several causes:

⟨ For some years the country has been in the process of making up the underinvestment of the depression and the war.

⟨ Scientific discovery and technological development have been occurring at a very rapid rate because of the rise in research expenditures to an unprecedently high level.

⟨ New products, new methods, and new equipment have accelerated obsolescence and the consequent need for replacement.

⟨ Intense competition has forced managements to install new methods and new equipment.

⟨ The tax structure operates to enhance demand, or at least to reduce the customary restraint of interest cost. The corporate borrower who is apparently paying a 4% rate actually pays less than 2% because of the 52% corporate tax rate; the cost to an individual is cut by an amount depending on his income, and the reduction is very large for many.

⟨ The labor shortage stimulates demand. This shortage is produced by two factors—the low birth rate of the 1930's and the growing cost of labor imposed by the powerful labor organizations. So business management has increasingly turned to the use of labor-saving devices which both are more economical and upgrade the skills and incomes of employees.

What about savings? It is true that the figures on savings are among the least satisfactory in economics, but we can be sure that the total is below the volume of investment desired. Furthermore, there is evidence that some forms of saving are declining and perhaps even that the motivation for saving may be weakening.

This is scarcely surprising considering today's antisaving climate, which is characterized by the diminishing value of retained funds and the massive pressures to consume. Furthermore, the rewards for saving have been drastically reduced by the extremely heavy burden of taxation which has prevailed since the war. Even at low incomes, the tax authority takes 20% of current return, and on some forms of saving it imposes further penalties through premium and other taxes. The deprivation of reward is drastic for the middle- and higher-income individual who could be expected to do most of the saving. If, therefore, we have not thus far succeeded in impairing the motivation to save, an impartial observer from Mars might say that we certainly are trying hard.

Trimming Ship

So much, then, for the present situation. The demand for funds to finance investment is unusually high and the supply of saving is insufficient—we could use between $1 and $2 billion more—and the motivation for saving is under attack. What can we say about the outlook under such circumstances?

We might profitably discuss the future as one eats an artichoke —by dealing with one possibility after another.

Everyone would agree that if the volume of business activity falls off appreciably for any reason and unemployment rises to a noticeable degree, the relation of demand to supply in the investment markets would be changed sharply and promptly. The supply of saving is less subject to short-term change than is demand. Furthermore, the monetary authorities would doubtless change their position speedily. On the other hand, if we continue in an environment of labor shortage, inflation, and rapid technological development, a tight condition in the capital markets probably will continue more or less indefinitely, and at least some would-be borrowers will be disappointed.

If this combination of circumstances causes further damage to the motivation for saving, we will in time find ourselves in a very deplorable situation.

There is still another possibility. If the current acute labor shortage undergoes a significant change, we may find investment demand somewhat less intense. Finally, if the savings rate improves as present life insurance and savings bank advertising would have it do, and if this improvement is helped along by the often requested reduction in tax rates, an easier condition will prevail in the capital markets.

One can easily weave back and forth among these different possibilities. Over considerable periods of time, a strong case can be made out for each of these alternatives.

Comfort and Care

Even in face of the dangers, we can achieve some equanimity about the outlook for ever-higher living standards because the unprecedentedly beneficent economic system which this country operates has shown a remarkable and heartening persistence over a long period of extensively fluctuating conditions. As the Goldsmith study shows, the American people have saved and invested something like $12.50 out of each $100 of income through the decades.* Thus we have provided more and better tools for the production of goods

* Raymond W. Goldsmith, *A Study of Saving in the United States* (Princeton, Princeton University Press, 1953).

and services, which have made it possible to achieve an increase in productivity per worker of about 2% per annum compounded. Because of this tremendous accomplishment, we have doubled our standard of living every 35 to 40 years.

The fact that this trend has persisted for so many decades, of course, does not prove that it will continue into the future. But its long history indicates a very powerful set of cultural habits and a strong momentum. The institutions through which this system has so long operated still exist, and, thanks to the development of business education, they are better managed today than ever before.

However, if we have even a part of the wit that God gave geese, we will not blithely take it for granted that the system will continue to operate indefinitely, regardless of the amount of abuse to which we may subject it. The conditions which I have just discussed make it very urgent indeed that these massive and pervasive attacks on the motives and incentives for saving be reconsidered in the interest of our future welfare. There is some point at which the robbery of accumulated savings by inflation, the deprivation of current return from saving by taxation, and the penalizing of the savings mechanisms by imposts on its institutions can seriously curtail the extent to which people will forego the pleasures of present consumption.

The cry of "wolf!" has been raised in the past more than once without the appearance of the beast, of course. But let us remember that in the famous old story the animal did in fact eventually appear, and at a time when heedlessness had become pronounced. The result was devastating. It need not happen here, and I think we have the wisdom to prevent it from ever happening. But more of us had better join together more seriously to see that it does not!

QUESTIONS AND ANSWERS *

From the floor: How can you entice individuals to save more? Should they be urged to buy more life insurance, or might corpora-

* Businessmen present at the panel session on which this chapter is based raised certain questions which brought about the interplay of ideas reported more or less verbatim in this section.

tions be encouraged to establish more pension funds, or can business put out some new kind of obligation?

Mr. Woodward: The record suggests several things that can be done, within the general framework of a higher reward.

The most effective single move in getting individuals to save is direct solicitation, according to the results of a most intensive study, made during the war, of motives for the purchase of government bonds. People could be bombarded with literature and herded into pep meetings and exposed to big-names, without any significant effect. But, when somebody took them by the arm and said: "I want you to buy a savings bond now," the average of the purchases went up.

At the same time, new packaging of securities and new instruments have proved to be of some help. The "pay-as-you-go" plan in the stock market is an example. Under this arrangement, the customer enters into a specific program involving regular payments, and this specific commitment and practice may lead to habit formation. The mutual fund operations will prove to have an important impact, partly because of their flexibility.

But I think everything we are doing could be improved greatly. For instance, we could well make use of the kind of extensive market research that goes into the promotion of consumer goods; our information generally on the motivations for savings is inadequate.

Mr. Lintner: The insurance industry is clearly showing the great impact of a combination of solid solicitation and up-to-date packaging. With $90 billion-plus, accumulated in the life insurance companies and in personal savings, their record is an enviable one. By comparing the sales performance of the many companies that use salesmen with the showing of those who do not, coupled with a study of those firms which have adapted policies designed to meet the needs of more and more finely divided groups of savings, we can see the effectiveness of the double-barreled approach which Mr. Woodward mentioned.

From the floor: Let me carry this discussion forward one step. I am in the mutual fund business. Many of us feel that if we were allowed into a plant with a payroll deduction type of plan supported by your organization, we could increase the amount of money being invested in industry. But the fact is that we don't get much support from employers.

Look at the government bond program. It is backed up by payroll deductions for something like 80 million people. Yet I doubt if there are more than 50,000 buying mutual funds on payroll deductions.

How can we sell management on allowing us a chance to solicit in their plants?

Mr. Woodward: I am a director of a mutual fund, and I agree with all you have said. I think the answer is that the mutual funds are going to have to win by persuasion, just as the life insurance companies have done over a long period by getting group hospitalization and health insurance on a payroll deduction system.

From the floor: If inflation continues at the current level, how long will the government go on selling bonds to individuals at or near private interest rates?

Mr. Lintner: The statistics indicate that the market has been drying up for some time.

Mr. Woodward: The short answer is that the problem is already catching up with the Treasury.

From the floor: Mr. Reierson said that dividends had increased and were likely to increase even more in the future. If it is becoming increasingly difficult to raise funds in the equity market, we are going to rely increasingly on retained earnings, aren't we? Thus, dividends cannot increase.

Mr. Reierson: I don't know that it is increasingly difficult to raise cash in the equity market; actually, the reservoir is much higher than it was some years ago. The point is that business is relying more on the sale of equities than we have in past years. This policy automatically carries with it some dividend-payout implications, plus one unknown: the extent to which managements may find it necessary or expedient to be somewhat more liberal in their dividend distribution policy.

Granted that there is room for a difference of opinion, it seems clear that when you sell more equities, you have to pay out more earnings.

Mr. Woodward: But the use of stock dividends, which has become widespread, takes some of the pressure off retained earnings. Furthermore, the fact is that corporations are now distributing a far smaller proportion of their earnings than they did in the 1920's. In those days the slice was customarily two-thirds to three-quarters. The standard now is closer to one-half.

From the floor: When I raised the question, I was thinking about the development of the professional corporate manager who tends to divorce himself from the stockholders and consequently is less inclined to pay dividends and more interested in retaining earnings.

From the floor: I am disappointed by this material, and I am more pessimistic than ever. Is the future really that gloomy?

Mr. Lintner: That leads to a question of mine. This economy has grown at an impressive rate since the early 1800's. There have been cyclical swings, but even after the prolonged declines of the 1870's and 1930's we recovered to about the levels required to maintain our long-term records of growth. We have obtained the savings in various ways, either by producing more than we currently consume and transferring equivalent dollars to others to finance new investments, or by creating new funds to finance increased output and investments. Has this historical process really broken down now?

Mr. Woodward: In my section of the chapter, I pointed out that this historical process had gone on and said that we can get a good deal of equanimity out of that fact. To insure that it will continue, we must place more emphasis on savings. We can do this by selling savings, just as we do products.

From the floor: I am in the banking business, and I say that your idea is all right in theory, but it isn't practical. It is too expensive.

Mr. Woodward: I am in two businesses that do contact people— life insurance and mutual funds—and we do sell, and it is not too expensive. You fellows in the banks must simply wake up to the facts of life.

Mr. Reierson: What troubles me about Mr. Woodward's long-run portrayal and his equanimity is that I think this time we have a large new factor in the picture: inflation. We financed a husky investment boom in the 1920's, but after we got through with the price adjustment in 1921, my recollection is that the index of industrial prices was relatively stable during much of this period.

This time, however, we find the most rapid price increases in the capital goods sector. The upsurge in prices of building, construction, and machinery have been much more rapid over the past two years than the rise in the general price level. And those are the very sectors of the economy that are large users of credit.

What makes me pessimistic is my belief that our economy cannot generate enough savings to maintain a full-scale investment boom and continued inflation at the same time. Consequently, I am very much troubled by current trends, which, it seems to me, increase the political pressure for the wrong sort of decisions in the fields of fiscal, debt management, and credit policies. The wrong sort of decisions in these areas would contribute to an accentuation of inflationary pressures and to an acceleration in the rate of advance in prices well in excess of the 2% to 3% per year that is assumed by some to be the likely maximum rate of price advance, even under conditions of chronic inflationary pressure.

The problems encountered in financing a rising level of public works provide another example of the difficulties posed by a widespread investment boom and an inflationary environment. Rising costs, exemplified by recent sharp increases in the cost of road building, add to the financing problems of state and local governments at a time when they must meet the competition of other borrowers for a limited flow of savings. Also, the constant increase in the supply of tax-exempt obligations means that the value of tax exemption progressively declines as it becomes necessary to widen the list of prospective buyers for these securities to include those to whom tax exemption may have only limited value.

As a consequence, higher interest rates may have to be paid by the state and local borrowers, and this, in turn, brings forth plans to provide relief, frequently by transferring part of the cost of the facilities or the financing problem, by one means or another, to the Federal Government. Similar proposals are advanced to have the Treasury make funds available for home mortgage financing at rates below those prevailing in the market place. In both cases, of course, passing the burden to the Treasury is no solution; it only compounds the already difficult problems of the Treasury and the Federal Reserve, as pointed out earlier.

I think that the relief, if there be some relief here, is dependent on Mr. Woodward's artichoke leaves being proved correct. But, I don't see any relief, near-term. Maybe we will have a subsidence in business investment spending over the next two or three years. But, that is another subject. All I am saying is that it is not here yet.

From the floor: Is there any inherent danger in the increasing amount of consumer debt?

Mr. Reierson: I was very much concerned with the rate of increase in 1955, which, in my judgment, was closely associated with the liberalization of credit terms at that time. But I have not been so concerned at its behavior since then; it has been a much more tractable economic statistic recently.

THE LONG-TERM EXPANSION OF STRATEGIC INDUSTRIES

John G. McLean, Charles A. Anderson,
William H. Lowe, Don R. Learned, and John M. Kinard

AS A BACKGROUND for this chapter, I want to review one or two major changes which we may anticipate in our national economy during this coming decade and point out some of the general requirements which those changes are likely to impose upon the strategic industries of this country. Let me start with the population growth which has been mentioned so frequently in this book, because it is, of course, one of the most powerful of all economic pressures.

Note: Mr. McLean, who makes the introductory observations and prepared the section on the petroleum industry, is Vice President, Continental Oil Company; Mr. Anderson is Vice President, Magna Power Tool Corporation; Mr. Lowe is Treasurer, Inland Steel Company; Mr. Learned is Controller, Lincoln Division, Ford Motor Company; Mr. Kinard is Vice President, Riverside Cement Company.

During the past half-century, the United States population has been moving upwards at an annual rate of 1.4% per annum, and conservative estimates from the Bureau of Census and elsewhere indicate that we can expect at least 1.5% per annum in the decade that lies ahead. On that basis, our total population will be moving up from 168 million in 1956 to 196 million in 1966, which is a gain of about 17%.

These statistics are cold and do not mean very much until we stop to visualize what they add up to in terms of cities, houses, roads, automobiles, food, clothing, and all of the other luxuries and necessities of life.

Roughly speaking, this projection of population increase means that each year we shall be building and establishing the means to supply one city the size of the whole of the metropolitan Boston area. During the 10-year period as a whole we must look toward the constructing and maintaining of a string of cities roughly equivalent to New York, Chicago, Los Angeles, and San Francisco.

Along with the over-all growth in population will come some fundamental changes in its composition, including a reduction in the proportion of the people in the 20 to 64 age group from which the major portion of our labor force is drawn.*

Another major economic condition that I would like to mention is the increasing pressure from all population groups for a higher standard of living.

This pressure, of course, has long been one of the outstanding characteristics of the American people. It has distinguished us from other countries over the past century. Our real per capita gross national product increased about 1.8% per annum from 1929 through 1956; since 1947 the rate has been about 2.2% per annum. In terms of 1956 dollars, our gross national product per capita has grown from about $2,000 in 1947 to $2,450 in 1956. The gain in over-all output of goods and services per capita has thus been about $50 a year. While part of this increase has gone into large investment and

---

* For a more detailed discussion, see the Section of Chapter II by Mr. Eckler, entitled, "Significant Changes in Population and Income Over the Next Decade," p. 54.

defense expenditures, most of it has been available for consumers.

From a political and economic standpoint, we have every reason to suppose that the people of this country will insist on increases in their standard of living during the next decade that are at least comparable to, if not greater than, the $50 a year they have secured during the past 10 years. If we are to have political stability, therefore, it would be highly desirable for our economy to produce sufficient goods and services to yield a real increase in gross national product per capita of about 2% per annum. By 1966, then, our gross national product per capita should be about $3,000 per annum (1956 prices).

Putting these figures together, we get a picture of the task that lies ahead for the strategic industries with which we are concerned in this chapter. If we do nothing more than keep pace with the growth in population, our gross national product will have to move up from $412 billion in 1956 to $480 billion by 1966, an increase of 17%. If we are to provide for the very modest increase in real income per capita to which we have been accustomed, we will have to have a gross national product of $588 billion— a 43% increase.

At the time we are attempting to perform this feat, the 20 to 64 age group, which provides most of our labor force, is going to represent a declining portion of the over-all population, growing only about 9%—from 92 million to 100 million people.

The extent to which we are successful in closing the gap between an estimated 40% to 50% increase in our total requirements for goods and services and a 9% increase in the most productive segment of our population rests in large measure on those strategic industries, accounting for roughly one-third of our national output, that are represented by the authors of this chapter.

TOMORROW'S CONSUMER APPLIANCES*

As Mr. McLean indicated in his introduction, the basic elements of strength underlying the consumer appliance industry are a de-

* By Mr. Anderson.

mand for a higher standard of living with commensurate resources to buy and a steadily growing number of consumers. Consumer appliances—large and better refrigerators, television, hi-fi, home freezers, power lawn mowers, power tools—are clearly important items in our increasing national standard of living.

Indeed, an important characteristic of our domestic economy during the past 10 years has been the increasing rate at which these appliances have become commonplace in our homes. I know a Boy Scout troop that recently was given an icebox for their camp. The boys were greatly intrigued with the strange-looking box, for it seemed that most of them had never seen or heard of an "icebox." And perhaps you have heard of the boy who explained to his young brother that radio was TV without a picture! A little reflection on these examples will indicate the tremendous rate at which new consumer appliances are being assimilated by our economy.

Nevertheless, during recent months, many major appliance manufacturers have announced significant reductions in their production schedules. In the face of a strong basic demand for consumer appliances, how do we explain these examples of market weakness and consequent production dislocation, and what are the implications of this apparent contradiction?

New Products or New Features?

Actually, there really is no such thing as a single consumer appliance industry. Rather, there is a series of industries embracing hundreds of product lines. At any given time, the demand for some of these products will be increasing, for others it will have leveled off, while for still others, it will be declining. Therefore, making generalizations about the consumer appliance "industry" can be exceedingly dangerous.

Within this framework, we can expect increasing emphasis on the new appliance because of our great and seemingly increasing capacity to produce and assimilate consumer durable equipment. The product that performs a new function or very dramatically improves an older unit can show rapid or even "explosive" growth. And, perhaps because of this rapid initial growth, demand may level off at a relatively early point in time.

For example, look at television, the clothes dryer, and power lawn mowers. Each started as an innovation and has become a commonplace in a phenomenally short time. However, once we as consumers own these appliances, we seem relatively content with them and look for other new ones on which to spend our money or make down payments. In spite of vigorous efforts, appliance manufacturers have not generally succeeded in making their products obsolete with yearly model changes. "Face lifting" does not do the same trick for refrigerators that it does for automobiles. The "sheer look," revolving trays, automatic ice cube dispensers, and other ingenious devices have not helped the home refrigerator manufacturers to increase their growth substantially.

Thus outstanding growth will come more and more from the new or dramatically improved products. Here is where we will focus more of our attention, for this is where the most significant profit opportunities lie. I suspect, unlike many industries, the small, fast-moving, creative company that can conceive and develop a line of new products will be an important factor in the appliance industry.

Luxury Market

What is the character of this market? It is basically a luxury market; we are catering to wants rather than needs. These "wants" are subtle, if not ephemeral, in nature. Prestige, pleasure, and comfort or the desire to indulge in creative or cultural pursuits become the significant buying motives. The logics of performance, service, and economy may be less important to the success of a new product than the pleasure or prestige the owner derives from it.

Dealing with these subtle buying motives and producing new or dramatically improved products to take advantage of the "luxury" market constitutes our principal challenge for the next decade. We will have to improve our ability to evaluate these motives, and we will have to be more creative in our product development. There will be an increasing premium on successful decision making in the selection of products, the choice of promotable features, and the determination of how and when and on what scale to undertake production. We will need to sharpen our abilities in these important fields, for they will be the important profit-setting decisions.

Marketing Channels

Another major management challenge will be the development of specialized distribution channels for many appliances. New devices are almost certain to become increasingly complex, and many will require specialized skill in demonstration, personal salesmanship, installation, and service. To give an example, more home appliances are now designed to be "built-in." Indeed, this is probably one of those dramatic developments which can produce rapid growth. Merchandising these items demands the traditional salesmanship, but it also requires adequate installation service. Unfortunately, conventional appliance merchants are not usually equipped to handle installation, while, on the other hand, organizations specializing in installation services are notably deficient in appliance merchandising. Full development of the built-in appliance industry, then, may well require the evolution of specialized distribution combining both merchandising and installation facilities. This same need for specialized distribution facilities will probably be repeated for many lines.

If we expect to develop such specialized distribution, we manufacturers will have to be more attentive to the profit opportunities extended to our distributors and dealers. We will have to allow for the important cost element in our price and discount structures and, where it is warranted, we should provide some protection for the dealer's profit. We should not expect specialized dealers or distributors to develop overnight to meet our market requirements. We will have to give more thoughtful attention than we have in the past to providing and respecting profit opportunities for them.

The next 10 years, then, afford unusual opportunities for us. We have a vast market of a "luxury" character. To take advantage of it, we will have to venture into new products on a very broad scale.

"Face lifting" efforts alone on today's products will not sustain satisfactory growth. This means more emphasis than ever before on creative efforts—in market studies, product development and distribution facilities. The stakes are high, and the organization that develops and refines its abilities in these fields can realize unusual profits.

LOOKING AHEAD AT STEEL*

What are the prospects for growth over the next decade in the steel industry? In order to arrive at an answer, I want to provide a perspective and set a basis for looking ahead.

Increased Consumer Demand

Let me start with the historical growth of the industry. In the year 1900, steel production amounted to about 11.5 million tons; by 1929, that figure had grown to 63 million tons; by 1940—at the beginning of the war—to 67 million; by 1950, to 97 million; and in the current period is in the range of 115 to 117 million tons a year.

Even in raw figures this growth is fabulous, but in relation to the population increase it becomes almost miraculous. In 1900 we used about 400 pounds of steel per person; by 1956, that consumption was up to approximately 1,400 pounds. This astounding increase reflects the wider use of steel and the steady expansion of the nation's living standards. We have used more steel in consumers' goods, like containers and cans, and in consumer durables, including appliances and other major items.

In 1924, approximately 85% of the steel output went into the capital goods industries, and 15% into consumer goods. By 1956, the proportion was approximately half and half.

Continued Rise

What about the demands over the next decade? I would estimate that with a population of 196 million people we will need about 135
* By Mr. Lowe.

to 150 million tons, or an increase of 13%. If you are really optimistic and believe that the standard of living will continue to rise in the future, you can move the per capita estimate to 1,550 pounds, or 165 million tons.

If you really want to be bullish, you can assume a faster rate of growth in the automobile industry and the steel industry—say there will be three cars per family and appliances are going to increase. Those who look ahead to such a society prophesy that steel consumption will be 2,000 pounds, or one ton, per capita, in the not too far distant future. If they are right, we will require a steel capacity of 215 million tons or an increase of 62%.

But whatever the figure turns out to be, we certainly can expect a substantial increase in the rate of steel consumption during the coming decade. The postdepression baby crop is now beginning to reach a marriageable age, causing a rise in the rate of family formation. That statistic is as significant to steel as it is to many other industries because new families mean new houses, and these homes are increasingly going up in the suburbs, where cars and appliances are a necessity. On top of this growth, we can expect another bulge when the postwar youngsters start to marry and have children.

Raw Materials Sources

With these increased steel requirements in the offing, what is the raw material situation going to be? Over the next 10 years, we will see a continuation of two recent developments: foreign explorations and mining projects, like those in Canada and South America, to provide iron for the industry, and the benefication of low-grade domestic iron ores. Despite recently expressed concern over depletion of our high-grade ores, the low-grade reserves which we can now use appear adequate for the foreseeable future.

Problems Foreseen

Steel will expand over the next decade, but that growth will not be problem-free. In the first place, the construction of new facilities is extremely expensive. According to our estimations, the cost of providing an additional ton of integrated steel capacity is in the neighborhood of $350. Based on the 1956 figures for the steel industry, the value on the company's books for the present capacity is a little less than $100. The 1955 earnings for the industry, which are the latest available and which cover the earnings of 94% of the steel producers, averaged $9.40 per ton of capacity. This means a return on investment of 3.7%, at today's costs, which obviously does not compare well even with the current rates on government bonds. Therefore, the steel industry has real trouble showing the investing public why they should make this particular use of their funds.

The second problem is the growing labor shortage mentioned by Mr. McLean and other authors in this book. If we are to continue the desired rise in living standards, we must undertake more mechanization. So I would predict that there must be certain significant technological changes introduced into the steel industry over the next 10 years. There will be production process improvements as well as product improvements, and, of course, the mechanization of clerical functions that all of us are studying so closely today.

All of these steps will be aimed at increasing the output per man-hour, reducing the investment, and, we hope, significantly cutting costs. Coupled with these programs will come product improvements and a search for additional markets for steel.

The kind of process improvement that I am suggesting will include the use of continuous casting and an increasing use of oxygen converters. In addition, the industry is trying to master the direct reduction of iron ores, and I look for very significant developments in this field during the next decade. Finally, we are turning to more automatic, faster rolling equipment. These innovations will not come overnight, but I feel sure that they are on their way.

Impact on Industry Patterns

What is the implication of these changes for the organization structure and management of the industry? The trend is to larger companies because of the heavier investment required, and this tendency will continue over the next 10 years. It is already impossible for a new steel company to start in the business today because of the high cost of investment required. I do not foresee any significant change in the next decade in the methods of financing our needs in the raw material field. A group of companies will associate together in order to share the cost, which no one company alone can afford. I do not expect any breakup of the traditional corporate organizational pattern, although ultimately the expected developments in the direct reduction of ores at the mine by gas piped in from the coal field may force some changes.

Thus, I look for continued growth and constant technological innovation in the steel industry. I am distinctly bullish about the prospects.

THE AUTOMOBILE INDUSTRY: 1958–1966*

Assuming no major change in world conditions, the continued economic growth of the United States as projected by Mr. McLean seems assured. In the next decade, a repetition of the 40% growth in gross national product that has been achieved in the past 10 years is a realistic objective. As in the past, this growth rate will not be at a constant rate, and there will be occasional interruptions to forward progress. The projected growth in total output and the 17% increase in population in the next decade are obvious stimulants to demand for both consumer and industrial products.

More Car Owners

Certain factors within the broad economic projection are of particular importance to the automotive industry, and consumer durable products in general. As a result of projected population growth and age distribution, it is reasonable to expect the number of spending units to approximate 64 million by 1966, 9 million

* By Mr. Learned.

higher than the 1956 level. The projected increase in gross national product should yield an increase of approximately 22% in the income of these spending units.

The proportion of the increased number of spending units that will fall in the $5,000-and-over income group will have a substantial impact on automobile demand, for car ownership rates increase significantly as income rises. In the $5,000-and-over income group, about 91% have at least one car and 17% have more than one. On the other hand, for those income units under $5,000, the ratios are only 58% and 4%.

With the projected increase in the number of consumer spending units and the higher income per unit, spending units with incomes of $5,000 and over should increase from the 1956 level of 20 million to nearly 31 million by 1966, if the present pattern of income distribution remains in effect. From these statistics we can easily see the underlying factors indicating continued growth in the car market, not only for the one-car family but also for the two-car family. Underscoring this growth is the expected continuation of the present trend toward suburban living and a relative decline in public transportation, both of which increase the requirement for car ownership.

Replacement Market

In addition to the growth element in automotive demand, a total projection of car needs for the next decade must deal with the probable size of the replacement market. The passenger car scrappage rate is one of the more important measurable trends. It is primarily a function of used car prices and the cost of repair versus new car prices. In the postwar period, scrappage rates were held down below prewar levels because high used car prices and a shortage of new cars made costly repairs to older cars necessary and desirable. Scrappage rates rose as used car prices returned to normal, and today scrappage rates are approximating prewar experience. In 1955, 4 million units were scrapped, and in 1956, it is estimated that scrappage was somewhat higher, with the over-all average scrappage rate approximating 8%. It is expected that the current scrappage rates will continue in the next decade.

Taking into account the underlying economic forecasts and scrappage rates, the automotive industry should be able to sell, on an average annual basis, from the current rate of 6 million units to a rate of 8 million units by the end of the next decade. Of course, in a dynamic economy such as ours, there cannot be a wholly smooth flow of demand, and we do not anticipate that sales in any specific year will be right on the average.

Attainment of the 6 to 8 million average annual production during the next decade should place total car population at approximately 70 million by 1966. This is an increase of 19 million over the 1956 car population and represents an average annual growth rate during the decade of approximately 3%. This growth rate compares with a rate of 6% during the 1949–1956 period, which was, of course, somewhat abnormal due to the pent-up demand created by the shortage of the war period.

Truck demand for the next decade is projected from 1.1 million currently to nearly 1.4 million by 1966. Attainment of this projection would produce a truck population of 14 million in 1966. The growth rate implicit in this projection is approximately 3% per year, the same as in the years from 1949–1956.

Labor Short

I would now like to turn to a brief consideration of some of the major developments and problems that the automobile industry faces in the next decade. The first of these is the projected disparity between the growth of the work force, 9% for ages 20–64, and the 40% increase in gross national product, as mentioned by Mr. McLean. One source of potential relief is increased participation in employment by the 20–64 age group. While this may partially offset the indicated shortage, most of these people will be women entering service industries. The principal means of overcoming the forecast labor shortage for our industry will be by increased productivity per worker through further mechanization and automation. This action in itself creates additional problems. It increases the need for highly skilled workers, already in short supply, and points to the necessity of intensive employee training to raise the general level of skills in the labor force.

Automation

Automation, while highly developed for certain manufacturing areas, is not yet a panacea, as some would wish us to believe. The labor saved by automation has been used elsewhere in building our cars of today. It has helped us to do more things better. In the future, it must continue to give us a better mass-produced article, it must continue to reduce man's physical effort in accomplishing a given task, and it must also free labor for the enlarged requirements of the economy.

Automation in the office is yet in its infancy. Many of the skills necessary to apply our presently available electronic devices to business problems are hardly taught in our schools and universities at all. In addition, we in industry have much to learn. Certainly, automation in the office offers one way of meeting the indicated labor shortage of the next decade. Before leaving the problem of increased output, it is perhaps worthwhile to note that the labor-consumers' share of increased output may, by their choice, take the form of reduced output and increased leisure time rather than spendable income.

Better Design

In the highly competitive product race, the automotive industry has improved the efficiency, safety, power, and styling of its cars many times, and yet, the average consumer today works only 27 weeks for a low-priced "dream car" as compared with 31 weeks back in 1941 or even 1949. For the future, the scientist, engineer, and stylist have promised us better suspension systems, safer and more comfortable seating, and the car may be lower or perhaps give the appearance of being lower, while providing improved entry and exit facilities. New products from the metal, glass, textile, and petroleum-chemical industries may well revolutionize styling and manufacturing techniques in the coming decade. Engines of the reciprocating type will be developed further to give more power per pound of weight and greater economy. And these engines may, in time, be replaced by the gas turbine and free piston engine.

Investment

Styling, engineering, tooling, producing, and distributing the car of today is an extremely costly process. The industry begins these activities three years before the first unit is sold, and the cost for a single car line can range from $25 million to over $200 million. Failure by any one company to judge correctly the consumer acceptance of its product obviously proves very costly. Furthermore, this risk is taken annually in order to produce a fresh line of products to satisfy consumer demand.

Because of the tremendous investment required in developing and manufacturing automobiles, there does not appear to be any reasonable basis to project a change in the present industry pattern of a limited number of large firms. The relatively smaller firms can exist profitably as long as they serve the specialized and relatively small markets. As long as the small car market continues to remain limited, we can expect some rise in the importation of foreign cars.

Sales Techniques

Another significant task for the automobile industry in the next decade will be the continuing modification of its distribution methods to conform with the requirements of the mass market. The independent dealer system has been successful to date in adapting to the changing requirements of the growing market. Nonetheless, there has been some discussion of a shift to a supermarket type of distribution similar to that in the home appliance industry. This is typified by the large multibrand retailer and so-called discount houses.

While such a major shift in distribution methods can never be wholly ruled out, it is pertinent to note that an independent automobile dealer requires a relatively heavy investment in service facilities and needs an inventory of some 6,000 to 10,000 parts to service a single line of cars.

Such a sizable investment, along with a reasonable inventory of new model cars ranging in cost from $1,500 to $6,000 each, would tend to discourage any move to a supermarket type of distribution. In addition, there is no indication to date that a change in the basic method of automotive distribution would better serve the needs of the growing market.

Perhaps the most pressing problem of industry, including the automobile industry, is management itself. Securing and developing a sufficient number of personnel of management caliber who are willing to assume the responsibilities of management is our greatest challenge for the future.

I should also mention the fact that the automotive industry is affected by the results of its own growth. With 70 million cars and 14 million trucks on the road—as projected for 1966—we are going to need improved highways, urban and suburban parking facilities, and the like.

But, all in all, we look to the future with confidence, despite the serious problems with which we are faced.

PROSPECTS FOR THE CONSTRUCTION INDUSTRY *

The next ten years will offer a challenge to the construction industry. Traditional problems will be intensified, and a new and

* By Mr. Kinard.

different competition will develop. Basic demand will tax the industry's ability to expand; we will need better solutions for the usual problems of rising costs, transportation, and labor-management relations; the advent of heretofore impossible designs and new materials will require versatility to a degree as yet unexperienced.

In the next few pages I want to discuss briefly each of these conclusions in some detail.

Basic Demand

Basic demand will pose a real challenge to the construction industry. The estimated 1966 gross national product of $588 billion will force a level of growth for our industry which will exceed that of the economy as a whole.

New construction has ranged from a high of approximately 17% of gross national product in the late 1920's to a peacetime low of 6.4% in depression years. Currently, it is running at about 11%, in figures adjusted to 1947–1949 dollars. A gross national product of $588 billion denotes prosperity. If the trend of the late 1930's, interrupted by the war, or its resumption as evidenced during the past five years is conservatively projected, total new construction in 1966 can reach $82.8 billion (1956 dollars) as compared to an estimated $47 billion in 1957. To this we must add approximately 37% for maintenance and repair, bringing total construction in 1966 to well over $100 billion!

These specific figures may be open to question, but no one can doubt that a substantial increase must take place over the next ten years, when they look at these facts:

⟨ New net household formation will increase from approximately 1 million in 1957 to an average of 1.3 million for the period from 1960 to 1965. Although, as has been pointed out, the proportion of people in the 20 to 64 age group will decline through 1965, the number of young people reaching marrying age will increase starting in 1960. Meanwhile, increased longevity will cut down the number of housing units available for new families so that the past ratio between residential construction and new family formation will increase.

⟨ This surge of youngsters is now passing through the grade school period and is overtaxing existing facilities. However, elementary school enrollment will be higher by 30% in 1965 and high school enrollment will be up 50%. The 3.2 million college students today will increase 60% by 1965 and will double by 1970.

⟨ The record in recent years shows a relative stability in downtown metropolitan areas, while suburban areas have grown. Decentralized shopping areas, commercial establishments, and industry have resulted. Armed with this knowledge, business planning today is allowing for the construction of all these facilities concurrently. The growth in the commercial and industrial segments will parallel the development of new surburban communities in large part.

⟨ National projects, some of a size hitherto unknown, will not only bolster construction during this period but will lend impetus to the development of these new communities. Foremost in this group is the President's 13-year highway program, but the St. Lawrence Seaway, the Glen Canyon flood control irrigation and power projects on the Colorado River, and the Feather River projects in California must be included as well. The highway program alone calls for 40,000 miles of four- to eight-lane interstate highways, linking almost every city of 40,000 or more population. As you know, its estimated cost is $27 billion. To this we must add at least another $5 billion to cover the cost of regular, secondary, and rural roads, financed on a fifty-fifty state and federal basis.

Every billion dollars in this program calls for 16 million barrels of cement, 510,000 tons of steel, 18 million pounds of explosives, 123 million gallons of petroleum products, 16 million tons of aggregates, thousands of units of equipment. Hundreds of thousands of production workers and thousands of engineers will be required. New residential and industrial sites will be made accessible to major markets and for major markets.

Incidentally, the rate at which this program has been launched has been criticized recently. At the present time, contracts for less than 3% of the project have been let and actual work has started on probably only half of the 3%. I cannot help noting, however, that the construction industry has made some progress over the years.

The roads of Rome covered some 50,000 miles and took over 500 years to build; the St. Lawrence Seaway, a $600 million project now under way, took 50 years just to gain legislative approval.

❡ The population growth noted earlier will be a further stimulus to the construction industry. To reach the goal in national production when the gainfully employable group is increasing at such a slow relative rate can be accomplished only by an expanding output per man-hour. We can achieve this growth only through an increased tempo of technological change and increased capital expenditures. During this period business expenditures for new plant and equipment must actually increase.

The impact in terms of sheer volume can be illustrated by the effect on the cement industry. At the 1956 usage level, over 567 million barrels of cement would be required in 1966 compared to 303 million barrels consumed in 1956, an increase of almost 90%. In 1956 the industry operated relatively near its rated capacity. At the present cost of new plant construction, over $2.6 billion in new plant and equipment will be needed to finance expansion in this one industry. The current capital investment cost in the cement industry is in excess of $100,000 per worker. If man-hours per unit of output are to be reduced still further, larger capital expenditures will be required or new methods must be introduced.

Meeting the Challenge

Up to this point I have been dealing with demand and problems generally applicable to the construction industry. I would like to touch on the implications for the cement industry as such. Some of the problems—to a degree—will be faced by others of our friends in the construction industry.

Availability of Funds. Funds for all new construction must be derived from savings, and the possibility that insufficient savings will be available to finance future expansion has long been of concern.* A shortage of funds not only impairs the cement industry's

* See chapter entitled "Financing Investment in a Larger Economy," p. 104.

ability to expand but a general lack of capital affects the market for cement directly. This impact on cement is greater than on consumer goods, or semidurables, or even steel.

The availability of funds for the expansion of cement capacity is obviously related to profitability. Many of us believe that profits in the industry are overstated because of traditional concepts of depreciation. Depreciation based on original cost does not approach the cost of replacement. Recent revisions in depreciation regulations do not pertain to equipment placed in operation prior to 1953. The cement industry and others in which capital investment is great and the basic facilities are old are not self-sustaining. Retained earnings at 50 cents on the dollar place an extra burden on dividend policy. To the extent that overstating earnings increases the price of shares, new capital can be brought in to maintain existing capacity. This, in the long run, is hardly satisfactory to the investor, however, and increases the difficulty in securing funds for enlarging capacity.

Rising Construction Costs. A second major problem lies in the constantly rising costs both of construction materials and of fabrication and erection. Though a great deal has been accomplished, we have not offset the rising tide, particularly in the area of labor rates.

Building costs in 1957 stood at 139 (on a 1947–1949 base), average hourly wages in the building trades at approximately 141; over the past two years cost per man-hour increased about 9½% while output per man-hour rose only 5%. Meanwhile concrete products stand at 127. We have been able to hold the price line partly by shrinking profit margins (a fact that is not always evident in the profit-and-loss statements as noted above) and partly through improvements in processing and manufacturing techniques and equipment. Today's cement plant can operate on .12 to .15 man-hours per barrel as compared to .25 to .30 for plants constructed 20 to 25 years ago. The utilization of larger equipment and the substitution of kilowatts for man-hours has been largely responsible for this growth.

Increased size has also had incidental advantages, like improved fuel consumption:

Since 1955, the cost of residual fuel oil has increased almost 55% in our area. This rise has stimulated additional research and in the last two years we have developed a variety of preheaters using exhaust kiln gases heretofore wasted. These products have reduced fuel requirements by between 33% and 50%.

A considerable amount of control instrumentation is used by the industry, but the concept of total automation has, as yet, not been generally accepted. Since cement making is basically a chemical process, I believe it is well adapted to this concept. Thus automation shows great promise for sharp cost reduction, improved quality, and the manufacture of a variety of cementatious products which are presently uneconomical.

Significant innovations in the erection field have helped to reduce field costs substantially in the last five years. It should be noted, however, that innovations come slowly here due to the atomization of responsibility for building codes, the strong influence of trade unions on procedures, and the lack of a unified vehicle for stimulating change and gaining public acceptance.

Straws in the Wind

The problems I have mentioned involve the production and sale of our traditional products. Recent signs point to innovations which may result in a deviation from the familiar methods of doing business and lead us into new patterns and techniques.

New Design. Engineers and architects generally design to the qualities of basic building materials. These designs usually have not exploited the characteristics of the products to their greatest extent simply because calculations of impractical complexity were required.

A year and a half ago a crucial bottleneck in the highway program was the shortage of engineers. But today, with the cooperation of state highway officials, the electronics industry has produced devices which, coupled with aerial photographs, can not only designate the most appropriate routing for a new highway but will also calculate cut and fill. Today we have every reason to think that the lack of technical personnel will not be a delaying factor.

In 1957 the first handbook on design of thin shell concrete roof structures developed for use by engineers with desk calculators was completed by the Portland Cement Association. Requiring 250 man-days to compile, it shortened design engineering computations from months to approximately 3 days. Computers now available would have cut the time required to put together this basic manual from 250 man-days to 4 man-days. Slight modifications making the manual acceptable as a program for a computer further slice the design engineer's time from 3 days to 10 minutes.

A normal arch span can be designed by qualified engineers using the conventional trial load method in 485 man-days. Using a computer it can be designed in 10 man-days.

Such illustrations show how this historic limit on design has been overcome in a brief period, so that now some specialists claim that any building which can be conceived can be constructed.

New Materials Available. Since building design is the analysis of sheer, bending moment, torque, and so forth, and since such elements can now be analyzed economically for a building of any imagined shape, the most promising immediate prospect is for the utmost utilization of the traditional building materials. Already we have examples of this: prestressed concrete employing high-strength steel and high-early-strength cement; thin shell structures using plastic forms and thin shell concrete for basic structure; gunite producing high density concrete on hollow cardboard cores for load-bearing walls. In addition, there are special cements for use under extreme heat and pressures for mass structures such as dams; for resistance to corrosive elements; for sanitation, with disinfectant qualities; for better weight to strength ratios; for special acoustical or thermal qualities, made of manufactured aggregates or naturally porous aggregates.

Materials must still meet standards of durability, strength, stability, and appearance, but in addition they may be required to provide light transmission, transference of heat and coolness into interior atmosphere, adaptability for stamped circuitry for power transmission, or other extraordinary needs.

Already producers of traditional materials are improving their products to the end that this combination with new design techniques will further expand the outer limits of their ability to construct.

Economy. With new concepts of design and new materials possible, the major discipline remaining appears to be that of economy. While many of these traditional and new qualities might be produced in materials at present, costs are prohibitive. For instance, United States Steel Corporation is currently engaged in a research project investigating the possibility that the crystal structure of steel may be so oriented that in thin sections light may be transmitted. Present costs would undoubtedly be prohibitive of its general use, however.

This pressure for economy is also at work, forcing changes in production practices. Much construction has moved from field to factory, as evidenced by a growing volume of prefabricated wall sections, precast beams, girders and slabs for buildings and bridges, and prestressed concrete. In the field, tilt up, lift slab, gunite and hollow core, structural frame, curtain walls, suspension roofs, inverted domes, thin shell (represented by barrel, folded plate, hyperbolic paraboloids, space frames, hollow mast), all utilize existing materials, and all fundamentally aim at reducing costs. Many forms could not have been designed to their extreme dimensions as recently as five years ago.

Under study are prefabricated-prestressed highways; greater fire resistance; stability; improved strength to weight relationships; electronic control of precast element sizes; and a host of unknown products, the result of an expanded program of research into molecular structure and compound characteristics.

A New Approach. A survey of the problems and opportunities ahead would not be complete without noting the chemical industry. In 1954 a number of major companies announced their determination to invade the building material field. Hard melamines, light styrenes, moisture repellent vinyls and silicones, strong polyesters, have been developed. Each has one or two of the characteristics required of good building materials. When combined with other materials (as cement has been with asbestos or with steel) the results could be building materials with new qualities. The results of this move are as yet unknown, but it is only reasonable to assume that an industry with a gross income of $20 billion a year, expending close to $1 billion annually in capital additions, and spending $500 million on research will contribute to the building material field if, as appears at present, it is determined to do so. This could well mean a reversal of emphasis. Where heretofore we have primarily designed for a given building material we may, in the future, produce materials for a given design.

Implications for Management

As these trends develop, the building material industry must continue to face today's problems of rising costs (both operating and capital) and its traditional forms of competition with undiminished vigor. However, individual managements within the industry must maintain a farsighted outlook on markets and new competition. Research must not only proceed more rapidly on basic materials but must reach related products and extend toward the market to the end that the ultimate in design for specific products be explained and understood throughout the architectural and engineering professions. More cooperative exploration of the possibilities of combined materials must be undertaken. This, as in the case of high-tensile steel and high-compressive-strength concrete (resulting in a new product—prestressed concrete) should culminate in new applications and better conformity to the requirements of the structures which can now be designed.

Individual companies in the cement business will undoubtedly have to increase in size if they are to undertake the research programs on which the necessary diversification must rest—or even to meet cooperatively the stiff competition from their counterparts in other industries. The cement industry is still made up of a great number of small companies. (Of the total number of firms in the industry, 84% produce less than 12 million barrels each annually and in total have only 48% of the industry's rated capacity.)

To continue to produce and sell the most widely used plastic in the world at less than 1 cent a pound and to insure that it continues to meet the needs of changing design will require foresight, tenacity, and an organizational atmosphere capable of dealing with change as the normal state of life.

OUTLOOK FOR THE PETROLEUM INDUSTRY*

During the next 10 years the oil industry will be characterized by five major developments:

1. Continued rapid growth in demand.
2. Increased dependence of the United States on foreign oil.
3. Gradual development of a single world-wide oil economy.
4. A large number of new technological developments.
5. Certain fundamental changes in the structure and business practices of the industry.

Let us take up each of these matters in turn.

Growth in Demand

Throughout almost its entire history, the petroleum industry has been favored by a strong growth record. During the past quarter of a century, consumption of petroleum products in the United States has expanded at an average rate of 5.2% per annum, with very few significant interruptions in the general trend. Petroleum demand has thus been doubling every 13 or 14 years.

In the next 10 years, we anticipate that the annual rate of growth in petroleum demand will be somewhat slower than in the recent past. The annual rate of growth in gasoline demand, which ran about 7.5% per annum in the years just after World War II, has declined in recent years to 4.5%. This lower rate of growth is likely to continue because the percentage rise in total cars on the road will be somewhat less than in recent years and because a larger share of the new car additions will be in multiple-car families, which typically consume less gasoline per vehicle than single-car families. Some slackening in the rate of growth in middle distillate de-

* By Mr. McLean.

mand, which has been about 6.6% per annum recently, is also expected because (a) proportionally fewer coal furnaces are left to be converted to oil, (b) wider distribution of natural gas has provided strong competition for oil in the home heating markets, (c) increased oil burner efficiency and better housing insulation will continue to reduce individual burner consumption, (d) new housing starts will not be particularly strong until the middle 1960's, when the rate of family formation will increase, and (e) the dieselization of locomotives has already been 80% to 90% completed.

Demand for residual fuel, the third major component in total petroleum demand, has shown no major growth in recent years. Future growth in the market will depend on the general level of economic activity, price relationships between residual and competitive fuels, and the rate of progress in the development of atomic power. Only modest increases are expected.

All things considered, it appears that the rate of growth in domestic petroleum consumption during the next decade will be about 3.7% per annum—which is still a satisfactory level of expansion in comparison with other major industries. If this pace is realized, total domestic demand for petroleum products in 1966 will be approximately 12.6 million barrels a day, or about 44% more than in 1956.

Petroleum demand in Free World areas outside the United States is expected to grow much faster than here at home because present per capita consumption is far lower and the markets are less saturated in terms of their potential consumption. Moreover, the economies of these other countries are generally less advanced in their utilization of all forms of energy. The efforts of these countries to industrialize rapidly will cause energy consumption to grow at a faster rate than in the United States.

During the past 13 years, petroleum demand in Free World areas outside the United States has been growing at a rate of about 11% per annum. An annual growth of at least 7.5% may be anticipated in the future. On this basis, total demand in such areas in 1966 will be approximately 13.3 million barrels a day or double what it was in 1956.

On the basis of the foregoing projections, total Free World demand will expand during the next decade from 15.5 million barrels a day in 1956 to 25.9 million barrels a day in 1966, an over-all growth of about 66%.

Looking Abroad for Oil

A second major economic development during the next decade will be our increased dependence on foreign sources of supply.

Currently, the Western Hemisphere (principally the United States and Venezuela) contains about one-quarter of the Free World crude oil reserves and accounts for about three-quarters of the Free World petroleum consumption. The Eastern Hemisphere, on the other hand, has about three-quarters of the total Free World reserves and accounts for roughly one-quarter of the total consumption. In 1956, crude oil reserves in the Western Hemisphere represented about 14 years' supply at current rates of production, whereas those in the Eastern Hemisphere (principally the Middle East) represented about 100 years supply.

On July 1, 1956, crude oil reserves in the Western Hemisphere were about 17 billion barrels greater than on June 1, 1948. Eastern Hemisphere reserves, on the other hand, increased about 109 million barrels in the same period. Moreover, Eastern Hemisphere discoveries were made at a fraction of the cost of those in the Western Hemisphere, and particularly of those in the United States. In the history of the oil industry to date, approximately 60% of the world's crude oil production has come from the United States, and in the process, much of the cream has been skimmed from our domestic reserves, leaving only the more costly, harder-to-find deposits available today. For example, it is not at all uncommon for a single Middle Eastern well to produce as much as 8,000 barrels a day, whereas a good well in the United States will produce only a few hundred barrels, and the average production for all wells in this country is only 13 barrels a day.

In view of these circumstances and the very large increases expected in our energy requirements in the future, it seems quite clear that we shall need increasing supplies of foreign oil to supplement our domestic production. A recent study prepared by the Chase Manhattan Bank of New York contains estimates indicating that approximately 25% of our total petroleum requirements will come from foreign sources in 1966 as compared with 16% in 1956.

One of the major economic problems of the industry in coming years will be that of making an orderly transition to a larger volume of foreign oil imports. This transition must, of course, be made in such a manner that our military and political security will not be jeopardized by undue dependence on foreign sources or disruption of our domestic oil finding efforts.

World-wide Oil Economy

As a corollary of the circumstances I have just been discussing, it is reasonable to suppose that the next decade will witness the gradual emergence of a single, comprehensive world-wide oil economy to replace the several somewhat independent, regional oil economies which have existed heretofore. Generally speaking, many of the European and Far Eastern countries, spurred by a persistent drive for a higher standard of living, have been expanding their energy requirements and potential for consuming petroleum products far faster than their indigenous crude oil production. Meanwhile, certain of the economically undeveloped nations in the Middle East have been enlarging their production far faster than their capacity to consume.

From a geological and economic standpoint, we have reason to suppose that these disparities in rates of growth will continue throughout the next decade. From 1948 to 1955, the volume of crude oil moving in international commerce increased from 1.9 million to 4.7 million barrels a day, a gain of 145%. In the next 10 years, world oil traffic could easily increase to as high as 7 to 8 million barrels a day.

In the future, therefore, it may be anticipated that demand, supply, and price conditions will be closely interrelated in all the

major petroleum markets throughout the world and that developments in our domestic industry will be subject in increasing degree
to the influence of circumstances in foreign countries. It is also
reasonable to suppose that the next decade will witness the development of large international pipelines out of the Middle East and of
large tankers capable of traveling around the Cape of Good Hope
on an economical basis, in order that the world oil traffic may not
be jeopardized by political disturbances in a single country, as they
were in the Suez crisis of 1956.

Technological Developments

A fourth major characteristic of the petroleum industry in the
next decade will be the appearance of many significant technological
advancements.

The steadily increasing difficulty of locating domestic oil reserves
will put domestic producers under powerful pressures to find better
tools and techniques for locating new oil deposits and for drilling
deep wells at lower costs. The new turbo-drill recently developed by
the Russians and brought to this country by Dresser Industries is
perhaps indicative of some of these new developments.

Similarly, offshore operations will require a large amount of new
equipment and open up a whole new field of oil industry technology.
Already we have platforms which permit us to drill wells in over
100 feet of water. On the West Coast, free-floating barges now in use
make it possible to drill wells through a hole in the bottom of the
barge. Since there are no connections to the ocean floor, other than
anchors, drilling may be undertaken at depths of about 600 feet.
Along with this equipment, marine television cameras are being used
to observe what is going on at the bottom.

We will also be giving increasing attention to secondary recovery
methods, like water-flooding and in situ burning. Historically, the
oil industry has recovered only about 25% of the total oil in place.
With some of the new secondary recovery techniques now in the
experimental stages, we have hopes of raising this ratio considerably,
perhaps to as high as 40% to 50%.

The next 10 years should also be marked by much technological progress on methods for recovering oil from oil shale and on new refining techniques to obtain the high octane gasolines required by the new automobiles, at a lower cost. Some of the new processes will undoubtedly utilize waste materials from nuclear reactors as energy sources.

Structural Changes

Finally, it is not unreasonable to suppose that there will be a number of important changes in industry structure during the next 10 years.

The increasing importance of foreign oil, offshore operations, and deep drilling in the domestic onshore may curtail somewhat the opportunities that have heretofore been available to the smaller independent producers. All of the developments I have cited tend to increase the risks and raise the cost of the ante in oil's poker game. Small producers will continue to have opportunities to exploit individual situations and will, of course, be able to operate offshore and abroad through partnership arrangements. In general, however, their field of opportunity may be somewhat smaller than in the past. The changing characteristics of the oil industry are likely to demand that an increasing share of the world-wide operations be conducted by large companies with substantial financial resources.

Similarly, it would appear that the economic opportunities for small refiners may continue to decline. In 1956, 24 plants with capacities of over 100,000 barrels a day accounted for 46% of the total United States capacity, whereas in 1947 plants of this size held only 26% of over-all capacity. On the other hand, the number of plants with capacities under 20,000 barrels a day decreased in the period 1947–1956 from 288 to 180, and their share of the total United States capacity shrank from 29% to 13%.

These trends, which are likely to continue during the next decade, may be explained by such things as: (a) the clear economic superiority of the larger plants in operating costs and product flexibility, (b) the growth of products pipeline systems which has extended the area that a single plant can serve on an economical basis, (c) the increasing concentration of population in metropolitan areas, (d) the accessibility of industrial markets for refinery by-products in certain metropolitan areas, and (e) the regulation of production by state authorities which has removed the opportunity to buy cheap crude oil in flush fields. Notwithstanding these circumstances, however, there may always be some areas and situations in which small plants can be used more effectively than large ones.

A number of changes may also be expected in the marketing field. Ordinarily, new capital funds do not flow into any industrial activity on a smooth, uniform basis. Usually a surge of investment to provide for growth in demand is followed by a slackening in capital input when the new facilities exceed immediate needs. When demand has a chance to catch up, money is available again.

During the past few years new investment has poured into retail marketing facilities until there is considerable evidence that the market has become overcrowded with new service stations. As a result, some moderation in marketing investments may be anticipated in the near future.

The so-called cut-price, independent marketers are capturing a steadily growing share of the retail gasoline market. We may, therefore, be entering an evolutionary period in gasoline marketing not unlike that which took place in the retail grocery business with the advent of the supermarkets.

The development of products pipelines, better roads, and new truck transport facilities has made it possible to supply a growing number of service stations directly from pipeline terminals rather than via bulk plants. Moreover, the growing concentration of population in metropolitan markets has slowed the growth in gasoline consumption in rural areas. In the future, therefore, we may see a decline in the "middle-man function" (i.e., bulk plants) in the oil business, paralleling its lessened role in many other lines of trade.

The pressure on companies to offer three grades of gasoline, providing that octane numbers continue to advance as presently projected, will probably increase. As the proportion of the cars on the road requiring the highest octane fuels grows, it now appears that the total market can be satisfied more economically, and at lower prices to the public, with three grades instead of two. Increasing the number of octane grades permits closer conformance of product specifications to customer requirements with resulting cost savings.

Our prospect, then, is for continued growth, but with a widening focus as our international relationships come to play an ever more significant role in our business.

QUESTIONS AND ANSWERS*

From the floor: Nobody seems at all worried about where they are going to get the money to finance these great expansion programs.

Mr. Learned: We hope to continue to finance the bulk of our cost through earnings over the next 10 years. We have demonstrated our ability to do that for the last 10 years.

From the floor: Will the economy as a whole be able to do this?

Mr. Learned: The economy may have some difficulties, but I am confident about my own industry.

Mr. McLean: Europe has recognized that growth requires more savings. Some countries have developed fancy schemes to induce a higher rate of saving for capital accumulation. Perhaps we too shall need some special kind of inducements here, as well.

From the floor: Isn't it likely that some companies may have to restrict production simply because of a lack of credit facilities? And won't that make some of those figures for the future look rather foolish?

Mr. McLean: It could be. I think there is another factor, mentioned very briefly by Mr. Learned, that would also interfere with the accomplishment of the objectives: this business of a shorter working week. How do we handle the desired expansion of output in the face of only a 9% gain in our work-force population, a shorter

---

* Businessmen present at the panel session on which this chapter is based raised certain questions which brought about the interplay of ideas reported more or less verbatim in this section.

workweek, and capital shortages which make it difficult to construct new plant facilities?

Mr. Learned: I don't think the country would allow a shortage of money to stand in the way of attaining the necessary production for expansion.

Mr. McLean: But the problem is getting an adequate supply of funds to finance expansion without aggravating inflationary pressures.

From the floor: When you break down your long-range forecasts, don't you run into a lot of duplication? For example, Mr. Lowe figured that the container of the future is going to be tin plate, but a paper industry forecast might assume that it will be paper, and the aluminum people think cans will be aluminum. If you added all these increases to the container industry, they would expand 500%! Is that overlap offset by new products so it will balance out, or are we kidding ourselves in some of these industries?

Mr. Lowe: My projection is based on the assumption that there will be a continuing need for steel in most of the major areas it now enters. Further, I am assuming that the steel industry will be progressive enough to maintain its relative position. If we don't, then my projection will obviously be way over the actual figures.

But the growth of everything has been fabulous, and that is really the underlying factor in our projections.

From the floor: Are the steel companies going to continue to pass wage increases along to the consumer, and continue to grant such pay raises?

Mr. Lowe: I hope so.

From the floor: God save the steel industry and the heck with everybody else. Is that the attitude of the steel companies?

Mr. Lowe: No. If you project these increases in the demands for steel, which I think should be met by private industry, and if you have the problems I outlined, you can't afford to have a shrinking profit margin. Thus, we have to lay these wage increases onto the backs of the customer. As to rising pay scales—none of us have the courage to stand up to a powerful labor union to try to stop that.

From the floor: There are three main industries represented here that can stop it: steel, oil, and automobile. What are you guys going to do about this thing?

Mr. Lowe: It is not an easy one for any of us. Essentially it gets down to the exercise of counterbalancing power on our part. We have to do everything we can to resist the pressure for wage increases that are not justified by equivalent gains in productivity. But the pressure has to be generated by the consumer—he has to resist price rises—and then management can pass this pressure on to labor. Management can't start the process—we can't make the first move.

Mr. Learned: Some significant cost increases in labor contracts have not been passed on to automobile customers. As to the problem of wage hikes—I don't see any clear answer in the automobile business. We have a union which has grown very large and powerful, and can apply extreme economic pressure on a particular company that is improving its position in this very competitive business. At such a time, the particular company has too much to lose in the short run by a strike to withstand every inflationary demand.

Our industry cannot successfully stand against the pressure of one big union, especially when it is hitting the competitor with the most to lose. I trust that when consumer prices are too high, this process will be self-correcting as Mr. Lowe has indicated. But until the consumer says, "No, this is enough!" the industry can only lessen and not completely stop inflationary trends.

From the floor: Why do you insist that it is up to the consumer to take the first step? It seems to me that it is management's responsibility to explain to its workers why they should sit tight. They should be helped to look at the long-range goals, not just immediate advantages, and the public relations people should show what inflation now will mean to pensions, insurance, savings, and so on. Furthermore, you should do something *now* and not wait until 1966.

From the floor: I agree. If we just wait around until the consumer stops buying because prices are too high, what is going to start him buying again? Are we going to reduce the price?

Mr. McLean: I shall not try to make any very elaborate summary of this chapter, but it seems to me that all of us have fully agreed on two major points:

(1) Each author has told us that the next 10 years in his industry will be a time of major growth and expansion. If this proves so for these five basic industries, it will surely prove to be true for our industrial economy as a whole. Therefore, the next 10 years could easily prove to be a time of unparalleled economic prosperity for the country as a whole.

(2) These men have indicated that the problems which lie ahead of us in accomplishing the predicted expansion of our basic industries will be solved largely by innovations: new technical developments, new processes, new materials, new merchandising ideas, new ways of satisfying consumer wants, and new management methods in all areas. It seems to me, therefore, that the future will place an even higher premium than in the past on the creative capacities of management.

There is one further thought I would like to express by way of conclusion. The growth potential of the United States during the coming decade offers a great business opportunity. In addition, it lays heavily on us all a great economic and social responsibility. We must find the ways and means of making some of these dreams for our economic future come true! If we fail to do so, we shall not be able to provide adequately for our growing population, to say nothing of achieving the rising standard of living which can contribute so significantly to social and political stability.

Part Two

BASIC TOOLS FOR THE MANAGER
OF TOMORROW

CONSUMER MOTIVATION IN A LARGE MARKET

Samuel A. Stouffer, Ernest Dichter, Charles Winick, and Paul F. Lazarsfeld

ABOUT ONE HUNDRED YEARS AGO an experiment was performed which passed more or less unnoticed at the time. Nevertheless, it was perhaps one of the most important in the whole field of human behavior, because it led to the discovery of posthypnotic suggestion.

Most of us are familiar with posthypnotic suggestion in the guise of a parlor trick. For example, a hypnotist putting on a show in a living room before a somewhat stuffy audience may place his subject in a trance and then tell him that he is to respond to some prearranged signal by taking off his shoes and putting his feet up on

Note: Mr. Stouffer, who makes the introductory observations, is Professor of Sociology, Harvard Business School; Dr. Dichter is President, Institute for Motivational Research; Mr. Winick is at the School of Industrial Management, Massachusetts Institute of Technology; Prof. Lazarsfeld is Chairman of the Department of Sociology, Columbia University.

the piano. He further explains to his subject that his feet will hurt but that they will feel better once they are comfortably settled on the piano keys.

This stunt works almost infallibly. After the person wakes up from the trance he dutifully puts his feet on the piano. Quite oblivious to the bizarre pattern of his behavior, when he is asked about it he provides an elaborate, rational, consistent explanation.

But this extraordinary discovery is no mere gag for our amusement—it has colossal significance. Long before Freud, it blasted the simple notions about the rationality of man and eventually forced the assumptions of the Age of Enlightenment to give way to a new kind of approach to the nature of the human animal.

In view of the fact that a century has passed since this discovery, it is astonishing that until fairly recently its significance was apparently missed by a great part of the human race, who continued to believe that after all people were rational and that they did make thoughtful decisions. The distinction between rationalization and rationality was only rediscovered a few decades ago, and has been applied in research only in the last 10 or 15 years. Thus we are in the early stages of understanding the implications which this significant experiment revealed.

The whole field of psychology and sociology is, then, a field that is still very much in the making. There are innumerable theories of personality. Some of them are completely contradictory. Some are complementary and therefore not contradictory. In the face of all these theories, each with a fairly solid claim to validity, it is obvious that we are not dealing with a full-blown unified science as yet.

To talk about applied social science, when social science itself is still a very shaky business, may seem ill-advised. But in the past couple of decades we have acquired some very superior methods for finding out whether certain aspects of our theories are right or wrong. By the use of a variety of techniques we have begun to learn something. For example:

⟨ The mathematics of sampling has made it possible to deal with moderately small samples in a known and calculable area, to deal with a representative sampling, and to develop the probability sample.

❲ The mathematics of analysis has equipped us to deal with scale and measurement problems of various kinds, to work with the theory of panel operations, and to set up adequate statistical controls for experiments. The new high-powered electronic computers are making possible certain kinds of analysis, like vector analysis, which would have been physically inconceivable even five years ago, and the rate of progress in this field is likely to be geometric.

Thus we do have here and there—we are beginning to pin down —some psychological and sociological theories; and we are beginning to demonstrate that we can make predictions which have at least a little better than chance value about how people will behave by the use of some of the techniques of questioning. And the person who has the little edge, who uses these predictions that have a little better than chance value, is in the long run going to be a lot better off than the person who does not have that edge built into his prediction system. The fact that the margin is small *now* does not reduce the potentialities of the new research techniques, which are exciting indeed, even though they are still little more than potentialities.

IMAGINATION IN MOTIVATION RESEARCH*

Every so often I am asked: "Why has this whole motivation research thing become so popular in the last few years?" The answer, I think, lies not so much in the ingenuity of motivation researchers as in the fact that many of the advertisers and advertising agencies came to us out of desperation. They did not want to turn to applied social science, but they had to because they had tried all the other possibilities.

Here is a concrete example:

If you are selling a General Electric refrigerator, one competitor is selling a Westinghouse, and another is selling an International

* Dr. Dichter.

Harvester, the customary step is to find out how your refrigerator is better than the other two. That is all well and good, so long as you can discover real technological differences—nuts-and-bolts differences.

But what do you do if you suddenly wake up from a nightmare which makes it clear to you that there really are *no* differences between your refrigerator and the ones sold by your competitors? What do you tell the public then? You start looking for a psychological story.

In other words, the advertisers have rediscovered that after all it is the sizzle rather than the steak—or in addition to the steak— that sells. If the word sizzle sounds undignified or unscientific, we can turn to a long list of much more technical-sounding, intriguing words for it. But it exists, no matter what we call it.

No Gimmicks

In my personal experience, I have fought for a few specific approaches to finding the right psychological story, a few specific ways of thinking that people should accept if they are in the business of persuading the public—for good ends or for bad. I do not mean research techniques, like interviews, projective tests, psychodrama, and so forth. They all smack of a panacea: "If I only use the right technique I'm going to find the right answer." The answers cannot be found in the "right" technique, but in the right kind of thinking and approach, as I shall demonstrate in this chapter.

Don't Believe What You See

Some of us still seem to believe that all we have to do in motivation research is go out and observe people: if we only watch enough individuals and ask them direct questions we will get the answers.

We have suffered from this principle for at least 2,000 years, as from many other axioms that we are having to throw overboard these days. It is easy to show that our observations deceive us. For instance, put a pencil into a glass of water and look at it. The pencil appears to be broken.

That is *observing*. You can observe it 2,000 times, but you cannot rely on your observation.

Play Your Hunches

What you need instead of observations, then, are intelligent hunches and intelligent hypotheses. Unfortunately, the average American is frightened by the concept of a hunch and hypothesis; it sounds like the antithesis of science and controlled procedure. Yet no scientific procedure is possible without an intelligent hunch or hypothesis to start with.

In other words, you almost have to know what your findings are going to be before you start your research. You have to *guess* why this particular person buys or does not buy—or, better, you have to make a series of guesses, because there may be six or seven or eighteen possible explanations. I do not mean wild guesses, of course; a social scientist or psychologist should have enough background from previous analyses and observations to form intelligent hypotheses on possible explanations for a particular phenomenon.

Here is a concrete, practical example:

> We had an interesting job for the NSU-Werke Aktiengesellschaft in Germany, a firm that manufactures Mopeds, or motorized bikes. There are 50 million bicyclists in Germany. Having suffered a serious sales slump, NSU asked us to help them reach these 50 million bicyclists, their natural market.
>
> They wanted to say, "You won't get a heart attack from pedaling," "It's easier," "It's more streamlined," "It looks better than the regular bike," and "It doesn't cost much more."
>
> We took a different tack altogether. We asked: What does the German want out of his future? This was not so impractical and academic as it may sound. Using the specific projective technique, we found that every German wants a car. He dreams of owning a Mercedes.

The Moped was no Mercedes, but we could *make the consumer think of the Moped as the first step into the motorist world.* The German resisted buying a Moped because he felt that pretty soon he would get his Mercedes. Therefore, what was the sense of buying a motorized bike, which cost almost one-fourth as much as a good car?

The problem had actually been aggravated by advertising which stated: "This Moped is wonderful. It is practically indestructible"— exactly what this consumer unconsciously feared. He was afraid that once he bought it he would not be able to get rid of it.

Consequently, we advised NSU to describe the Moped in automobile terms and to say, not that it was indestructible, but that if, after two years, the owner discovered he had enough money saved up to get ready for an automobile, they would be glad to take the bicycle as a down payment for the car. The new approach got results, because it was aimed at a dream in the hearts of the German people.

Thus, there is far more involved in doing a market study, in trying to find out what really motivates people, than just observing, although that sounds very scientific at first glance. You have to do some thinking. Too often people rush into the design of a questionnaire and spend weeks or days worrying about correct sampling but very little time in thinking about what could conceivably be the solution.

Let the Diagnosis Fit the Cure

Almost every client we talk to presents his problem in this fashion: "I want to know why our sales have gone down." That approach makes sense only up to a point.

We answer: "We really don't know that. What you want to know is how to get your sales up again. If I studied your problem very carefully and told you, with all the decimal points, why your sales have gone down, you still would be very dissatisfied, and I wouldn't blame you."

This is not just sophistry; it involves a wholly different way of looking at the problem. It requires you to design your research to give you useful answers to your questions, not just diagnostic answers. In other words, we are interested in therapy as well as fact-finding. For example:

> The General Electric Company wanted to know why engineers would not buy D. C. motors for work that necessitated such equipment, such as jobs in automation. Since the engineers already had all the tables, all the illustrations, all the technical data to prove that these motors were really better than A. C., we decided that our problem was not the motor but the engineer. So we did a personal study of engineers, rather than of "why D. C. motors do not sell."
>
> We found that the engineer had been trained to seek definite answers to definite problems. He was precise by inclination and by training. He did not like having to revise his "well-founded," definite prejudice that the D. C. was old-fashioned and had been discarded 20 years ago. He did not like having made a mistake about D. C. motors.
>
> The answer was plain: redesign the outward look of the D. C. motor to develop a face-saving device so General Electric could say, "This isn't the same D. C. motor that we used to talk about," even though it was. "Remember the old one was blue? This one is red, so it can't be the same one. We changed it."
>
> General Electric also wrote a booklet, which told the engineer: "You are a very ingenious and creative engineer. Look at how many of your opinions you have changed in the last 20 years. All we are asking you to do now is to change another one, as behooves a creative, ingenious fellow." And it worked.

The Longest Way Round

Another objective—and an extremely important, though elusive one—is the development of a nonmaterialistic attitude toward the problem in the clients' minds. In this connection, I am reminded of a very famous psychological experiment:

> Some apes were put into separate cages. Outside each cage, just beyond reach was a banana; inside the cage were some sticks. Only

one or two of the apes were smart enough to turn their eyes away from the banana, put the two sticks together, and go back and get the banana. The majority only stretched out their arms for the food itself.

Many of the people we are dealing with are like these apes. We say, "Will you permit us to go into an analysis of cultural trends? Will you permit us to study things that are not apparently your immediate problem?" "No, we want you to study how to get the banana. Please don't turn your head away from the banana. We won't pay you for the study if you start talking about something else. We told you our problem is the banana."

Take advertisers, specifically: in working with them, we find that they go back again and again to, "What can we say about the refrigerator that will convince the consumer that our product is really better and different?"

Only recently, for instance, I had a most disillusioning experience. After a two- or three-hour discussion of our findings, one of the clients came back and said, "Well, you haven't quite told us whether we should run our advertisement in the *New Yorker* or *Life*." Our answer had been, "In neither one. You have to change your whole philosophy, your whole approach." They might as well have asked a social scientist to find out how permanent peace could be established in the world and then responded to his detailed and profound analysis by asking whether the passports of the future should be two or three inches wide.

Thus, we have found all along that it is the personality of the company and the image of the product that is important, rather than the size of the lettering or the number of colors in the advertisement.

Need for Spiritual Satisfaction

We are living in an era of abundance and prosperity, but few of us have started to worry about what this abundance will ultimately mean. The perspective, after all, is not uniformly bright. Continued good times involve many important, and perhaps dangerous, psychological implications.

One of the gaps that is generally apparent is an ever-increasing need for spiritual satisfaction. By this, I do not necessarily mean religion, although the church is certainly involved. In many, many studies we find people asking the same question: "What is it all about?" They have their cars and their television sets, but this does not appear to be enough. Whatever it is they want next, it does not seem to be anything material.

Here may be one of the most important facts that we should report to a client, because there are many products that will survive or will be sold competitively only by that company which is quickest to recognize this growing need for spiritual satisfaction and do something about it.

A very important aspect of this trend is the new role emerging for the American businessman. In trying to find out what is responsible for the happiness of workers, we are beginning to think that it may be management's responsibility to meet this need, which simply did not exist 20 years ago or even 10 years ago.

After voicing this thought to the executives in one company we studied, we were asked, "What do you mean? Are you saying that we ought to replace our office with a church?" Our answer was, "No, but maybe you should bring many of the characteristics that we think we can find only in church, and perhaps not even there, into the day-by-day business world."

In other words, the businessman may be required to fill a new and completely unsuspected role, which may sound hypocritical or arrogant at first glance, in which he concerns himself more and more with a new morality that goes beyond persuading people to buy bigger and faster cars. Thus, the modern business leader may have to learn not only to wait for an analysis as to "where are we going?" but even to accept the fact that he himself must contribute fundamentally to the direction we take, in a fashion that goes deeper than economic development.

A REALISTIC VIEW OF MOTIVATION RESEARCH*

I should like to begin by clarifying the image I believe many people have of motivation research and to show just how accurately or inaccurately this image reflects what is really going on. Even though the repetition of these misconceptions and canards gives further currency to them, I think they are sufficiently widespread to deserve critical attention.

Old Hat

The first component of the popular image of motivation research is that it is something relatively new. Actually, it was "new" a half-century ago:

⟪ In 1903 Walter Dill Scott said, "How many advertisers describe a piano so vividly the reader can *hear* it? How many food products are so described that the reader can *taste* the food? How many describe an undergarment so that the reader can *feel* the pleasant contact with his body?" †

⟪ Over thirty years ago, a psychoanalyst was asked by a German cigarette company to provide advice on how to sell cigarettes. The company made Tufuma cigarettes. Tufuma means "everybody smokes," and the advertising theme was: "Everybody smokes Tufuma" and "You must smoke Tufuma." The cigarette was not successful, and the company wanted to know why it had been such a failure.

The psychoanalyst pointed to the remarkable success of the Ab-dullah cigarettes in England. In every subway station, under the large "No Smoking" sign, almost as if it belonged to the official message, was the statement, "Not Even Abdullah." The psychoanalyst pointed out that smoking is related to unconscious feelings

* By Mr. Winick.

† Walter Dill Scott, "The Psychology of Advertising," *Atlantic Monthly,* Vol. 93, p. 34.

of protest, like thumb sucking and chewing. Smoking was still somewhat forbidden, which was part of the fun, and Tufuma failed because there is little fun in doing something you must do.

❡ In 1926 Dr. John B. Watson prepared a memo on the subject of applying psychology in advertising that is as modern today as if it stepped out of last week's issue of *Printers' Ink*.

❡ In 1930 Dr. Lazarsfeld made his brilliant and justly famous study of why the steam laundries in Vienna were not getting the customers they should be getting.

❡ By the mid-1930's a steady stream of such studies, relatively unnoticed by either the social scientists or the advertising fraternity at large, had begun.

Great Variation

Therefore, this application of psychology and other social sciences to marketing has a considerable historical background.

The second component of the image I want to talk about is the myth that there is some entity called motivation research. There is no such unified, cohesive science. Rather it is a collection of individuals, companies, schools, and the like, working in various ways to apply different social sciences to various marketing and advertising problems.

Motivation research is not only what Dr. Dichter, Dr. Lazarsfeld, Dr. Stouffer, or anybody else does. It is a vastly varying collection of different kinds of activities ranging from mathematical and psychological techniques to psychoanalytic interviews.

The Direct Question

The third dimension of the image I want to comment on is the belief that motivation research requires not only complicated people but also complicated ways of asking questions. To ask a simple question with a relatively untrained interviewer, according to this view, is automatically to admit you are not looking for a really important or definite answer.

This is, of course, completely untrue. There are many matters which you can ask people about directly, and they will be able to give you an intelligent answer. Also, it is extremely difficult to ask even simple questions well, and complicated ones are even worse!

Magic

The fourth component of this image is the idea of the magic solution.

Many seem to think that there is one button which can be pressed to traumatize the hapless consumer and send him off to the store asking for your product—and, further, that no other combination of ideas or words or notions will get him to do so.

This theory is contrary to everything we know about human motivation, which, in fact, is so complicated that no textbook in the field has appeared since 1933, when Young wrote the only textbook on the subject.* It is so baffling and so complex, that no one has had the courage to bring together a new description of the field of motivation. In 1924 L. L. Bernard listed 5,759 *classes* of instincts which have been held responsible for human behavior.†

My point here is not to indicate whether we have 6,000 or 6 instincts. We know so little and what we do know is so ambiguous and complex that we can never even begin to think of any one magic button.

An illustration of the number of levels on which it is possible to understand human motivation is the famous series of advertisements featuring a man's shirt:

> This group showed a gentleman in his fifties, with graying hair and a moustache, wearing an eye patch. The shirt company involved tripled its sales within a few years after this campaign began in the 1940's. Its low advertising budget, under $75,000 a year, is often

---

*Paul T. Young, *Motivation of Behavior* (New York, John Wiley & Sons, Inc., 1933).

†Luther L. Bernard, *Instinct: A Study in Social Psychology* (New York, Henry Holt and Company, Inc., Publishers, 1924), p. 220.

cited as an example of how powerful a tool advertising can be if only you use the right motivational approach, although motivation research was not used in preparing the advertisement.

What angle did this advertisement hit, and why was the campaign successful?

First of all, the man is wearing a patch. In other words, the sight of one eye is gone. It is well known in psychoanalytic literature that the eye is a symbol of virility. Therefore, a reader of the advertisement who has qualms about his virility may say to himself, "This man looks very distinguished, he looks very soigné, even though he has lost an eye. Maybe I can look as distinguished as he does, if I buy one of those shirts."

That is the depth level of interpretation. Another such interpretation is that the man is mutilated, and so gets our attention and empathy. On another level, the advertisement appeals to the interest of women in men of the age of the person in the picture. We know that women buy about half of all the men's shirts.

Other explanation might be that this brand is the only one which has any real national coverage in its price range, that this particular shirt company has a good sales force which has been with the company for a long time, that it has more styles than any other, that it is the best shirt in its price range, and, finally, that the text of the advertisement is compelling.

Furthermore, it is the only mass-produced shirt with square cuffs in all models, and square cuffs are found on all expensive and custom-made shirts. Therefore, in addition to being the best-made shirt, it carries the mark of being expensive, and people who want to pay this much for a shirt are likely to be aware of the importance of square cuffs. There is one more possible reason: it may be a good shirt! Now, which of these reasons was responsible for the shirt's success?

Just as there are supposedly magic buttons, there are supposedly magic words. At the present time "communications" is a magic word in social science and in industry. About 10 years ago dynamic psychology was *the* term in psychology, until everybody began saying, "Wait a minute. My psychology is dynamic, too!"

Motivation research shares some of the overevaluation of the communications field. When we look at the general concept people have of communications we find a high foam rubber quotient. When you push and squeeze a little it seems to fade away in your hands.

In the same way, psychology and psychoanalysis are believed to be magic weapons. (It is perfectly true that Freud wrote that the major use America would make of psychoanalysis would be to incorporate it into its advertising.) Even though both psychoanalysis and psychology are involved in advertising to a great extent, sociology and anthropology and insights from several other sciences enter at least as much into what we call motivation research as do psychology and psychoanalysis.

The Truth of the Matter

Motivation research *is* used to create interesting themes for advertising. It is used, for example, to develop the kind of unusual symbol we find in the salty character scenes of the cigarette advertisements to differentiate relatively similar products from each other.

Interestingly enough, this job is often done not through complex research but simply by picking up a textbook. For example:

> One Chicago agency took an introductory psychology book, looked up "human motivation," and found "self-love." Following this clue, they developed an apparently successful campaign showing women looking at their stockings in the mirror.

Why should these social science techniques be lifted so crudely from the textbook? The reason is the complexity of human motivation. If research alone were used, it would have to be very extensive. A textbook can provide the basic campaign theme, while supplementary research can help in such ways as these:

- By determining whether to search for people who might be new buyers for a product or to try to sell more to those who are already its primary consumers.
- By inventing provocative names and slogans and ruling out inappropriate ones.

- By discovering how people communicate their preferences about various products.
- By learning the cultural differences affecting the market in different areas of the country; by learning the personality differences of occupational groups.
- By isolating and identifying a company's marketing problem.
- By defining the "personality" of a store, a magazine, or a television station and by finding out how much of a carry-over there is from one medium to another.

Developments Ahead

These are some important projects being undertaken today in social science as applied to marketing. What can be hoped for from all this activity?

There are several drawbacks. For one thing, we are not working in a scientific field, partly because we are not communicating our results to each other. The essence of the scientific community is the free communication of results, so other people can study them. The better a motivation research study is, the more advantage it gives its sponsor and the less likely he is to want to communicate it to anybody. So long as this condition prevails we shall be operating in a subscientific area and our knowledge will not be optimized.

Another drawback is the lack of feedback from marketing to social science. Unfortunately, the process has been one-sided. Social scientists bring their talent, insights, and the like to marketing, but their professional knowledge and skills are seldom improved in the process, and their armamentarium usually remains static after the kind of experiences they have.

Conflicts of Opinion

The most promising signs are the wide differences of opinion within the field. The fact is that there are many specialists with different, not necessarily converging, points of view, each presenting his ideas in whatever media are available to him. This is an indication that the field is reaching for a certain kind of maturity, though some observers might construe it as proof of just the opposite trend! But no area is complete—no one has all the evidence on anything— and the fact that this profession suffers from gaps in its knowledge which make disagreement possible is no reason to set it apart for any special condemnation.

We now have available, or are trying to perfect, various methodologies for piping in on and influencing the process which leads to the purchase activity at different points along the way. Further, we seem to be developing more points at which we can tie up to the long series of behaviors, thoughts, contacts, conversations, anecdotes, and experiences with media that the consumer has had and which form his image of the product. The procedure for getting in on the whole process is, of course, not yet complete. The mere fact that we now have so many opportunities is a sign of health and a harbinger of good things to come.

Let me close, as other authors in this book have done, with a quotation from Alfred North Whitehead: "Operations of thought are like cavalry charges in battle," he said. "They are strictly limited, they require fresh horses, and must only be made at decisive moments." *

At its present stage of development, the application of social science to marketing faces just such a combination of circumstances. The extent to which it selects fresh horses and acts at decisive moments will determine the degree to which it will develop into an even more fruitful tool for industry.

COMPLEXITIES OF CONSUMER MOTIVATION†

It may seem impossible to agree with both Mr. Winick and with Dr. Dichter. But I do go along with both of them on a number of points.

I agree with Mr. Winick in two areas especially. The problem

---

* Alfred North Whitehead, *An Introduction to Mathematics* (New York, Henry Holt and Company, Inc., Publishers, 1911), p. 61.

† By Mr. Lazarsfeld.

with which we are dealing is indeed very complicated, much more complicated than Dr. Dichter made it appear. Secondly, we must take care to avoid remedies that have more the character of slogans than of realities. On the other hand, I agree with Dr. Dichter that ingenuity and imagination are essential.

No Simple Problem

So far as the complexity of the problem goes, let me start with an incident that happened to me when I participated in another conference on motivation research:

> One of the participants from a telephone company indicated that he was very concerned about how they could sell second lines, since nearly everyone had one telephone by now.
>
> It had occurred to him, as the result of this conference, that if he were to concentrate on families with 14-year-old children he could tell them with certainty they needed a second line. Anyone who has 14-year-old children knows it is impossible to use the telephone!
>
> But I discouraged him. There are more complicated psychological factors involved, I pointed out. If the family had two lines, the parents still would not want the 14-year-old on the telephone all the time because they would be envious. "That teen-ager should not have all this fun," they would say, "when poor father has to work all day long. People shouldn't waste their time like that." So they would finally give up the second line, and if they needed to use the telephone, they would have the fun of chasing the children off the line.
>
> My friend was very impressed. He immediately said, "What would it cost to do such a study and devise an appropriate campaign?" I figured a little bit, and replied, "Well, for half a million dollars I could do something."
>
> I was not really joking.
>
> First, we know from studies that "Puritan envy" probably varies by social classes. In general, poor people are willing to let other people have fun and to have fun themselves because what little pleasure comes their way is very precious to them; the rich people are willing to live and let live because they have the means.

It is the middle class that has this Puritan idea that it is sinful to be entertained. I do not know exactly how far down on the economic scale this envy would go or how high. It would require a very careful large-scale economic sampling to find out.

Then, I would have to know whether this 14-year-old was the first child or the fourth child, for instance. With the fourth child one of two things may happen. Either by then the parent is already so beaten down he does not try any more, or he feels he should be easier on the last child. I would also have to study families with one, two, or three children.

I would have to examine personality differences according to how the father was treated by his parents. If he had been badly treated, his attitude toward his children would be affected. And so it goes; the half million dollars would be quickly spent.

Such a survey would still not necessarily answer all the questions. Anyone who just says "a survey showed" makes me uneasy. The whole question of what is evidence in this field has to be watched very carefully. Whenever I have been near an idea, there has still been the possibility that another personality factor, another economic factor was playing an important role.

It is true that in many situations it is not important whether you are right or wrong; it is just important to have some leads on which to act—to try one thing one day and something else another day. It *is* a mistake to spend huge sums on evidence that cannot be used; they had much better be spent on ideas. But at least you should know your particular likes and dislikes. You should not believe "you have evidence" or that any survey "has shown" something.

Method, Not Madness

Secondly the tradition behind motivation research should not be forgotten, because it gives us systematic methods more useful in the long run than brilliant slogans.

Not just in the past 50 years but since 900 B.C., everyone has wanted to find out why people act the way they do. The unique contribution of the last 30 or 40 years is the number of techniques that have been developed to approach the problem a little more systematically.

There are dozens of such techniques, which can be classified into four major groups:

- Factual information.
- Structured questionnaires—definite questions with "yes" or "no" answers, statements with which one must agree or disagree.
- Open-ended interviews—more complex questions, asking reasons for preferences, and so forth.
- Projective techniques—such as ink-blot tests, which present such a vague stimulus that the only way a subject can comment is by projecting his attitudes into the situation.

Next, let me characterize the whole situation in the most primitive way because another distinction has to be made. There are three kinds of problems in which we are interested:

1. The attractiveness of the product, in the largest sense. What is it about the shirt, the airplane trip, or the second telephone line which might or might not be attractive to people?
2. The influences that are important and act on people.
3. The goals people have.

The minimum way a purchase decision can be analyzed has to be "For what purpose does a man buy what product and under what influence?"

These distinctions remind us of one of the major confusions which develop in motivation research discussions: Are we trying to give the product a new appeal by a word or packaging, or are we trying to satisfy a new desire, which we have not yet uncovered? What is right or wrong about a product has to be uncovered by experiments or by observations. When we want to get at the hidden goals of people, we usually have to use projective techniques. They often do not know or cannot communicate these reactions directly.

Probably Dr. Dichter's work is in the area of goals, and his methods are extremely successful there, but his opinion that the experiment or the carefully worded questionnaire should not be used to find out the effectiveness of advertising is not correct. The techniques used depend on the purpose in mind. By overemphasizing any one goal or technique, the others will be obscured and harm will be done.

I would like to add one more remark. There is a possibility that we can conduct large-scale sampling in the goals area—the field with which Dr. Dichter is mainly concerned—by translating projective topics into standardized questionnaires. That is the most interesting development in motivation research at the moment. In effect, we are combining Dr. Dichter's and Mr. Winick's views.

Let me give an example, from a study made by Mr. Stouffer:

> When he worked for the Army, he wanted to know at what period the draftee began to feel like a soldier rather than a civilian. He could have found out by very complicated projective tests, but he had to study nine theatres of war and half a million soldiers. So he thought of a way to do it by using just one test, just one question: "When you are on furlough and go to a party, do you prefer to wear civilian clothes or military clothes?" He found the most important differences between the people who answered one way and those who answered the other.

This is a projective idea, a basic desire, a basic attitude, a basic disposition, but it has been moved into the category of observation. There are many examples of success in the use of this approach. It is possible to combine careful statistical data to obtain large breakdowns, to compare rich and poor people or different ethnic groups.

Triangle Situation

In conclusion, I would like to introduce one more complexity. The notion that the research man should be the one with all the good ideas on what to do lies at the root of one of the difficulties in our present situation. Actually, this business is a three-cornered matter: We have the manager with a problem, the research man who works on it and comes up with the best information he can, and a translator, a public relations man or copy writer. This profession, unfortunately, does not yet exist, and it is sorely needed. When research people have to operate under the continual threat that businessmen will not buy their services if they cannot present their ideas well, very little good work is done. It has been my experience that the best research work is produced if everyone forgets the immediate applications for a while.

Analyze why people do things, why someone has lost his sales, and then let another professional take the research data and translate it into practical advice. There are unusual people who can do both, but most people cannot. The businessman will get more out of researchers in terms of practical application, and researchers will get more out of businessmen in terms of interesting data and peace of mind, if there is a translator, than either will if they have to be analysts and business advisers at the same time.

QUESTIONS AND ANSWERS *

From the floor: About 10 years ago I left school and disappeared into a department store. I spend most of my working day watching goods being sold to customers and sometimes selling them myself. What about this link in the chain—the actual purchase itself? What impact does the salesperson on the spot have in this process?

Dr. Dichter: I didn't mean to slight the salesman by any means. When we talk about advertising and communicating with the public, the salesman is one of the communicators and one of the most important ones. All the things we may find in a total study, of course, have to be used and can be used by the salesman.

From the floor: I agree that the man on the firing line is the key person in selling. If we don't solve the basic fundamental problem of improving the caliber of salesmanship at the retail level in this country, our booming population and other factors to the contrary notwithstanding, we are going to embrace our next depression— motivation research or no motivation research!

* Businessmen present at the panel session on which this chapter is based raised certain questions which brought about the interplay of ideas reported more or less verbatim in this section.

PLANNING FOR AUTOMATION

Emil F. Gibian, Edward D. Kemble, and Jay W. Forrester

INTRODUCING AUTOMATION—A FRONT LINE REPORT*

INSTEAD OF PRESENTING a theoretical discussion about the organization of a program for automation, I want to describe two or three typical problems as they occurred in our company, in the hope that I can thus clarify both our mistakes and our successful decisions. Then I want to draw some general conclusions on the question of how to make automation a success.

Note: Mr. Gibian is Staff Director, Industrial Engineering, Thompson Products, Inc.; Mr. Kemble is Manager, Management Research Service, General Electric Company; Dr. Forrester is Professor of Industrial Management, Massachusetts Institute of Technology. James R. Bright, Associate Professor of Business Administration, Harvard Business School, acted as moderator for the panel session on which this chapter is based.

* By Mr. Gibian.

Ours is a decentralized company, with 13 autonomous divisions. Each one has separate automation projects. I am going to compare two of these projects as they worked out in the Valve Division, which has undertaken a number of automation programs. The first was launched in 1946, before the term "automation" was coined; the second one was started in 1955 and completed in 1957.

Strung Together

Let us look first at the 1946 project, an automatic line which involved feeding forgings into line, straightening, grinding and machining operations, and inspection. When we started, we viewed automation in the wrong way: we took the existing operations and tied them together somehow in order to make the whole line automatic, instead of realizing that automation is a complete system. Although we did incorporate some ingenious features and advancements, our basic pattern was unchanged. Thus, all we really had was automation of existing operations.

This project was organized like any other method improvement program. One man who knew how to handle mechanization studied all the possible ways of conveying, and of automatizing certain machine tools, and put his findings together. The results were satisfactory: the line operated exactly as we had expected it to and made possible real savings in labor costs.

But the final outcome reminds me of the story of a graduate who came back to his Alma Mater to visit:

> Just for fun, he listened to a lecture by his old professor who used to talk on the principles of electricity. He was disgusted to find the teacher saying the same old things about electricity, static, and so on that he had years before, without ever mentioning electronics, radio, or television. So he approached the professor afterwards and said, "I am amazed that you still teach the identical information that you used to. A lot of new ideas have been added since then!" The professor replied, "Is that so? Well, I would like to talk about it. Let's go have lunch together."

While they ate, the graduate bored in and told the professor about the many wonderful advances which the teacher had not covered at all. At the end of the conversation, the professor said, "I guess you are right. I should change my lectures. As a matter of fact, I am going to make the change right now. The title of my next lecture will be 'Old Principles of Electricity.' "

We had done the same thing in our Valve Division: we were using the same old principles of electricity and automatic processing, and trying to tie them together. By 1955, we had learned our lesson. We planned a project not as an automatic line, but as an automatic system.

"Set the Goals"

Once you think about automation as a system, you do not limit it just to technical improvements. You start thinking of everything right from the ground floor, and begin fresh. You think about organizational approach, accounting, and possible future changes in materials. Most important of all, you say to yourself, "Set the goals."

The chief goal is always cost reduction, which has to be accompanied by space saving, by improved and guaranteed quality, and by flexibility. Therefore, almost everybody associated with the organization has to participate in the project: salesmen, engineers, cost accountants, manufacturing men, vendors, and so forth.

There are five possible organizational approaches:

1. A division management committee—the most common technique.
2. An automation department.
3. An automation coordinator.
4. Outside consultants. Incidentally, we have had disastrous results with this technique because the people we called in were not intimately acquainted with our particular problems.
5. A council of outside suppliers—machine-tool suppliers who have plenty of experience.

In considering these approaches, some companies seize upon the last one as the most likely possibility. Personally, I think the machine-tool suppliers have only recently begun to wake up and discover that they have to do some original work in order to stay in the automation field. It is true that the machine tool people are going full speed ahead now—in this most recent project of the Valve Division we had some excellent cooperation from a number of machine-tool manufacturers. But they are all handicapped because automation projects are of such a specific or specialized nature that it is difficult to produce a ready-made package for anyone. They can help by cooperating with the customer, but it is still the customer's job to develop automation for his needs.

An Automation Department

For our part, we settled on approach number two and created a separate group which was charged with full responsibility for automation. Five of our best men were selected, a sixth was put in charge, and the entire group was completely divorced from any routine duties. Its job was simply to think, dream, and propose automation. Called the Special Equipment Design Group, this committee reported to the factory engineer, who is an authority on automation. The administrative cost was an overhead item, charged up to the division. Finally, we backed up this group with a team of three of the key people in any organizational project: the factory manager, the division factory engineer (a supervisor, too), and the division industrial engineer.

As a first step, the committee compared various projects, selected those which looked attractive, and assigned them for preliminary testing by a task force made up of two men: an industrial engineer and a manufacturing engineer. It was their job to study such matters as cost reduction potentials and to discuss the plans with the various people who would be involved in the change. After careful research, they took their findings to the committee of three, who checked them over. If the results looked promising, the committee of three explained the project to the division managers. Programs approved at this stage were assigned back to the Special Equipment Design Group, which worked out the preliminary design of the system and assembled pertinent data. They prepared a complete set of preliminary drawings and made a project report to the task force. Here the necessary cost factors were added, and the whole package was referred to the committee for its decision. Assuming the committee thought it was economically justified, the proposed system was submitted to the central staff for their review, approval, and release of money.

To get the funds, automation projects had to be justified in exactly the same way as any other capital expenditure. These projects have to pay for themselves if they are to be approved by the Central Staff on the basis of over-all corporation needs. They receive no special dispensation. Incidentally, only about 20% of the projects make their way successfully through all these screenings.

Four Ground Rules

The whole process was governed by a set of clear ground rules, which carefully defined the objectives to make sure that everyone knew exactly where we were and what we were doing. All four of these ground rules were quite ambitious:

(1) The line had to be viewed as an automated system. We demanded a fresh approach which would discard the established concepts of valve finishing operations, if necessary.

(2) We wanted the maximum reduction of direct labor.

(3) We insisted on the greatest automaticity possible for each operation.

(4) We had to have automatic material handling between stations, postoperative inspection, and feedback control to keep the machine in adjustment.

In short, our Special Equipment Design Group had to build a line with no operators. They did so, in this case, so we have only technicians, whose sole duty is to make the system operate by itself. They do nothing to make the line go—they only correct it if something goes wrong.

Methods and Materials

To accomplish this, we had to survey the possibilities and determine the requirements of future designs and possible future materials. We had to decide whether we were going to machine valves or grind them—a basic decision, incidentally, and a fundamental one in organizing for automation.

In our case, we determined on grinding, which forced us to recast all our thinking and redesign both our valve forgings and forging methods. We made the choice so that we would be able to handle any type of material which might come along. Furthermore, by grinding we could put the product through from start to finish without removing it from the line, because grinding permitted us to heat treat the forgings prior to their entering the automated line. Thus no subsequent heat treatment and straightening between operations was necessary. Finally, we found that we can maintain tools which are used for grinding much more easily than those needed for cutting.

This matter of tools proved to be especially important. In selecting the machine tools to do the job, the Special Equipment Design Group had three choices:

1. To take existing machine tools, where possible.
2. To modify existing machine tools to meet our needs.
3. To design completely new tools.

Of course, none of these decisions are frozen. In his chapter, Mr. LaPierre discusses artificial diamond and borazon cutting tools, which have an indefinite life. Because of these new materials, we may perfectly well have to change our thinking again and go back to machining.

In addition, the group had to develop a completely new system of gauging and feedback, with memory-built-in automatic devices to fit into our line.

I mentioned the importance of discarding axioms and accepted methods and designs for automation and production. We found it constantly necessary to do just that. For instance, here are two examples:

> One so-called law says that you should take hold of a piece and never let go until it is through the line. But we do just the opposite—we never grab a piece, and we always let go of it—because that is the only way we can handle grinding machines. So we use a whole new concept of conveyors. We can pick up a valve in any position, distribute it from one operation in one machine to three operations in the next, and then back two stations to the next step, and so on. To do this, we have developed a chainless conveyor which uses ball-bearing balls as a means of propulsion. By feeding bearing balls through slit tubes to solid tools, the product can be moved anywhere. Incidentally, we tested this conveyor for 6 months, 24 hours a day, 7 days a week, to find out whether or not it would stand up, before we adopted it. You have to be very careful in dealing with untried devices!

> When we decided on grinding instead of machining, we were faced with a real problem on centerless grinders in that the presently designed rest blades wear out, produce a taper, and have to be replaced. This means stopping production and making adjustments. But you cannot afford to do much adjusting in an automatic line; it has to be running all the time to justify itself economically. So we had to work out a new type of rest blade, a design which, incidentally, has been patented.

After all these obstacles—and many others—were worked out and final approval was obtained, the staff set up two check sheets: a timetable for engineering, purchasing, erection, and grooming, and a table of costs. We figured out that it would take a minimum of 21 months to do the job: about 6 months for engineering, 12 months for delivery of machine tools, both gauging and conveying, and about 3 months for what we called grooming and putting into production. We established a very strict schedule, with a minimum of 21 months and a maximum of 24. That calendar was watched very closely by management to make sure that we would always have the

necessary manpower to hold to the schedule, because all the de-
liveries for the whole year were geared to come together in order
to have the line operating as of 24 months.

Our cost breakdown was as follows:

> Out of each dollar we spent about 73¢ for machine tools and
> equipment, and about 12½¢ for gages and material handling. Al-
> together this adds up to 85½¢ for capital expenditures. In addition,
> it cost us about 10¢ for preproduction and depreciation during the
> "de-bugging" period. This included the cost of depreciation for
> machine tools which were delivered and "de-bugged." The other
> costs were surprisingly low: 4½¢ for engineering.

Problems Encountered

Needless to say, there are some management problems in planning for automation. For example, we were faced with the fact that
when we were finished we would have no operators, but only technicians. So we had to re-evaluate jobs and shift personnel. The impact of machines on the work force is, of course, a basic question in
automation. In our case, no one had to be laid off because our business is growing sufficiently to take care of any displaced people. Our
sales, for instance, increased from about $300 million to $400 million
in one year. If you enjoy such a growth, you do not encounter problems which might become very serious if the level of sales or volume of business remains constant. Thus our employment in the
Valve Division actually went up instead of down, and all the people who lost their jobs were retrained—often with an upgrading
in classification.

Then, our work-in-process planning changed. At each station on
the automated line we keep about 10 minutes of work-in-process, or
about 210 minutes for the whole system, as against about 10 days'
work-in-process in the conventional type of operation.

Still another example is the need for quick maintenance and
servicing. We cannot afford to have one portion break down, because within about 10 minutes the whole line behind it or ahead of

it stops too. A shutdown costs us $150 an hour, and that runs into real money.

Or take cost accounting. We find that we cannot base our expenses on overhead and direct labor anymore, since the manpower factor is so small, but have to use machine-hours instead. In other words, it is not the number of hours spent by men that is important—it is the number of hours spent by the machine. Finally, the system demands a very rigid operation timetable preset and controlled by the factory manager. Maintenance of machine tools and equipment, change of wheels and fixtures, setups, and servicing of instruments are rigidly planned and scheduled for the third shift when the line is not operating. This procedure is essential so that the system can operate and run during the two working shifts with as few interruptions as possible.

Thus all these decisions and questions overlap and interlock. One change sets off a chain reaction, with ramifications in many other areas. To cope with such a complex and delicate system, careful planning is required. For us, it has paid off—after only three months we were getting about 92% of theoretical capacity, which we think is a good result.

Link by Link

Automation has to be approached as the United States Air Force handles the development of a weapon system. It has to be looked at as a system, and not as a line. It demands skilled engineering in both manufacturing and production. It calls for a careful study of sales and a close tie-in with cost accounting, chemical and metallurgical laboratories, job evaluation, training, and many other fields.

In my opinion, success depends on the creation of a group of specialists with no other responsibility, people who are applying themselves 100% to automation. Top management has to insist on very strict justification for every part of a project like this, based on detailed economic and engineering studies.

Finally, it requires extraordinary flexibility. It is usually impossible to make the series of relatively slight changes which are characteristic of an ordinary line, so a system has to be designed in such a way as to enable it to keep up with foreseeable technological developments. Furthermore, no matter how carefully it may be planned, the moment the project is in operation it is already obsolete. I think that our system is one of the very few examples of absolutely complete automation in the country. Yet already we see how it could have been done differently.

Finally, it costs money. A company thinking of automation has to be prepared to put a great deal of cash into it. After all, you cannot get anything worthwhile without spending money for it. Perhaps I can illustrate that basic fact of business life by closing with a story about a traveling salesman:

> This particular gentleman was alone at a hotel for a week end. When he went down to the bar he came across a very beautiful blonde, so offered her a drink, and then dinner. Finally he propositioned her and asked her to go up to his room. She agreed, but said that her charge would be $100. He was somewhat surprised, and told her that he had never paid that much in his life—his maximum was $10. "Oh, no," she said, "I'm sorry. That's impossible." The next week end he came back again, but this time he had his wife with him. While they were having dinner, the same beautiful blonde appeared and sidled up to their table. "There," she said to the salesman, "See what you get for $10?"

AUTOMATION AND LONG-RANGE TRENDS*

In my section of this chapter I want to put principal emphasis on the relationship between basic, long-range characteristics of our economy, and automation. How does the kind of question discussed by Mr. Drucker,† for instance, fit into planning in this area? What sorts of interactions exist, and how can a corporation analyze

* By Mr. Kemble.
† See the chapter entitled, "Social Changes—What They Mean to Management," p. 3.

them in a way that will be meaningful and helpful to those who deal with the manufacturing process firsthand?

I have selected two of these trends—expanding technology and scarcity of capital—to illustrate my point and to show the direction of our thinking at the General Electric Company. I say *thinking* advisedly, because we cannot claim to have any real answers.

But I do not want to give you the impression that General Electric Company is waiting until we do a lot of planning before we start using automation—or that I think anyone else should adopt such an approach. There are a great many obvious chances to use automation all around us and a considerable amount of past experience to go on. So we have been automating for some time, thanks to the natural response of sharp-witted production men to some very good opportunities.

Brain Trust

To assist and service this inevitable development, one of our vice presidents has established a pool of knowledgeable men in an organization which we call Manufacturing Services. It is their job to distribute data and ideas to the company, based on their own experience. In addition, they study the experience of other companies and make it available to our people. Together with electronics men in other parts of our organization, they develop new ideas and go so far as to design some new automation systems and mechanisms in the Manufacturing Services Laboratory. These devices have general company-wide applicability, and are available for study by our manufacturing engineers, who come from some 140 plants to examine the entire process from the new thinking involved to the actual nuts-and-bolts presentation.

Further than that, these men sometimes encourage, sometimes sponsor, and sometimes actually assist in the formation of other pools of men around the company to take care of more limited applications. This step is necessary because we conduct such a wide variety of businesses that there are some techniques which apply to a whole group of intracompany business, though not to the entire company.

Basically, then, our central group is concerned with the development of skills for automation. Only very occasionally and incidentally does it actually do a job for a division, because the basic theme of our company is decentralization. We believe in the delegation of every kind of work that can be delegated, especially of all creative projects. To accomplish this goal, we have to decentralize the responsibility and the necessary authority as well, so the headquarters' role becomes one of assistance and guidance, not operation.

There are, of course, limits to this format as an exclusive approach. Several specific ones come to mind:

(All manufacturing engineers are not equally sharp-witted, so we do not have equally good projects coming through all 140 shops.

(The enthusiasm that these men have for imaginative and workmanlike production jobs sometimes obscures their good judgment. They may seize on automation, rather than capitalize on other easier and less expensive opportunities.

(A similar enthusiasm for the use of new skills clouds the possibilities in other, less glamorous, technological developments, which may not demand brand-new know-how. It is never as rewarding to play out everything that you know as it is to start on something really untried.

So my first point—before I get into the long-range planning aspects of automation—is this: the primary requirement for a company interested in taking advantage of modern technology is to get going and start trying out some of it!

On first glance, this direct and obvious approach to automation might appear to be sufficient. But the trouble is that we live in a "rapidly changing economy," as the theme of this book makes clear. We cannot afford to be content with any one set of modern techniques for too long, or the world will pass us by. We have to look at automation, along with anything else in business, against the background of the kinds of issues raised in every other chapter of this book. This is what we are trying to do at General Electric.

Now let us turn to these two examples of the factors that we feed into our planning for automation: technological advance and capital scarcity.

Technological Advance

Mr. LaPierre has dealt with this matter extensively in his chapter, but I want to look at some of the premises underlying what he had to say. In the first place, knowledge of technology must be in men, not in books or machines. Until men develop the necessary under-standing and the required know-how, all this scientific progress just is not usable. Thus, if you want to use the new technology, you have to provide the right people with the requisite skills—and that de-mands a terrific amount of effort and money.

Furthermore, as fast as we break through one frontier of knowl-edge, we find we are confronted with another which we have to conquer. So the expenditure of effort and dollars has to go on and on. We cannot call a halt to the process of developing men if we want to stay in front technologically.

Needless to say, trained research personnel are of no value if we fail to use their ideas—and this implementation involves us in a con-stant collection of new costs and new demands on our supply of human energy and talent. Thus we have two sets of requirements: the training of men and the exploitation of ideas. Obviously, neither of these can be fully satisfied—a practical balance that we can afford must be struck. The task of planning is to find that balance, and work out the necessary steps to achieve it.

But the planning does not end there: more than cost is involved. These highly skilled professional men impose new requirements on an organization, as Mr. Drucker points out in his chapter. The manager must deal with a far higher proportion of men who can think, who will think, who must think.

Given the host of intricate problems which will rise up in business firms in the next decade—both in the laboratories and in the ex-ploiting and marketing of the scientists' discoveries—we have no choice about the kind of personnel we will need. They must be intelligent, self-disciplined, and responsible, the sort of men whom we often think are to be found exclusively in the executive group.

Therefore, our management philosophy and all the ramifications of our planning have to take into account that running the company of the future will not be like the job our fathers faced in the first industrial revolution. These people have special attitudes, expectations, and incentives. They will not produce unless they actually participate—and I am talking about something much more real than simply letting them have the "feeling" of participating. They have to be in on the planning.

From our viewpoint, incidentally, this is one reason decentralization continues to be our basic approach to this elusive task of appraisal and decision-making with respect to the technological frontiers.

Capital Scarcity

Let me start by saying that actually there are more funds available now than there ever were. Our problem arises from the fact that we *need* more money than we have ever needed before. Thus, it has become *relatively* scarce, because of our expanding population and rising standard of living, based on an ever-widening choice of products for the consumer.

More people wanting more things creates a larger potential market, and this would seem to be the first condition for automation. But with this expanding number of products vying for the consumer's dollar, the whole concept of competition changes. You are not only contesting against items in your own field—you are faced with competition from many other kinds of products as well. We find, for instance, that the automobile is as great a competitor to our refrigerator business as are the directly competing products in the appliance field. So the *total* business competing for the consumer's patronage has to be taken into account in market surveys—not just the specific product itself.

In a period of relative capital scarcity, a company needs a high rate of flow of funds. This rate will be affected by two factors in a

high volume market—the kind of market which automation requires. One of these elements is price, and the other is inventory.
Thus, we have to make sure that we understand the effect of price
on volume and the amount of inventory that is going to be tied up
between the line and the end customer in a national market. The
combination of a low profit margin, the normal characteristic of a
mass market, and a high inventory financing cost may mean that the
product which seems appropriate to the normal and nondiscriminat-
ing production man with his eye on automation may not turn out
to have a lucrative market at all. It may not be the item that we
want to automate from the viewpoint of the business as a whole.

One other consideration is important because of the need for a
flow of funds. As Mr. Gibian pointed out, in a period of rapidly
moving technology, any given project starts to become obsolete in a
hurry. This fact has to be taken into account in pricing policy.
Prices should produce a return on investment which is rapid enough
so that a manager's profits are not all eaten up by a premature
obsolescence. Thus pricing strategy must be a major concern, at least
for the coming 10 years, in the development of criteria for what is
good automation and what is bad.

In summary, then, if a major company is going to plan on how
to achieve automation, the obvious first step is to get going on all the
really good opportunities. In view of all the technological possibilities,
the generation of individual projects cannot be centralized but has
to be spread out on a wide front if they are to be productive.

But some kind of common criteria of valuation is necessary if
the relatively scarce funds of the total corporation are to be applied
with the greatest wisdom on the best of the projects that are available.

WHAT CAN AUTOMATION DO FOR
MANAGERS? *

I want to reverse the direction of our discussion from what
management can do to prepare for automation and look instead at

* By Mr. Forrester.

what automation can do for the practice of management itself and how recent technological developments can help us understand the principles which underlie the art of administration. We will look at the way the principles of automation can contribute to our knowledge about the operation of an industrial organization, and even extend to our understanding of national and international economics.

All this, of course, is a large order. We must consider automation in a very broad sense, as the interrelationships of information flow, feedback control systems, and communications. When we put these together, I think the effect on management processes may have a far greater impact and significance for industry than merely the physical handling of materials in production lines.

I am speaking of an area we call "industrial dynamics"—a long-range development that will take a decade or two to prove itself. In five years or so we may very well see conferences like the one on which this book is based which are devoted entirely to the topic of industrial dynamics.

Let me point out why automation and the broad practice of management have a very closely related future. You have already read in this chapter about some of the elements that go into the consideration of automation: the need for the systems viewpoint, the importance of studying the entire scope of what a company wants to do, the necessity for re-examining methods and taking a new look at the business as a whole. Furthermore, most of us fully realize that automation devices and practices depend fairly heavily on what we call feedback control systems.

Information Flow and Feedback

If we note the similarity between information flow in an electromechanical feedback control system and in a company, we perceive a new picture of business organization. A company in its entirety, including its distribution system, material supply, manpower, cash flow, and information channels, is very much like a physical process control system, such as you might find in an oil refinery. The company has channels of information flow which modulate the flow of materials, cash, and manpower. And in this fabric, which interlocks the information flow and the flow of materials and money, lies the key to industrial fluctuation, to growth, to cyclical behavior within the company and within the national economy itself.

All this becomes significant at the present time because the tools and the techniques needed for a better understanding of this whole process are beginning to be available. The study of feedback systems and the relationship between communications and control provides a foundation for understanding the management process.

Up to now, management education and management practice have been a highly fragmented affair. People concern themselves with finance, or with manufacturing, or with advertising, or with sales, or with research. Most of us specialize in these areas to the exclusion of a real understanding of how they are related to each other. Only at the top of our organizations, where it becomes necessary to view the operation as a whole, do we consider how these parts are interrelated.

Management education and practice are on the verge of a major breakthrough like that in engineering education and practice during the last 20 or 25 years which produced our present interest in automation. Just as engineering and research have taken on a new vitality, so we will see a new attitude toward management a decade or so hence. Looking back at the engineering precedent:

> A quarter-century ago, engineering tended to be a textbook, handbook, trade-school affair. One learned how to do certain things, but relatively little attention was paid to fundamental physics and the principles underlying engineering practice. But beginning about 1940, two things happened. First, there was an increasing emphasis on the underlying principles (the relationships between physical phenomena and engineering, and the relationships between information flow and control), and second, an awakening awareness of what has come to be called systems engineering (the interrelationship of the parts of a physical system with each other, with the

people who operate them, and with the economy in which they must be built).

The same sort of rebirth can come in management, giving an awareness of some of the underlying principles and a quantitative understanding of the over-all system interrelationships. To give you a picture of the universal importance of the feedback concept in this process, let me digress at this point to describe it a little more fully and then go on to a specific example.

Simple Analogy

The concept of feedback control systems is universal to everything that we do. When we reach for a pencil on a table, we do not miss it and grope for it because our eye observes the difference between our hand position and the object. A feedback control system operates when we drive a car: hand, to steering wheel, to front wheel, to road, and back to eyes and arm muscles.

But this is too perfect a feedback control system. Let us modify it a bit. Suppose the driver is blindfolded and has a companion in the front seat who can see where he is going and issues instructions to the driver. Then the driver guides the automobile on the basis of the instructions from his front-seat companion. What is the result? The driving is going to become considerably more erratic. And why? Because there is an information distortion from sight to voice, and, very much more importantly, a time lag has been introduced into the system. There is a delay between what the companion sees and what the driver does.

To make this system even more representative of an industrial enterprise, let us imagine that the companion who is issuing instructions is restricted to looking out the rear window so that he can see where the automobile has been but not where it is going. Here we have a very nice analogy to the feedback control system that we are using in managing an enterprise on the basis of past and present information which must somehow be applied to future behavior.

Feedback in Industry

Looking specifically at a company situation, what are some of the feedback control systems in the industrial environment? Every act, almost without exception, affects the environment and the conditions on which the decision was based. In other words, we make a decision on production rate in order to change inventory levels which, in turn, will lead to new decisions on production. Likewise, policies on research and development expenditure will manifest themselves in a change in current technology, leading to a new set of circumstances and a new environment in which fresh decisions are demanded. In other words, each choice affects the conditions on which it was based, and so, by definition, is an information feedback control system.

We must consider the company in its entirety, and look at the impact of these forces on one another. In presenting an example, I have to depart from that rule because going the whole way and looking at all the ramifications of a company would be too complicated to handle in these pages. Thus, I must restrict the situation to a manufacturing operation and a distribution system and look at how decision policies and delays can lead to rather dramatic and unexpected behavior in the operation of a company. But even this limited illustration should clarify what I mean.

Charting a Course

In *Exhibit I,* with months across the bottom and factory orders plotted against time, we have a fairly ordinary type of production chart for a company making consumer durable goods. In recent months we find a fairly consistent picture of about 1,000 units ordered per week. But here it is the end of June, and orders received at our factory have gone up as shown, so we must make some prediction about the future. We can ignore the uptrend, we can extrapolate it, or we can assume that it will level off. But we must make some sort of a deduction as to what it is going to be in the future. Probably most assumptions would lie somewhere in the dotted area, either being extrapolated upward further or leveling off.

A month or so later, we see the picture as shown in *Exhibit II*. There has been a little leveling off. Because of the factory lead time of perhaps eight weeks, we are just now beginning to get an upturn in output from the production line. It has taken us some time to plan a new, higher production level, and this is just beginning to materialize.

In *Exhibit III*, we are looking at the same situation around the end of October. Orders have suffered a very considerable decline, but we are just reaching peak production in the factory, and production is beginning to level off.

Exhibit IV shows operations for the period of about one year. Production rose from 1,000 units a week to something like 1,300. Then it dropped to 900, and now seems to be leveling out at about 1,100.

All this represents the story as it looks to the factory manager. Let us now delve into the situation and see what might be causing the ordering and production fluctuations. To start with, we ought to know something about the system in which we are operating.

Exhibit V represents a schematic diagram of the context in which this snapshot of production orders was taken. At the bottom we find the consumers, who place orders as indicated by the dotted line and the retailers, who deliver goods as indicated by the solid line. Retailers, in turn, order from the distributors, who order from the factory warehouse, which is replenished from the factory production line.

To see what the dynamic characteristic of this system might be, we need to know a couple of things besides the organizational structure which is shown here. We need the time delays in the system and the policies which govern the placing of orders.

The time delays are shown on *Exhibit V* in weeks. The customer gets the product he orders the week after he places the order. The retailer takes two weeks to process sales records into purchase orders for replacement stock. There is about a week of mailing time between retailer and distributor, a week of processing time at the

Exhibit I

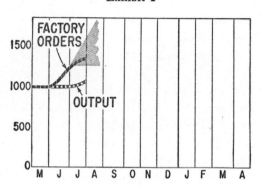

Exhibit II

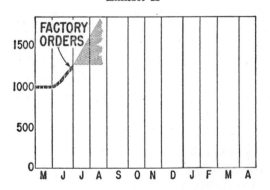

Exhibit III

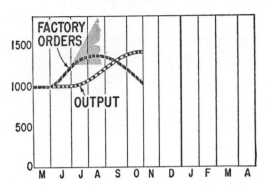

Exhibit IV

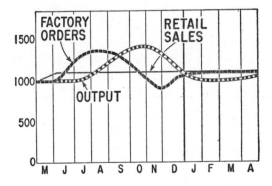

distributor, and a week of railroad or trucking time before the goods appear back at the retail store.

Likewise, the distributor faces a similar set of delays in placing his orders with the factory. And the factory, in turn, has the eight-week production lead time which I mentioned before.

In addition to time delays, we need statements of the policies followed in placing orders. To keep the example simple, let us say that both the retailer and the distributor order to reflect any increased sales rate, plus goods to replace inventory depletions caused while waiting for the new increased supply rate to start arriving, plus orders for any desired change in previous inventory levels.

On the latter point, it may be desirable to increase the previous inventory levels when total sales volume goes up.

In *Exhibit VI* we can see the previous factory order and production curves and the consumer sales from which they result. Consumer purchases went from 1,000 units a week to 1,100 a week over a one-month interval and remained constant at this 10% higher sales level thereafter. The delays and ordering policies in the distribution and production system converted the small increase in consumer purchasing rate into the factory production oscillations. This is an ordinary kind of factory and distribution organization, and we see that it can amplify a small external influence (here consumer purchases) into serious changes in production and employment stability.

Different time delays and changed ordering policies produce the situation shown in *Exhibit VII*. This second system is only slightly different from the first: a few changes in time delays, a 1,300-units-a-week ceiling set on maximum factory production rate. Here we find the factory unable to respond to the demands on it, because of this limit on capacity. The consequence is a leveling off of factory output; at the same time, factory orders, due to some minor changes in time delays, come into the plant looking very unlike *Exhibit VI*. Factory inventory for the period of a year drops to 50% of its initial value, rises to something like 140%, and then levels out. Total inventory in all levels of the system (not plotted) varied only 10% during the year; its locations shifted up and down between distribution levels.

One of the causes of unstable behavior is, obviously, the time lags. But, one can jump very easily to the unjustified conclusion that electronic accounting and data processing will solve the problem. Speeding up today's procedures in today's organizational structures may produce improvements that are slight compared to those from changed information flow patterns and changed operating policies.

Exhibit V

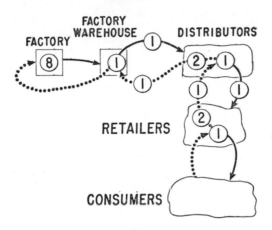

Use in Automation

This discussion is closely related to automation in two ways:

(1) The techniques used in studying this interrelationship of information to the flow of materials and to the flow of cash are very similar in concept to some of the techniques being applied in the automation field.

(2) The problem I have described on the company level will have to be solved hand in hand with the trend toward automation. Modern technology demands more stability in industrial operations—less fluctuation, less difference between minimum and maximum demand—than we have customarily seen over the last few decades.

In summary, I think we are going to see the development of a new approach, which considers the flow of information as a constant

Exhibit VI

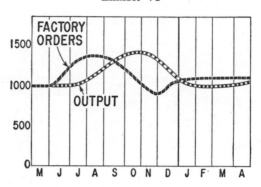

Exhibit VII

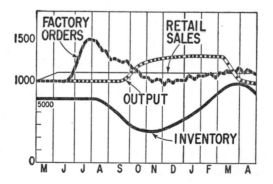

process modulating the other characteristics of a company, with a fairly sound philosophical and quantitative basis underlying it. Many of the routine, day-to-day decisions which are made by management at the present time can be modified and made a matter of policy, freeing the manager to look further into the future, study new developments, focus more on the human side of enterprise, and examine the problems of innovation and change.

QUESTIONS AND ANSWERS*

From the floor: What kind of steps can an average person in a company take to stimulate present management to understand the new management techniques?

Mr. Kemble: I doubt if the individual can do much. I feel that the further development of the profession of management is the best long-term answer. In the meantime, the ones who are smart enough to see these things but are not in a position to make decisions will probably just have to sweat it out.

Mr. Forrester: We have to remember that it is very early in the development of industrial dynamics. The techniques do exist, and problems of this sort which are too complicated for strictly mathematical solutions will be approached through the use of simulation on our high-speed digital computers. In the military world, of course, the approach has been used extensively in the study of military weapons systems.

But there are probably only a few hundred people in the country who are conversant with the techniques, and it is up to them to see that there is a steady flow of understanding into the management area.

I suspect that it will take about five years for demonstrated success in a few areas. But the impact on the operations of a company will be so important that it will represent a competitive advantage which

---

* Businessmen present at the panel session on which this chapter is based raised certain questions which brought about the interplay of ideas reported more or less verbatim in this section.

cannot be overlooked. Even now, I know two or three companies in which top people believe that this kind of approach will spell the difference between the ultimate success or failure of their companies.

So I have real hope for the future, though I admit it may be some years before the awakening occurs very widely.

Mr. Gibian: If some one says to me, "I have some good ideas, but management doesn't want to listen," I always wonder where the fault *really* lies. After all, this is not a one-sided matter. If an employee is capable of developing new ideas, he should also be able to persuade management that they should be tried out and accepted. If he is not capable of persuading management, it is likely that the ideas are not very good, or he would be unable to carry them out.

From the floor: These new techniques—advantageous as they may be—require very complicated machinery and a heavy investment in funds. How can a small business survive in a situation which is dominated by the need for such large allocations of time and money?

Mr. Forrester: The approach I discussed is a matter of principle and knowledge as much as it is a matter of machinery. The particular curves in the exhibits were calculated by hand on about three average-size sheets of paper. It takes about half a day or a day to do one of them. When a company reaches the point of using machine solutions for their systems studies, they will need people who have spent a few weeks, a few months, or even years studying the techniques. But even so, this is not too expensive.

Nor is it true that the techniques are applicable only to the very large, nationwide companies. Multiple-stage inventories exist in the small manufacturing companies as well. When you have an inventory of finished products, an inventory of raw materials, and an inventory of processed material, depending on how they are controlled, you may get precisely the fluctuating situation I described.

Mr. Kemble: Furthermore, programing takes up the large part of the cost for this activity. But you don't have to own a machine, or be leasing a machine, if you can do your own programing. Centers where you can feed in the material and get it back on a regular basis already exist.

From the floor: What is the best source of study material on the area that Mr. Forrester has discussed? Where can an individual find out about it?

Mr. Forrester: So far, this is very new. Our job at M.I.T. is to interpret a fair body of information coming out of military laboratories, apply these methods to management problems, and work up examples and principles during the next five years. We are going to work with industry on cooperative projects to develop know-how and ways of applying the theory. The work will gradually grow, so that we hope material for publication and teaching purposes will soon become available. The first such is a paper I have in the June 1957 issue of the M.I.T. *Technology Review.* In the meantime, I would say that people who have experience in feedback control systems and the simulation of military control systems have the main tools that are required. Some are already beginning to apply them in the management area.

THE GROWTH PROBLEMS OF
SMALLER BUSINESSES

*Paul Donham, John Peterson, Henry Blackstone, and
Ansel M. Kinney*

WE MIGHT SPECULATE as to what would have happened had the title
of this chapter been "The Survival Problems of Smaller Businesses,"
for it is survival that one hears most about in the halls of Congress,
in its committees, and from articulate small business lobbyists. Yet
these professional flag wavers who hold small business, with mother-
hood and the American way, as something sacred and inviolate
completely miss the point.

Survival is a negative objective. It implies running a losing race on
a treadmill, racing ever faster but never getting anywhere. These

Note: Mr. Donham, who makes the introductory remarks, is Associate Professor of Business Administration, Harvard Business School; Mr. Peterson
is Vice President, Scientific Instrument Company; Mr. Blackstone is President,
Servo Corporation of America; Mr. Kinney is President, International Register
Company.

prophets of doom fail to realize that the only way to survive is to set growth as the objective. When we put our minds, our skills, and our hearts on growth, survival becomes an automatic by-product.

So in this chapter we will deal with growth, and we will see that the successful entrepreneur is one who has converted problems into opportunities. This is a positive approach, and it is by accentuating the positive—corny as that may sound—that the best small business-men have been able to progress toward their goal. The problems are many: keeping ahead or at least abreast technologically, attracting and motivating the best management team, securing adequate funds, and maintaining financial resilience. Yet they all become opportunities through the exercise of ingenuity, courage, and daring. For these are the qualities which make for entrepreneurship—the ability and the willingness to set a course into uncharted seas, the spirit which enables men to move into the unforeseen and the unforeseeable.

One overriding factor insures survival, makes for growth, and holds the promise of vocational happiness: the ability to carve out a competitive niche for one's business, to maintain that niche against all opposition, and to enlarge and expand it over the years. It is in these terms that the authors of this chapter have written their sections.

A PLAN TRANSLATED INTO ACTION*

To me, the fascinating aspect of small business is the satisfaction of sharing quickly in the success or failure of your own plans and decisions, and doing so with maximum independence of action. Furthermore, I wholeheartedly believe in the general theme of this chapter as expressed by Mr. Donham: in an expanding economy, smaller companies must grow in order to survive.

We all recognize that businesses, large and small, share the same basic problems. The fundamental difference lies in the degree of pressure exerted by certain problems in today's economy, and in the

* By Mr. Peterson.

relative point in time or "phase" in the growth pattern of the business. We must remember that all businesses were small once and are hence only the lengthened shadows of one or more men.

The small business I represent is somewhat different, perhaps, because it has been established almost 70 years and has not grown at all. It is a manufacturer of test and industrial process control instruments and has been conducted throughout its history as the hobby of one or more individuals, rather than as a dynamic business enterprise.

Why, then, did it survive? Apparently it is still alive because it filled a specific need. The company manufactured a standard product of superior quality, which was modified in small lots to serve the specialized needs of a few prominent equipment manufacturers and process industries who were delighted to obtain custom-built instruments at standard prices. Also, it provided outstanding service in the repair of competitive instruments when the original manufacturers were unwilling or unable to do so.

Taking Over

In 1952–1953 I spent approximately a year finding an established business—which had to meet certain predetermined specifications—to purchase. After I had investigated more than 300 opportunities, it became clear that most healthy businesses could be liquidated for about twice their prudent purchase value. Hence, I redirected my search to companies with sound, established product lines which, due to internal problems, were making no progress and could be bought for a realistic price. I obtained the company under discussion as a result of that search.

My first step was to initiate the following five-year program:

> *First year—1954:* Diagnose the problems and learn the business.
> *Second and third years—1955–1956:* Continue above and initiate changes.
> *Fourth and fifth years—1957–1958:* Emphasize growth and investigate merger.

Acute problems were pressing in from all directions, some of which are still with us. Diagnosis revealed that the following basic measures had to be taken if we were to achieve our objective of vigorous growth:

1. Establish a sound sales organization and step up sales promotion.
2. Determine product costs and improve shop efficiency.
3. Re-engineer parts of the product line.
4. Effect basic personnel changes within the organization and seek out and attract additional executive talent.
5. Rewrite product literature and issue new general catalogue.
6. Reduce overhead costs.

Methods of Attack

All these steps had to be undertaken with inadequate working capital, since the funds simply were not available.

A brief word about the methods and status of each of these major projects may be of interest.

Sales organization is a continuing problem, now about 20% solved. In surveying our company from a marketing standpoint we discovered that we were in four different businesses. The products of each operation require different marketing channels, and sales literature and promotion have to be brought into line with the way marketing actually is done. We cannot simply lump all our products together into one large catalogue for general distribution.

Like all small manufacturing businesses whose sales volume is too low to support high fixed sales overhead we find it necessary to distribute our products through agents rather than through company salesmen. The selection and proper leadership of a good agent in order to ensure yourself a fair share of his time is a never-ending challenge, and the basic argument of distribution through agents or through company salesmen is one which could consume an entire book, including outstanding examples on both sides.

Costs and Efficiency. We now know what it costs us to make our products. This analysis has resulted in some price increases and in the elimination of certain noncompetitive items from the line. We cut 42% of the man-hours from the work force and now are about 60% as efficient in shop costs as our large competitors. However, our overhead, in terms of direct labor charge, is under 200% as compared with approximately 600% for our competition. This area of inquiry can yield further fruitful results, particularly if we can move into new quarters and change certain manufacturing methods —all of which requires additional capital.

R&D problems are nearly beaten. Our basic need was to restyle the instrument cases, since the working parts were competitive or superior in design to those of other manufacturers. In addition, two new products have been launched, one designed in our own plant and one designed and built outside. It now appears that a small company must plan to rely on design engineering purchased outside for some of its new products, since the internal costs of a complete engineering department are prohibitive.

Personnel. Certain personnel conflicts were solved by termination as soon as they were conclusively defined, while others were brought under control by changes in job assignments. The most difficult problem has been to attract additional young executive talent with more interest in opportunity than in the illusion of security. At least six young men working with large companies have offered to join the organization to escape from the high pressure and boredom of a restricted scope of activity, but only when they could move without any reduction in their income. Their timing naturally means that the real fun of solving the pressing problems will be behind us, and their services will not be needed when they are available.

Catalogues. This project is under way on a spare-time basis and is about 40% complete. I discovered that professional catalogue writers require that most of the difficult technical writing be furnished them; they supply merely the layout and art work. Therefore, we are doing the writing ourselves and will subcontract the art work as required, thus saving about 75% of the cost.

Lower Overhead. Building rental has been substantially reduced; punitive local personal property taxes on inventory were eased by vigorous protest and sound facts; the traditional 2% cash discount, when most vendors sell us on net terms was eliminated; purchasing procedure was changed, overtime work in the shop was cut out, and other cost-saving actions were initiated.

Getting Results. Progress is evident on all sides. Operating results have shown a change from a serious five-figure loss to a realistic profit, and sales are up approximately 20%. The trend is in the right direction; additional sales effort and more executive talent to serve existing customers should step up our rate of improvement. We have been continually short of working capital, but bank and vendor support has been forthcoming when we needed it.

Refusal to Sell

That is my story. In addition, I want to mention a problem which will become increasingly important to all small manufacturing enterprises: refusal to sell. If not carefully watched, this can be devastating to a small manufacturer who has standardized on a component made by another manufacturer who suddenly brings out his own competitive end product. In this era when mergers are an accepted and often necessary corporate way of life, old suppliers frequently find themselves—to their embarrassment—competing with their best customers.

The "refusal to sell" problem manifests itself in devious ways such as unrealistic price increases, unreasonable shipping time, the requirement of absurdly high quantity orders, and just plain refusal to fill an order. This problem can be a vicious, two-edged sword, and I am sure thoughtful management will consider it carefully.

Growth and Merger

I am a firm believer in the premise that manufacturing businesses which endeavor to serve more than a local market must grow to survive. I also believe that they must grow much more rapidly than the normal 5% annual growth of the economy. Depending on the nature of the business, a company must reach a certain critical size quickly if it wants to maximize its potential markets. How big is that critical size? Surely it must vary among enterprises, but in the instrument business it should be large enough to support nine or ten capable men, including perhaps three in general management, three in sales, and four good engineers.

My studies reveal that a minimum annual volume of $500,000 is required to support three capable men in a competitive industry; hence, an annual volume of $1,500,000 to $2,000,000 is needed to reach the critical size at which one can compete on almost equal terms with big industry. Although I do not feel it is necessary to merge to *survive,* it does appear essential if one's primary objective is to achieve *maximum* growth potential.

We are following a policy of aggressive growth from within, and at the same time are watching for suitable mergers. The real solution still lies ahead of us.

THE PROBLEMS OF RAPID GROWTH*

The famous scientist, Lord Kelvin, once said, "When you can measure a thing and express it in numbers you know something about it." Consequently, I want to use some numbers and charts to show the dimensions of my company's growth.

Exhibit I reflects the growth in terms of employment level. The figures show that there has been no single year in which average employment has not increased.

Exhibit II measures the magnitude of our growth in comparison with other well-known companies. The percentage increase over the nine-year period is noteworthy.

The two columns on the right need further explanation. On the bottom of the chart is a simple equation which represents e^{xt}. This is the growth equation, and column X in the table represents the growth exponent.

The right-hand column of *Exhibit II* indicates what would re-

* By Mr. Blackstone.

sult after an adjustment in dollar figures, assuming a two to one decrease in the value of the dollar over the past 10 years. Under these circumstances, the growth of the larger corporations appears less extreme, while our figures still remain rather large.

The problems engendered by this rate of growth center in three areas: management, finance, and marketing.

Training and Recruiting

In the management of a growth business, no problem is greater than recruiting and training people. We have 370 employees in our company today; 10 years ago we had 3. There were years when several major functions in the organization were covered by only one man. The small business, therefore, can be extremely vulnerable to the caliber and performance of one individual. In a larger corporation these risks are smaller; a serious error in the choice of one man can affect only a portion of the performance of a whole department.

A successful corporation has consciously or inadvertently been building its management structure for the preceding 40 years—Bell Telephone Laboratories, Incorporated, has skimmed the cream off the engineering crop each year for decades, for instance. But the rapidly growing small business simply does not have this kind of time. It must find ways of compressing time itself.

We learned the hard way that we had to add something to standard personnel procedures, so we have consciously developed and augmented our methods of psychological testing. Necessity forces us to grope as we advance toward a better management tool. Of course, like all new tools, testing can be dangerous—the airplane was dangerous 30 years ago, but that did not stop executives from using it.

Under these circumstances, some strange situations have arisen:

> We hired one man—let's call him Mr. Foster—who had been a department head in a large company for over 10 years. On checking with the vice president of the company, I found that he was furious at the idea of our "pirating" his personnel. "You can't do this," he

Exhibit I. Servo's Employment Record

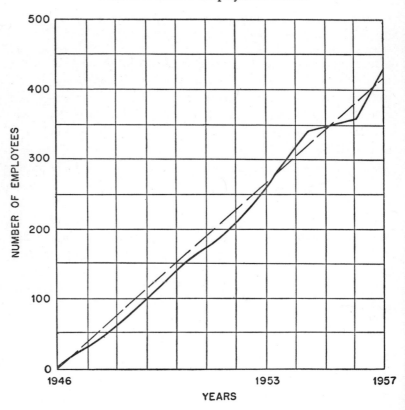

said. "You are taking the best man I have." His reaction surprised me, since I thought Mr. Foster had already submitted his resignation.

One day several months later, I received a telephone call from the purchasing agent for one of our best customers. "Henry," he said, "doesn't Mr. Foster work for you?" When I replied that he did, my friend went on: "He's in my office now." "Good," I answered. "We're bidding on that new equipment of yours and I'm glad to know he's in there pitching."

My friend tried to let me down gently: "But Henry, this man isn't representing you, he's representing another company on this bid." Needless to say, that was a little disappointing to us!

We are making sales managers out of engineers and production managers out of accountants, but just changing titles does not begin to do the job. With adequate time and a sufficient pool from which to select, the problem of executive development is clearly defined.

Exhibit II. Servo's Growth Record

	1947	1956	% increase	X	Assuming a 2:1 decrease in value of $ % increase
I. Sales:					
Servo	$120,000	$3,600,000	3,000%	.378	1,500%
Motorola	$50 million	$220 million	340%	.165	170%
Cutler Hammer	$40 million	$80 million	100%	.077	0%
II. Equity:					
Servo	$10,000	$1,400,000	14,000%	.797	7,000%
Motorola	$10 million	$60 million	500%	.199	200%
Cutler Hammer	$13 million	$34 million	161%	.107	31%

$$s_t = s_{47} \, e^{xt}$$

But the matter becomes more complex when there are no standards and no previous performance record, and when the products are new, untried, and unproven. Our efforts in this situation have focused on three areas: encouraging men to attend outside training programs, special recruiting activities, and overcoming prejudices.

Outside Training. The key requirement for the executive in small business is flexibility. He must be able to handle several kinds of assignments. To develop this talent in our people, we encourage them to participate in evening courses and help them with a scholarship program which pays 50% to 100% of the expenses for an approved candidate.

Aggressive Recruiting. Shortages in the engineering profession are hurting the growth businesses more than their larger competitors. Page after page of advertising in the Sunday newspapers underscores the frightful squeeze in which American industry finds itself. At a time when engineering help is in desperately short supply, 20% of those available are being wasted in an extravagant turmoil.

My company is meeting these situations with vigorous measures. We have a liberal profit-sharing plan: after deducting a growth factor of 15% of our capital from our earnings after taxes, we divide our income fifty-fifty between the company and the participants. In addition, some 60 people, or 15% of our personnel, hold options to purchase stock at favorable prices. From the inception of the company, we have followed a firm policy of fifty-fifty on all fringe benefits such as insurance, hospitalization, and educational support.

Furthermore, we actively merchandise our company. For example:

> To open up one campaign, we sent out a jig-saw puzzle to a selected list. When the recipient pieced the pattern together into a picture, he ended up with a list of questions as to why it would be wonderful to work at Servo. Along with the puzzle we included a post card on which they could request the next item—a hi-fi record. On one side of this platter was a high-frequency test recording that went all the way out to 16,000 cycles with which they could test their own sets.
>
> Interspersed, and on the other side, was a somewhat dramatic recitation of the possibilities for them if they worked for us.
>
> Following this we sent a letter from our personnel manager to each person to whom the jig-saw puzzle was mailed. About a month later we dispatched a copy of our profit-sharing booklet to all of the

original people on the list. And so it went, in a planned and organized campaign.

Backing up a systematic program like this, we have instituted other approaches. One of the most effective is to enlist the help of every person in our company to sell the firm. We give each one a regular memorandum which tells him specifically what jobs are open and what kind of people we are looking for. Then we urge the reader to talk it over with his next-door neighbor.

Overcoming Prejudice. One important observer of our social scene has quoted a typical American youth as saying that the big corporations try to do what is best for the employee. He felt that there are no backstabbing and politics in them as there are in smaller firms, and that the big corporations recognize the worth of the individual. Unfortunately this youth was completely wrong. This attitude, commonly held by American young people today, represents a major impediment to the growth and progress of smaller businesses.

Money Grubbing

Rapid growth generates a constant struggle for working capital. No sooner is one accretion of capital completed than additional funds are needed for further expansion; there is no end to this nagging need—it is the price of growth. Obviously, it creates exceptional demands on the time and energy of management.

The financing burdens on small growth businesses are excessive. At the very moment when the demands on our time for building an organization, developing new products, and cultivating markets are at their greatest, we have to consume precious days and weeks in the search for financial support.

Three sets of inequities make the problem even greater: costs of stock issues, tax laws, and interest charges. Looking at each one briefly, here is the picture:

⟨ For large stock issues, the cost to established firms runs from 3% to 4% of the issue; the financing costs for small businesses, particularly "Regulation A" issues, can run from 15% to 25%. The limit of $300,000 under Regulation A financing should, in my judgment, be raised to $1 million if we seriously want to attack the problem.

❡ My corporation has made a profit every year, and we have paid $750,000 in taxes to the federal and state governments. I do not ask that small businesses be excused from carrying their fair share of the tax burden, but it is elementary business prudence on the part of Uncle Sam to revise drastically these onerous tax laws. The idea that any business in its third year of existence should pay the same tax rate as the General Motors Corporation is illogical to the point of being destructive. The tax law as it stands is killing the goose that is intending to lay golden eggs. A graduated tax structure for smaller businesses is clearly necessary as a minimum contribution toward equalizing the many additional costs which a small business faces.

❡ The large corporation can borrow money at 2% to 3% interest; a small corporation pays up to 18%. This prevents us from accumulating a reserve strength and damages our growth to the extent that someday we might have a serious problem in our economy.

Servo's Story. In the face of these problems I founded Servo Corporation of America in 1946 with $10,000 which I had saved and received as proceeds from the sale of my house. Once in business, I established it as my number one priority to strengthen the capitalization of the company. I was able to negotiate a private investment with a Boston firm which added $75,000 to my capital in exchange for a 45% interest in the business.

A contract with Willys Motors, Inc. (then Willys-Overland Motors, Inc.) to design the guidance systems for a missile provided us with an arrangement for monthly advance payments of all expenses against a fixed contract price. In another instance, a contract from the Specialty Assembly and Packaging Corporation to do engineering yielded an advance payment of one-third of the contract price. We were again able to benefit from advanced payments in accepting a contract to build complex electronic navigation equipment from Bendix International, a division of Bendix Aviation Corporation.

In the beginning, we set about acquainting our banks with the activities of our company and developed a close working relationship with them. Our first local bank had a statutory limit which we rapidly outgrew, so we turned to a large institution which gave us the help we needed to run our current business on a more profitable basis. In addition, it provided us with the opportunity for continuing sound growth.

Over the first nine years we strengthened our financial position by retaining all earnings in the business. Further, we augmented our capital strength with a public issue of securities in 1955; we sold $400,000 worth of common stock and $600,000 worth of 20-year subordinated debentures. Finally, we have a line of bank credit of $1 million.

We have not yet come to the end of this struggle for working capital, and since this is a manifestation of growth, we probably never will. But at least we have strengthened our position immeasurably.

Two Markets

Exhibit III pictures our sales volume for the 10 years since our founding.

To start a new business one must have something to sell. We had engineering know-how in the field of guided missiles, and I had done experimental work for the Air Force on guided missiles in 1940 and 1941. During World War II, I was in charge of the first infrared guided missile that was put into production—the Felix.

In 1948, my company completed the first infrared guidance system for a powered missile which was known as the Navy's Gorgon. In 1949, we manufactured the radar guidance equipment for the first successful passive-radar, powered-missile flight which was made by the Skylark at Point Mugu, California. In 1950, the Air Force contracted with us to develop an infrared guidance system for Boeing Airplane Company's Gapa missile.

The outbreak of the Korean War demanded the manufacture of immediately available hardware, and these missile programs were

Exhibit III. Servo's Sales Record

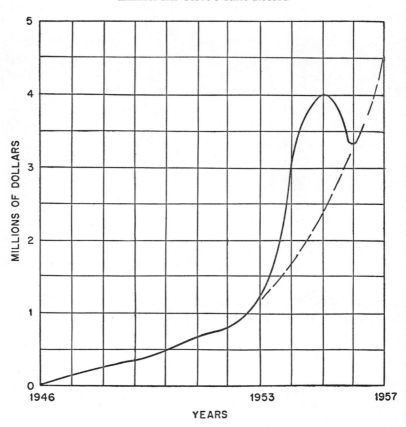

YEARS

slowed down. The Willys-Overland program was canceled, the Skylark was discontinued, the Gorgon was canceled, and Boeing's Gapa missile was called off. Thus, the market for our new know-how in the new missile field was seriously shrunken.

From the day we started in business, we worked to fill industrial needs in order to balance our otherwise all-government business. Work begun in those years culminated in several lines of industrial equipment, like our line of automation test instruments which is sold throughout industry and the scientific colleges. Other examples are:

- Our Servotherm line of heat measurement and control equipment for industry, based on pyrometry.
- Our patented Servosafe Hot Box Detective, which locates hot axle bearings before they can result in train wrecks.
- New activities in the fields of radio navigation and communication.

Even though lack of adequate capital has forced us out of a prime position in the missile business, we have nonetheless maintained our position in the field of military electronics. Thus, we have achieved a sound balance between our civilian and industrial market and the government.

But there are difficulties ahead in the government section of our operation.

The weapons systems concept developed during the past five years has added immeasurably to the burdens of the small company, because it has cut into the incentive to develop proprietary inventions and ideas for the military services. The patent concept is debilitated and ineffectual.

There is no adequate assurance of reward or production orders when proprietary inventions are taken to the military services. Unless serious attention is given to protecting proprietary rights, our national defense can suffer serious damage from loss of innovation over the years. Furthermore, military products are so expensive to develop that only the largest corporations can even consider doing it at their own expense. Profits are held low, and the costs of doing business with the government are high. The small businessman is becoming extremely discouraged.

Keep Competition Fair

These, then, are some of the problems of small business in America today. We do not need or ask for any handouts or unfair advantages, for they simply reward incompetence. But our society has placed many obstacles in the way of the progress and growth of smaller businesses, and these roadblocks should be removed. Although the Congress is doing a great deal to ease these problems, I do not believe that the government is fully aware of the precise nature of the difficulties. Consequently, those steps that are taken are less valuable than is commonly believed. The people who are dealing with these matters in Washington should consult with those who, as practicing small businessmen, are daily experiencing these problems and can contribute realistic solutions.

There are many ways in which we can rectify the inequities in our laws, in our tax structure, and in the general health of our industrial economy. These changes could solve most of the problems of the smaller growth business. Stated in its briefest form, our national goal should be to achieve and maintain a true condition of fair competition in a free economy.

THE NEVER-ENDING SEARCH FOR PRODUCTS*

Our company has faced three main problems, all of them characteristic of small business: securing funds, recruiting adequate personnel, and, above all in our case, developing a product line.

Few Money Worries

Of these three, capital has been the least worrisome. There have been times when we were church-mouse poor, but we have always been able to raise money when we really needed it, and we have paid reasonable rates. Furthermore, the owners of the business have

* By Mr. Kinney.

been far more interested in long-term growth than in immediate income. They have consistently approved plowing back practically all earnings into the business. So I cannot say that actual progress has been held up through lack of money.

Few Personnel Problems

Nor has the personnel problem, which has plagued so many companies, really proved a bar to our progress. Top management has considered the recruitment of young men as its first job. We pay relatively high salaries, offer fairly satisfactory fringe benefits, and try to make junior executives feel part of the management team. In addition, we have filled our executive ranks with men brought up through the company. Our policy has been to develop these people through a carefully planned program of rotation within the company and scholarships for courses in various universities.

Something to Sell

But the development of a product line has been a different story. By way of background let us start with a brief look at our company's history.

We were founded in 1891 to manufacture streetcar registers and fare boxes. Our business grew quite rapidly in the early years, but beginning with 1918—coincident with the decline of the streetcar industry—sales began to fall off. By 1929 total sales had shrunk to $258,000. We lost $19,000 that year, and owed the bank $40,000—not exactly a happy situation.

Fortunately, at this point management woke up, brought in new blood, and determined to find new lines of products, since it was obviously hopeless to try to expand the old line.

First, the Meter

As so often happens, Lady Luck came to the aid of the deserving. Two promoters appeared in answer to a small "products wanted"

advertisement which we placed in a Chicago paper. They had originated the idea of selling appliances, specifically refrigerators, on the
so-called "meter plan." In this method of merchandising, a refrigerator was sold to a customer for nothing down, but the customer
agreed to deposit 25¢, 20¢, or some similar sum in a meter every
day. These deposits were then applied to the purchase price. If the
money was not deposited, a timing device in the meter shut off the
supply of current to the refrigerator.

This plan was very appealing in the 1930's, and the sales talk was
highly effective. You could point out to a potential customer that
he could have a refrigerator costing $200 or so for cigarette money.

Others were in the field when these two men brought their idea
to us, though they had started the idea only to be frozen out. But
we built a good meter, we had some money, and we started in to
sell. In no time, International was producing 600 units of various
types each day, and making a satisfactory profit.

Marketing Our Meters

The key to our success was a sales plan that outclassed our competitors. The conventional method was to send salesmen from store
to store talking merchants into putting on a meter campaign. This
was both slow and costly, so we hit upon the idea of going to
Frigidaire, Westinghouse, Kelvinator, and some of the other producers and saying, "Look, if you will recommend our meters exclusively, if you will advocate the meter plan, we will sell you a
meter for half what your dealers are now paying."

This idea appealed to them, and we soon had the sales forces of
major manufacturers working for us on a scale which we could not
possibly have duplicated ourselves.

Then, the Timer

Important as the meter was to establishing our profits and our
volume of business, it was really more significant because it directed

our attention to a sales area which was very promising. We knew the appliance industry well, as a result of our contacts through the meter selling. In the mid-1930's this industry was expanding rapidly, and its products were becoming more and more automatic. Electric and gas ranges were being equipped to provide controlled cooking, and the invention of the automatic washing machine created a demand for an entirely new type of automatic control. The use of appliance manufacturers to sell our meters, which were basically coin-operated time switches, had brought us in close contact with the entire industry. Therefore, the design and manufacture of a line of timers for the appliance industry would put us in a field which was expanding faster than population growth, and increasingly demanded products we were equipped to make and sell.

The results have proved the soundness of our decision. In a little over 20 years (or 14 years, if the time when we worked exclusively on civilian products is considered), our payroll has expanded from 45 employees to between 800 and 900, and our sales volume has increased correspondingly. All of this growth has come in the timer field. We are, therefore, an example of a company which has not diversified but has found room for growth by intensively exploiting a relatively small segment of industry.

Our growth has not come easily. It has always been simple enough to design products which will operate satisfactorily; the real difficulty has been to develop a product at a price. In designing our timers, we have kept one definite plan in mind: we wanted a basic component which was common to all products and could therefore be produced in volume at low cost.

Since all our products are operated by a clock-type synchronous motor, our first problem was to develop a motor which would operate quietly for long periods of time and could be produced at rock-bottom prices. To train ourselves in motor manufacture we first bought motors, then made the same motor under license, and finally developed a product of our own which was both better and less costly.

We followed the same plan in designing our appliance timers. In 1939 we brought out an electric range timer which not only had new and novel features, but was much lower in price than competing products. As a result, it won immediate acceptance. Frigidaire, Kelvinator, Westinghouse, and many others became customers.

Small Fiasco

World War II nipped this business in the bud and interrupted our expansion, since we were quickly converted completely to fill military needs. In the postwar period of 1945, 1946, and 1947, our sales decreased appreciably because of the growth of competitors who had redesigned and reintroduced their civilian products more rapidly than we. To build up volume again we either had to attempt to recapture our position in the appliance timer field or enter a new and supposedly more promising area.

Unfortunately, instead of concentrating once more on the products which were responsible for our past growth, we chose to manufacture electric alarm and wall clocks, planning to merchandise them through chain stores and mail-order houses. Here an inherent disadvantage of a small company intensified our growth problem. We were not able to spend the tremendous sums of money necessary to compete with the major clock manufacturers, who had built up their product name with large advertising budgets through the years. Lacking public acceptance and a complete line, we had to sell on price with disastrous results. However, by facing up to the fact that we had made a mistake and by taking our losses promptly, we were able to return to the specialized field of appliance timers and to begin to grow once more.

Then, More Timers

Following our concept of a basic design which was simple and economical to make but could be modified readily to produce many versions differing considerably in appearance, we brought out a gas range timer, an interval timer, and a clothes dryer timer which were initially successful and which, in modified form, still command an important segment of their respective fields. The introduction of a line of clock-radio timers a year ago gave the company a complete line of appliance timers except for controls used in automatic clothes washers and dishwashers. We are now just starting production on clothes washer and dishwasher timers which complete our coverage of the appliance field.

Dangerous Customer

If our efforts turn out as we hope, we will have timers for all phases of the appliance industry. This is both good and bad. It is good in that all products are related and based on the use of the same low-cost synchronous motor. Also, selling expense is relatively low, since all sales are made to much the same group of customers. However, the situation is bad in that we are a manufacturers' manufacturer selling to the appliance industry, and are therefore subject to its vagaries.

Furthermore, the same trend toward concentration which has so reduced the number of automobile companies is manifesting itself very plainly in the appliance industry. We are selling more and more to fewer and fewer customers. In addition, it is logical to assume that suppliers of assemblies to the appliance manufacturers may well face the same fate that has overtaken makers of automotive parts, whose business has been absorbed largely by the automobile makers themselves. There are arguments that this situation may not develop to the same extent with appliances. The industry is smaller, and the assemblies it needs vary greatly. Appliance manufacturers, therefore, may not show the same enthusiasm for making everything themselves as their automotive counterparts. Nevertheless, a parts supplier in our position would be dull indeed not to appreciate the possibility of the fate which may await him.

Escape Hatch

We have been aware of this danger for a long time—in fact, since we first became a parts manufacturer—and we have endeavored to do something to protect ourselves. Our insurance takes the form of manufacturing and selling through jobbers a line of industrial and home time switches under our own trade name of "Intermatic." This phase of our business is growing faster than the appliance line, so that we have an escape hatch, but we realize that the proportion should be higher, and are now devoting the major portion of our new product development to the creation of items in no way related to appliances.

Developing new product ideas has not been easy, however. We have exhausted the ideas of the three men at the top level who run the company. The next level of personnel has added but a few more ideas. So we have started to try some "brainstorming." This system has not yet given us a product that I really feel happy about, but it has produced some good ideas and an excellent name for one of our items.

To date we have limited our search to products which fit our manufacturing and sales facilities—we do not want to diversify to the point of getting into whaling or peddling milk! Will this path lead to success? We can only judge the future by the past. In 1929 and again in 1946 we faced far more serious situations with success, so we have great confidence in our ability to continue to expand in new directions. Perhaps we may be forced to follow the example of many others and diversify into utterly alien fields, but for the time being we plan to stay close to the firm base of our present sales and manufacturing knowledge.

An Eye on the Record

Throughout our company history—right up to and including this search for new products—we have paid special attention to one of the key problems of the small business: the maintenance of good records.

When we were small, with one or two hundred people, I can remember the desperation that I felt when an accountant brought the January 1 statement to me about May 1. Somehow, I was supposed to have known in the meantime what had happened. Since

I am a great believer in prompt records, but do not remotely care about old ones, we developed a method whereby I know each day around 1:00 p.m. whether we have made or lost money the previous day and approximately how much within 10%. By 9:00 a.m. the next morning I have the data on all the scrap, in dollars and in parts, that has been made the day before. Similarly, production counts are maintained, while production line stoppages are immediately reported and the cause promptly determined and corrected. Since some of the operations involve 15 or 20 workers, real money is involved. This program has been extremely effective in reducing our down time.

All this accurate record-keeping does not involve anything like the cost and effort that might seem necessary. To illustrate, let me describe our daily record on profit and loss:

> First of all, we make the best guess we can as to what our sales are going to be in a particular month, based on actual backlogs and forecasts of variations. Then from experience, we estimate what our supplies and services are going to be. Our largest errors turn up in this category because we buy hundreds of thousands of dollars worth of tools in a year and a $50,000 machine can appear in one month when it is scheduled to come along at some other time.
>
> The cost of sales, labor, and material, is estimated on the basis of the product mix as determined by our sales forecast, and plotted at so much per day. Overhead is estimated for four days and corrected on the fifth. Putting together the various elements, we can arrive at a fairly accurate guess as to our actual profit on a particular volume of a particular mix.
>
> Surprisingly enough, doing all this work does not take our accountant 20 minutes a day. And it is clearly valuable, because when I see red figures coming up I can try to do something before we are in real trouble.

Some people have asked why we keep these records on a daily basis, instead of a weekly or monthly calculation. The answer is simple: we have to because of the nature of our business. While we attempt to standardize, we make something over 100 different types of motors. There are 65 or 66 different range timers of each basic model, and there are three models. Thus our product mix changes greatly, so it is often not clear at all whether we are making or losing money.

Furthermore, errors creep in quickly, scrap can grow, efficiency on assembly may go haywire, and production schedules can slip behind. If we try to control this a month later, or attempt to correct errors some time after they have happened, we are beaten. We can never find out the true story. But if something goes off the day before, we have a fighting chance of finding out what happened and correcting the error. Correcting mistakes quickly is important in a big company, but it is utterly vital in a small one.

Survival Means Adjustment

So much for our story. We cannot claim to have found the answers to our future—in a rapidly changing economy like today's we have no guarantee that we will be able to lick our problems and adjust to shifting markets. But this situation is typical of what will face many small manufacturers. Nothing that the government can do, nothing that any bank can do, will save a company such as ours. We have to stand on our own two legs and use our native intelligence. If we are not a really worthwhile economic entity, we will perish in the long run just like the manufacturers of buggy whips. It may be painful, but I am afraid that this is economic history and economic justice.

QUESTIONS AND ANSWERS *

From the floor: What use can be made of outside management help, either through professional consultants and professors, or through boards of directors?

Mr. Peterson: There are three ways that one can get help:

* Businessmen present at the panel session on which this chapter is based raised certain questions which brought about the interplay of ideas reported more or less verbatim in this section.

1. From associates and cronies.
2. From outside paid consultants.
3. From special connections.

In my own particular case—unique, to be sure—I had the advantage of having worked for three large companies. Because I was rather close to the top men, I have been lucky enough to have one of the most capable, unpaid, informal "board of directors" in the country (my formal board is the one I inherited). Probably I am buying $50,000 worth of consulting for free!

This general approach may prove to be a really practical help to the small businessman, who can't pay the professionals the rates they ask. Most of them want $1,000 for a look-see just to find out if they can afford to take on the job. Their cost problems are serious, and our outfit is really too small to make it worth their while. But forced retirement at 60 and 65 has driven some of the top men in the country into inactivity, and all it takes is a little grass-roots organization to put them together once in a while.

My old roommate in the Air Force, who is now a dean in the engineering department of a large university, started me off on this search for help when he said: "Since all men like to talk, you can get better advice for nothing than you will ever pay for, if you will keep the conversations off the record!" He himself sits on about 14 advisory boards, and he is closely acquainted with about six other men who sit on similar boards.

So I make it a point either to go through his home city or to get him down to my place with a couple of friends once or twice a year. I never feed them more than three problems at a time—it is usually only one. We try to work out these meetings when something is going on at the University of Michigan that we want to see. All in all I have about six sessions a year, lasting anywhere from an hour to an evening, not counting informal meetings with visitors from other countries.

Mr. Blackstone: We have used all of the usual sources of consultants: our general counsel is very active in the company, our senior partner is also secretary of our corporation, and the auditing

agency which audits our books is available for financial counsel.
Our board is most helpful, too, since it includes three financial
people, two of whom are substantial stockholders, the senior partner in the investment firm that handles our securities, and two
prominent corporation presidents.

But our bank is one of the best sources of help I know. This
sounds like a ridiculously simple solution to the problem and it
isn't as easy as it sounds. But this particular national bank is one
of the more progressive; it understands and intends to specialize
in the problems of smaller businesses.

As for the professionals, I have to confess that I have a little test.
It works like this:

> We have had callers wishing to sell us management counsel
> about two or three times a week over the last 10 years. Usually
> they take a look at our sprawling operation, which is in five differ-
> ent buildings. Then they go home and decide to write a follow-up
> sales letter. As a come-on, they tell me that they already have a
> solution to recommend for one of my problems. That "solution" is
> usually a suggestion that we must get all of our operations under
> one roof, which of course we knew before we spread out. That tips
> me off—and I dispense with that caller.

This last year, however, we developed a relationship with a
management consulting firm which is working out very nicely.
They have been in our plant for about six or eight months now
doing some general jobs.

Finally, I might say that I have learned one important fact from
experience: a management consultant is not likely to be helpful if
you treat him like a crash program. You can't wait until you have
a ring in your nose, and then rush out and tell him to come in
immediately to fix things up. So we are now learning how to work
with consultants, treating them as a part of the team even when we
don't specifically need them; we keep them abreast of our progress
and problems, so they serve as kind of a family physician for us.

Mr. Kinney: Basically, we are an ingrown company. There are
only four stockholders, all family. The board of directors is made

up of those owners, a professor from Harvard Business School, and the officers. We have stayed away from outside help purposely, because to date we have been able to generate from within ideas and policies which have kept our company prosperous. If we run out of ideas or if we are unable to solve some problem, then we would certainly turn to outsiders for help. Until then we feel that reliance and use of our own personnel to the exclusion of outsiders is a sound policy.

From the floor: I should like to make a comment on the use of consultants. The manager must distinguish between problem formulation, problem solving, and decision making. In the small business the chief man makes the decision, but he may need help in formulating problems and identifying alternatives because this process takes up time that he may not have.

Therefore, if he can find someone who is competent and can work on a "time spent" basis over a period of years, the cost of outside help can be kept down to maybe somewhere between $1,000 and $3,000 a year and the assistance can be highly effective.

From the floor: How can you select sales representatives effectively and then get your share of their time?

Mr. Peterson: This is the one problem I have been completely unable to solve. About four years ago when I started out I was carrying about 20 representatives for every one I found that was any good. This bothered me; here was a company with a high-quality product that was well known to only a few people, and I was disturbed not to see a representative in Cleveland, St. Paul, and other similar places.

So I went to the banks and asked them for an introduction to the top consulting engineering firm in town. If we had a good customer in the community, I would call on them and find out who would be a distinguished outfit to represent us. Then I would appoint the suggested group. But I soon found out that you don't get sales from a dignified reputation, and I would have to wait a whole year, out of fairness to the man, to find out for sure whether or not he was going to perform.

In short, I discovered that just appointing a man, having him cover the territory, and listing him in the telephone book wasn't enough, if he wasn't out ringing doorbells. It is better to have nobody in an area—at least then you have a free hand.

The second approach I took was to work through the engineering societies. That idea produced some results, but in most instances I was coming up with someone who was disgruntled with sitting at a drafting board and wanted to sell. Most of them had no native ability as salesmen, nor enough training.

Finally, I turned to the agents themselves. I soon learned that the Class A man knows all the other top salesmen in an area, and can pick up the telephone and help me convince one of his colleagues that he should take on our line.

This approach has been far and away the most successful. I have appointed about 35 agents in three years, and out of that group I probably got five good ones. But now that I am being selective and using my best agents to get other top men, I am getting about one out of four interviewed, instead of one out of ten or fifteen.

We have found that the key problem is to show an agent how your line can be made profitable for him. He doesn't give a damn about you; it has to be a money-maker from his standpoint. In some cases it won't be profitable for him. Under these circumstances, you are beaten. But even when it does fit his needs, the agent very often fails to see its possibilities. The natural step at this point is to write letters, send literature, work out a list of prospects, and so on.

But that isn't usually much good. Instead, we set up a division of six district managers. One of those men will go out to an important territory—not to all territories—and will live with the selected agent for a while. He will take him around and show him how the line can be sold. Sometimes he will go so far as to call on contractors and architects and actually get orders. Thus he can show the agent that our line can make profits for him. Needless to say, this takes plenty of time and money, but in an important area it produces real dividends.

Then there is another procedure which we follow when an agent has worked hard, but has not been able to crack a market: a crash program of selling. We send out a team of at least five, and sometimes as many as ten, men into an area and instruct them to put on a real drive. They visit every possible customer, and try to stir up the agent and his office people—especially the telephone girl, because she can sell a great many products if it is something that she can handle.

Finally, we institute contests between the agents, offering a trip to Mexico or Italy as a prize. The results are often amazing. In one case, the trip to Italy actually represented less money to the man who won it than his commissions on our products, but the vacation got him to work and the salary did not. His wife was of Italian extraction—maybe that's the answer!

Thus we have found out that the back stairs are sometimes much easier to climb than the front ones.

LONG-RANGE PLANNING FOR ECONOMIC EXPANSION

Edward C. Bursk, Robert C. Tait,
Charles T. Lipscomb, Jr., and Henry E. Crampton

IN INTRODUCING THIS CHAPTER, I want to point out one or two matters that have a bearing on long-range planning, particularly in times of economic expansion. One of these is increasing lead times; the other is the growth of the concept of professional management.

Longer Lead Times

One of the interesting phenomena of our economy has been the increase in lead times, which shows up in countless ways.

Note: Mr. Bursk, who makes the introductory observations, is Professor of Business Administration, Harvard Business School and Editor of the *Harvard Business Review;* Mr. Tait is President, Stromberg-Carlson Company, a division of General Dynamics Corporation; Mr. Lipscomb is President, the J. B.

Forty or fifty years ago the lead time of our dominant industries —textiles, for example—was perhaps a year or less. With the development of the automotive industry and its lead time of three years came obvious changes in the nature of our economy. But now we find that we have not reached the end of the process. In a very real sense, the dominant industry today is aeronautics, with its constellation of related industries—guided missiles, electronics, and so forth. Here the lead time, determined by advancing technology and increasingly complex production processes, is five or six years.* Thus, the whole trend of the economy is to ever-longer time lags between the conception of a product and its consumption.

But it is not only production that is characterized by this phenomenon. The same situation is developing in marketing. The magnitude of expenditures that have to be made to gain a share of the consumer market and the intricacies of market research, distribution channels, promotion, and so on have run the lead times for new products out as long as two or three years. Again, in organizational matters, the picture is the same. With business becoming ever more complex, it is impossible to shift an organization around overnight. It takes thought, preparation, communication, and gradual adjustments.

Finally, in management itself we see the identical situation developing: more and more companies are putting in time and giving thought to executive development programs that have a lead time of as much as 10 years. Most businessmen are concerned that the people who take over their jobs be able to step in with the necessary skills and abilities when the time comes for them to do so. Any management training system is designed for substantial time lags.

This whole tendency puts a new and greater emphasis on long-range planning. Obviously, we are being forced to think further and further ahead. Forecasting trends and finding ways to meet or

Williams Company; Mr. Crampton is Assistant Vice President, the Michigan Bell Telephone Company.

* See Eliot Janeway, "Tooling up for the Aeronautic Age," *Harvard Business Review,* November–December 1957, p. 103.

capitalize on them, and adjusting our organization to the future, not the present or the past, demands a degree of forward planning which has never been required of executives before.

Professional Approach

Another factor which fits neatly into the topic of this chapter is the increasingly intellectual approach which executives are taking to business. This professionalism shows up in the growing interest in books like this and in the conference on which it is based. It has led executives to lay a far heavier emphasis on the careful consideration of their problems and the rationalization of their decisions. "Seat-of-the-pants" management is less and less popular—and its effectiveness is diminishing rapidly.

To illustrate this point, let me refer to a survey which we did for the *Harvard Business Review* recently. To start with, we charted the number of men going into management from graduate schools of business administration all over the country during the last decade. The curve shows an increase of some 250%. Then we looked at the figures on businessmen who came back for a university advanced management or American Management Association type of training program. Here, again, we found a curve showing an increase of 295% over ten years ago. The best estimates of in-company programs for management development come up with even more of an increase, 340%. Finally, the circulation of the *Harvard Business Review* which is designed as we say on the cover, "for the thoughtful businessman," shows that identical curve. Since the *Review* seeks to reflect and foster the analytical, broad-gauge, professional approach in its articles on current administrative problems, its rapid growth is still another indication of the accelerating trend.[*]

Clearly, one result of this remarkable development is both the inclination and the training to do some careful thinking about tomorrow as well as today. The professionalization of management,

[*] See Edward C. Bursk, "New Dimensions in Top Executive Reading," *Harvard Business Review*, September–October 1957, p. 93.

in short, encourages and equips businessmen to look ahead and plan ahead.

A third factor which stimulates long-range planning today can be succinctly stated: since so many leading companies are already taking advantage of this approach and doing some planning, the laws of competition are going to force the rest of us into it in the very near future.

DEVELOPMENT OF AN LRP TECHNIQUE*

At Stromberg-Carlson we backed into long-range planning by accident, or rather, by necessity. We were forced into it by a crucial choice which we made several years ago: the decision to withdraw from the radio-television business.

Time for a Change

There is a memorandum in my desk written in August 1952. I slaved for hours on that document, putting together my thoughts about our future, and came up with the conclusion that we had to get out of the radio field. I said it was not even a matter of choice; we simply had to, or accept the other alternative of getting in whole-hog and selling a complete appliance line.

I based my position on the premise that the key problem in radio-television is not manufacturing but distribution. Anybody can make the products; as a matter of fact, production can be doubled simply by putting another mechanized line next to the first one, hiring a group of "cherry pickers," as we call them, and training them to handle a screw driver, a pair of pliers, and a soldering iron.

It was my contention that ultimately we would have to control our distribution, unpleasant as that sounds, in order to succeed. We would have to constitute enough of a dealer's business so we could tell him what to do. Otherwise we might make a dozen models at an expenditure of considerable time and money only to discover

* By Mr. Tait.

that one particular item was more popular than the others, and dealers wanted only that model. We could not know this in advance, of course. While we might increase the production of this one type, we could not very well throw away the others.

Under these conditions, when we comprise only 1% or 2% of the dealer's business, he can easily say, "I'll buy these and never mind those." Thus radio and television are really distributing businesses, and we decided—after about 30 days of discussion—that it was not for us.

In Transit

Having determined to get out of the field, we had to face the next question: How? It is easy to make a decision like this, but extremely difficult to carry it out. In fact, we finally got out of the business in the winter of 1956, four and a half years later, and we had to do plenty of hard planning in the interim. The company needed a substitute product, and the transition had to be made smoothly, or many of our people would be out of work, earnings would go to pieces, and our reputation in Wall Street would plummet.

Consequently, we decided to stay in the business for the time being and take advantage of the surge of sales which characterized the latter part of 1952. It turned out to be one of the best years we had, and Wall Street thought anything that had the name "television" on it had a great future.

The next year we called in our preferred stock. We were financing ourselves by our boot straps but at the same time were getting ready to get out of the television business when the time seemed right. When the day finally came and we did close our books on those products, we showed an uninterrupted upcurve in earnings and employment. We had no large inventories; there was no fire sale and no significant loss in the process.

This transition was our first lesson in the importance of timing and the need for some kind of long-range planning in a business built on rapidity of development. Since then we have worked assiduously on our long-range planning. We make mistakes and always will, but experience improves the technique. Our long-range planning today is infinitely better than it was when we made that first important decision in 1952.

Targets to Set

First of all, what do we plan? We program both our civilian and our government business, as well as the relationship between the two. It is true that government business is generally speculative, since it is subject to the whims of Congress and various political pressures. But in many respects the government electronics business is more stable than the commercial market and can be subjected to the same long-range examination. Furthermore, the balance between private and public sales can—and should—be carefully set.

Our own goal is to reduce our present percentage, which in electronics is about half our sales, to not over 25%. But we want always to maintain our total government business at somewhere between 25% and 33% of the total.

Long and Short of It

The key to our procedure is a five-year plan, backed up by a detailed one-year program, or more accurately, a one-year budget which is basically put together by the comptroller's department after consultation with the division managers. It is then examined by top management and coordinated in terms of the over-all company picture.

In considering this budget, we have worked out a custom which is time-consuming and a little exhausting, but highly productive. We take the top 15 or 20 executives of the company—division heads, officers, and so on—and go away, somewhere fairly nearby, for a week end. Our first session starts on Friday midafternoon, breaks for cocktails and dinner, and then continues until almost midnight. Saturday morning we start at it again, running through Saturday afternoon and evening, and closing on Sunday morning. In doing this, we get away from the telephone and the plant so that we can sit across the table from each other in an informal atmosphere. By Saturday night all the problems—including some we did not know existed—are out on the table, and we really make some progress.

Originally, we ran these sessions four times a year; now it is less often because quarterly proved too time-consuming. We are still unsettled on whom we should invite to these meetings. We have tried changing the general agenda to cover matters other than top management issues and bring in a secondary group like the sales or top engineering people. But this technique has been only fairly successful, for two reasons:

> (1) One such gathering got up to 30-odd people and required a formal agenda and somebody with a hammer in his hand to keep order. It lost its informality.
> (2) We found that the head of a division is more timid about speaking up with second-level people present because he does not want to look silly in front of a man who works for him.

Continuing Process

When we complete the detailed budget for one year, we knock that off our five-year plan and add another one. Thus we are always five years ahead, and planning becomes a continuing process.

Another important aspect of our planning procedure I call "bottom-up planning." We ask each one of the self-sufficient departments within our several divisions to tell us what they think they are going to do over the next few years. When we put these statements together at the top level, they are fantastic. But after we have leavened it all with the availability of capital, the practicality of some of the projects, products analysis, projected return on investment, and the outlook for the whole economy, we get down to a reasonably attainable goal.

Still another important planning area is product development. We have a Research and Development Committee of the whole corporation which is made up of representatives of each division, including sales people on an *ad hoc* basis, the research staff, and the vice president in charge of engineering. They attempt to evaluate all possible products from every division. Sometimes this process wastes the time of, say, the communications division when the matter under consideration is entirely electronic, but it does have the advantage of bringing everyone in on the decision. After all, this is where we make our decisions on allocations of funds, and that question is of vital importance to all the top division personnel.

The General Economy

All planning in industry today has to be set against the backdrop of the general economy. Only since the war have we had an atmosphere of stability, without which planning is impossible. According to every indication, this pattern is likely to continue with only minor changes. We have what we might call a planned or controlled economy, insofar as money manipulation can control it. In the near future we are going to be finding out whether we can expect it to keep up like this for an extended period of time. If we can continue to hold interest rates up to put a brake on inflation and still finance the national debt satisfactorily, we should move ahead confidently.

In addition, we have far better information than we used to. National statistics are generally improved, though some of them are still weak and too far behind the facts to be of much value. In our planning process we have paid special attention to the use of these figures, where they are sound.

I do not necessarily think that our system of long-range planning is the best method; there are all kinds of approaches. But we like this one, and it is working out well. We are learning something every day and are becoming increasingly convinced that there is no business that can do without some kind of planning under current conditions.

If this is true now, it is going to be even more true in the future. Every industry will have to program far ahead if it is to succeed against its competition. All of us are going to have to devote more thought, more time, and more skill to our long-range planning.

PLANNING FOR A SMALL BUSINESS*

As president of a small company, I believe I have two major responsibilities: executive development and long-range planning. The more I become involved in the latter, the more I wonder if it should not be listed as the first of these two principal functions, for only by looking and programing ahead can we achieve direction and purpose in what we do.

Seventeen-point Program

Two and a half years ago, when I first took over my business, which makes men's toiletries, it was run down in many ways. The first move I made was to draw up a list of jobs that had to be done immediately, which I presented at the first directors' meeting in November 1954. Let me list these 17 points, and then go on to show how they lead up to a long-range planning project in our firm:

1. See that all current production, advertising, and promotional jobs keep moving.

2. Meet all the people in our business. Get acquainted with key people fast.

3. Study each product. Look at its packaging, including the copy, printing, and colors. Check its quality, consistency, and performance, in relation to the competition. Examine our prices to distributors and consumers as compared with our competition. Check our trade policies, discounts, and terms.

4. Outline changes that seem necessary or desirable in formulas or packages. Plan the needed laboratory work and trade and consumer research, and find out the costs. Schedule the work at a rate the business can afford. Make emergency changes immediately.

5. Study past and present sales trend for total company sales and for each group of products in our three markets—domestic, export, and Canadian.

* By Mr. Lipscomb.

6. Analyze costs of administration, manufacturing, selling, and advertising to find out where they may be out of line.

7. Study and improve field selling policies and procedures.

8. Study recent advertising on our products and competitive products.

9. Define advertising policy for each of our products, specifying the consumers we want to reach, types of media and space considered best for our use, seasonal factors, and so on.

10. Decide on the "sales pitch" which will do the best job of selling each of our products against its competition. Have the advertising agency use this sales pitch as the basis for advertising.

11. Study recent merchandising plans of our company and of the competition.

12. Prepare merchandising and sales promotion policies for each of our products covering distribution, displays, consumer sampling, trade and consumer deals, and gift packages.

13. Prepare 1955 promotional plan and budget for each product.

14. Study the organization plan of the J. B. Williams Company and decide if we should make any changes in the reporting relationships and responsibilities of any job.

15. Study all key personnel and find out how we can help them to function better. Decide if any of them cannot perform their jobs properly and, if so, make fair plans for correcting the situation.

16. Make sure that there are bright, promising young men in the organization who have the capacity to fill my job and other executive posts when the time comes. If such men are not with us now, find them and train them.

17. Plan for expansion of the business through new product development and long-range growth objectives.

Plant Expansion

I soon found that implementing such a program demanded long-range planning in many areas—plant, finance, export sales, and so on. Take the problem of our physical facilities, for instance:

We had a top management consultant firm make a survey recently. They found out that our factory—the "new" building was built in 1895—is not only inadequate for what I gave them as a very rough rule-of-thumb projection of sales volume for five years, but is inadequate even today. It is costing us a penalty of $450,000 a year to operate this monster. So we have to make some changes in a hurry, and they will require some real long-range planning.

Money Problems

Then take our financing problem. Ours is a small business, with $12.5 million total consolidated and unconsolidated sales. We have $4 million in assets after deducting current liabilities. We have $2.4 million in long-term debt and preferred stock. According to the bankers, the ratio of our debt is not good, and we have real money problems.

To make the problem more difficult, some of our products are seasonal. Skol, Williams Electric Shave Lotion, and Conti show large seasonal fluctuations in advertising and merchandising expenditures, as well as in sales. For example, Skol sales come chiefly in May, June, and July; in September the dealers send back everything they have not sold. Thus we do not really know what our sales have been until the end of the year.

When we made up our cash-flow budget last fall, we found that we had to have a very serious heart-to-heart talk with the banks to get over the hump. With all new product formulas and advertising, we had to undertake types of expenditures that had not been needed in the past. This cost, the need for a new factory, and the existing debt have created a real need for immediate long-range planning.

Export Sales

Again, our healthy export business required long-range thinking. We have a $5 million business outside the United States, including large shaving cream businesses in certain countries like Brazil, with

$1 million, and France, with $600,000. With the world situation changing and foreign advertising, merchandising, and competition developing so fast, our policies, procedures, and organization go out of date very quickly unless they are based on at least a five-year projection.

Fresh Team

Then we have a new, young management team. Of our key men, 60% have come in during the last two years. They are very young indeed—28 to 35 years old.

At the President's Round Table at Colgate last summer I told a group that my main problem was the development of this team and someone passed along a suggestion to me which we put into practice: the establishment of a management committee. So on December 26 and 27, 1956, we held the first meeting of the Management Committee of J. B. Williams Company, with these three major purposes in mind:

1. To provide the president with a most important tool of management in all four major administrative areas—planning, controlling, appraising, and leading.

2. To aid our program of executive development by broadening and developing the management skills of our key executives who serve on the Management Committee.

3. To improve the operations of the business by requiring better planning and better assessment of performance on the part of all operating executives; by getting each committee member's ideas and suggestions on other departments; and by broadening each member's knowledge of the business as a whole.

At these meetings, each member presents his accomplishments in the past period, in relation to the goal set and the standards established, on the basis of a printed agenda he has circulated a week before. Then he states his goal and standards for the coming market and explains changes he has made in procedures or plans to accomplish his objectives.

Making a Start

It became immediately apparent that we would have to allow time in this Management Committee for the development and review of some long-range planning activity. Furthermore, it was clear that this group itself was going to become the long-range planning committee. So at our April 1957 meeting I had each one of the five key men make a recommendation as to what our long-range planning activity should be. The results were very interesting:

¶ Our Canadian Vice President analyzed the economy very briefly and set the general objective for the growth of Canadian business through 1962. He then went on to establish a 1962 goal for each product and the percentage of the business he wanted to attain.

¶ The International Division Manager outlined the general principles involved in long-range planning and the procedure they would follow in setting up a long-range plan.

¶ Our Director of Research and Development made some rather broad assumptions as to the growth and total sales of the company. He then estimated the increase in research and development and quality control, as measured in dollars and in percentage of gross sales for 1956–1961.

¶ The Operations Vice President simply dealt with the organization of the long-range planning activity, outlined the different areas which his department heads would be asked to analyze and set January of 1958 as the earliest date we could expect to have a framework for a five-year plan for the company.

¶ Finally, the Marketing Vice President gave us a book which he had prepared. It included an economic forecast based on expected market expansion and population growth; a company profit-and-loss sheet with sales, expenses, and profits for each year through 1962; personnel plans; and a long-range plan for each one of our products, which included a section listing the purposes of the product, present sales, future sales expectation, share of the market we can expect, costs, profits before taxes, and a discussion of advertising and merchandising plans.

Plans for Planning

So we are just at the beginning, working toward the next step, when we will reach an agreement on sales objectives for each one of our products for the five years ahead. These goals will be determined in the light of what we know about the products as we have developed them to date and the plans that we have in mind for them. In crystallizing these goals we keep in mind the competitive situation and the amount of money we think will be available to us for advertising, merchandising, and selling for each one of the products in terms of the sales we are seeking to achieve.

After we have reached a common position on these matters, each key executive in the business will set up a five-year plan for his own department, based on our total sales projection, and our costs will be worked out year by year for five years ahead.

Finally, we have to put all these costs back into the machine, grind it out, and find out if we will end up with more, or less, money for advertising and selling than we had thought. The marketing plans have to be re-examined in terms of the money available year by year for advertising and selling, and these plans may again change either our profits or sales estimates.

This procedure is very similar to the system we use to establish our one-year marketing plans, so it looks to me as though we are coming out with five-year programs constructed on our customary principles and in our traditional fashion. I do not know yet whether this is "right" or "wrong" according to the book—but I do know two things:

(1) It is a good activity, which is helping everybody, and the men are all excited about it. It gives them a sense of direction and purpose, and I am sure that five years from now we are going to be closer to where we ought to be because we have been going through this process.

(2) It is having a beneficial effect on our present performance because it is providing us with a target at which to shoot.

In conclusion then, our initial efforts at long-range planning have started to pay dividends in the attitudes of our key executives, the sense of direction instilled in the company as a whole, and the specific facts we have uncovered about the basic nature of our business situation.

PLANNING AND MANAGEMENT DEVELOPMENT *

In my section of this chapter, I want to describe a Bell System project which integrates long-range planning with higher-management development. This is a rather specialized aspect of planning, but it provides some general guides which can be of help to other firms interested in this important new management technique.

Bell System

To understand our program, a little background about the Bell System will be of value.

The Bell System is made up of the American Telephone & Telegraph Company and its various affiliates. There are 20 operating telephone companies which have the responsibility and the exclusive franchise to furnish telephone service in the territories where they operate. They serve about 50 million out of the 60 million telephones in the United States. In addition, we include the Western Electric Company, Inc., which serves as the manufacturing section and supplier, and the Bell Telephone Laboratories, Incorporated, which forms the research unit of the system.

Most of the interstate communications business in the country is handled by a department of the American Telephone & Telegraph Company known as the Long-Lines Department. In addition, the American Telephone & Telegraph Company maintains a small staff which coordinates the efforts of the Bell Telephone Laboratories, the Western Electric Company, and the operating companies, in

* By Mr. Crampton.

order to insure the orderly introduction of improved telephone services and equipment. This staff also acts as a medium of exchange for ideas that are continually being generated in the operating companies for the improvement of telephone service.

Rapid Growth

Since the end of World War II, the telephone business has been characterized by rapid growth and a very swiftly expanding technology. The number of telephones in service has doubled in the last 10 years. We have installed as many telephones in this decade as we did in the previous 70 years. Likewise, the number of long-distance calls that we handle has doubled, and we think that we will probably be able to double our business again in the next 10 or 15 years.

This same period of time has seen tremendous progress in technology. For example:

 ¶ Most obvious, of course, is the continued progress in the conversion of local exchange service from manual to dial.

 ¶ We have made great strides in mechanizing long-distance calls, by giving the operators facilities for dialing and by providing customers with the equipment to dial their own calls directly.

 ¶ The undersea cable mentioned by Mr. LaPierre in his chapter * and the transistor, developed by Bell Laboratories, which gives promise of an entirely new art of communication for telephones and many other electronic businesses.

Such great growth in the past and in prospect, coupled with the matter of lead time which Mr. Bursk discussed, makes long-range planning a fundamental part of the telephone business. It extends all the way from the manufacturing and installation end to operation.

There are, of course, many technical problems of a long-range planning nature, but I want to concentrate on the problem of inte-

* "Technological Change—What it Will Mean to Management," p. 27.

grating long-range planning with higher-management development which I touched on above.

Higher-management Group

First of all, what do we mean by "higher management"? In the Bell System we have about 780,000 employees. Of these, 300 are at the vice-presidential level or above. This is our top-management group.

Some 900 to 1,000 department heads report to the top-management people. When we use the term "higher management," we are referring to this echelon in our organization. Clearly, these men have attained substantial responsibilities in their functional duties: they are general plant managers, general traffic managers or commercial managers; they are chief engineers and assistant vice presidents with functional duties in public relations, personnel, or other areas.

In addition to their functional company duties, most of them participate in community or civic affairs at fairly high levels, many of them serving on boards of directors of community or business organizations. Furthermore, they are the prime source of talent for our top-management needs.

We recognize, therefore, that anything which can be done to help them continue their self-development is, in itself, a long-range plan to provide for the higher organizational requirements of the business. So in 1952 we decided to undertake a review of our higher management development program. We went about the job in this way:

> A committee of seven vice presidents from the operating companies, known as the Bell System Committee for Higher Management Development, was formed to consider the problem. A director was chosen, and he assembled a working task force which interviewed many of the department heads and company officers. The department heads were specifically asked what they felt would help them in their own self-development.
>
> As a result, we established the Bell System Executive Conferences, which have been held in Asbury Park, New Jersey, since the latter

part of 1953. The task force designed a conference program, and later became the conference staff. They were assisted by a group of consultants, including professors from leading business schools.

At Asbury Park

The department heads from the operating companies, Western Electric, and the Bell Laboratories come to Asbury Park in groups of about 40 to attend these conferences. The first series is known as the basic course and runs for four weeks. It is designed to give the conferees an opportunity to examine some of the basic social, political, and economic phenomena that are going on around us and to interpret the impact of these events on their personal and business lives.

The second course is known as the advance series and is two weeks long. It is set up to help the conferees study and evaluate economic, financial, and social trends, and to form judgments about the way these affect the telephone business. The last two days of the conference are spent in studying a comprehensive general management problem known as the Bi-State Telephone Company Case. The Bi-State Telephone Company is a fictitious firm that has been created from the statistical data of several real units in the Bell System. The material covers all areas of the operation, and the economic and social environment surrounding the company.

In discussing this case, the conferees are given the opportunity to evaluate current and future economic trends, examine the cost and service situation, determine what service and facilities require sales emphasis, decide on expansion programs and the availability of capital for financing them, consider future bargaining policies and their impact on earnings, and review and plan for community relationships.

We are now in the process of formulating a third series of conferences which will integrate long-range planning with our higher-management development. It will challenge the conferees to take a forward look at the problems that telephone management will be facing in the next 10 years. Consideration has been given to future growth possibilities with the realization that these changes will take place in a changing economy and society. Some of these changes can be foreseen fairly clearly, and their impact on telephone business merits serious study and consideration.

Some of the questions that these developments will pose for our business are:

⟨[What will be the effect of a continued creeping inflation on company earnings, wage structures, and relationships with regulatory authorities—which are very important to us?

⟨[What will be the result of some of the broader political and social changes in the world, like the drift towards more government regulation of other businesses, and government health, welfare, and security programs?

⟨[What will be the impact of advances in telephone technology on the wants of the public for telephone service, on our organizational requirements, and on our union relationships?

⟨[What would be the effect of a continued rise of per capita real income on customers' needs, and how can we increase our share of the customer's dollar?

In order to allow study of these influences on the telephone business, we are going to project the Bi-State Telephone Company Case to 1970. Throughout the two weeks the conferees will be studying what needs to be done now in order to prepare Bi-State for what may happen in the future.

Learning Limitations

One of the important objectives of this course will be to give the conferees some idea of what can and cannot be learned from a long-range program. Among the shortcomings of such a projection for the telephone business, or for any other business for that matter, is that it must necessarily be a projection into the future in terms of what we know now. For example, our present outlook is necessarily limited by the types of instruments and facilities that are either being manufactured at the present time or else are in a pretty advanced state of development. The projection must, therefore, reconcile our present concept of telephone service with the kind of service that will inevitably result from future innovation and merchandising.

Tracing Trends

Likewise the projections necessarily depend on general trends in wage and price levels, and the cost and availability of money for financing. Therefore, one of the primary purposes of the course will be to give the conferees an opportunity to learn how to deal with and reconcile general trends with the specific issues they face in their day-to-day work. This problem is one that all businessmen have to face, although the areas of operation which affect one business may vary from that of another.

In our business, some of the specific fields of operation requiring a knowledge of trends outside the business are these:

- Growth estimates.
- Types and quality of service required to satisfy the wants of the public in the future.
- Quality and structure of our organizational requirements.
- Financial requirements for plant expansion.
- Public and governmental relationships.

Teaching Methods

We have learned several lessons about methods of presentation, which we think may be of value to other organizations which are establishing management development courses. For one thing, we feel we have been successful in developing a high-level course based on the suggestions that the men themselves have given us. Secondly, we have found that the men feel they gain the most from their efforts when they are given both sides of a question and are able to form their own judgments. Finally, we obtain our best results from small discussion groups, rather than formal lectures. The case study method employed so largely at Harvard Business School and elsewhere is used extensively at the BSEC.

In summary then, the growth and rapidly advancing technology of the telephone business makes long-range planning a fundamental part of our organization. The third series of conferences at Asbury Park is, of itself, a long-term planning venture, because higher-management development is a necessary step in providing for the organizational requirements of the business. Further, the third series of conferences, focusing attention on the long-range program of the Bi-State Telephone Company, will give the conferees a renewed awareness of the importance of long-range planning and additional background to use in solving their current operating problems in light of what may happen in the future.

QUESTIONS AND ANSWERS*

From the floor: What use can be made of the newer techniques of business planning, operations research, and decision making such as the selection of specialized staffs, mathematical programing, and the new electronic devices?

Mr. Tait: We have not gone as far as we would like in this direction. We do have an I.B.M. which we are chucking things into as fast as we can, and we have mechanized nearly all of our accounting procedures. Right now we are trying to give the machine some problem to solve that will really help us. But we have no centralized system management as such.

Mr. Crampton: In our Michigan company we have formed a business procedures group which has representatives from each department. They take up projects which can be programed for the larger machines. For example:

> When a customer gives us an order, we have many things to do with the information he furnishes us. In addition, we have to

---

* Businessmen present at the panel session on which this chapter is based raised certain questions which brought about the interplay of ideas reported more or less verbatim in this section.

assign facilities for him, find a wire to his house, and assign him a terminal in the central office, which is determined by his calling characteristics. We can investigate the use of computing machines to work out the most direct and economical path to his house, given the facilities we have; we can pick out the terminal by mathematical calculations and perform the clerical operations associated with the order.

Mr. Tait: As for operations research, we have system and procedure groups who study nothing but these areas, but they aren't up at the level of planners. The division managers utilize their own staffs for this purpose.

EXTERNAL COMMUNICATION
IN A MASS ECONOMY

*Raymond W. Miller, Howard Stephenson, and
Paul Wickman*

MODERN PROFESSIONAL MANAGEMENT, with its growing concern for public relations, is largely a product of corporate enterprise. In the days of the carriage trade, each entrepreneur did his own managing, and his sphere of need and perhaps influence was usually bounded by the borders of his town or city or county. Those few who did grow beyond their own areas paid so little attention to their responsibility for external communications that they almost brought about the downfall of capitalism.

Note: Mr. Miller, who makes the introductory observations, is a Member of the Faculty, Harvard Business School, and President, Public Relations Research Associates, Inc.; Mr. Stephenson is Chairman and Professor of Public Relations, Boston University. Mr. Wickman is Director of Public Relations, Schering Corporation.

Thus, the age of the moguls was largely the result of nonfeasance, not malfeasance. The blame cannot be laid at the door of the "petty capitalist," who dealt largely with people whom he knew and with whom he lived and necessarily made his decisions with an eye to the problems of the individual customer. Rather, the culprit was the large company, set up principally to make money, get customers, and hold competitors in line, which gave little thought to the external public as anything more than just potential customers. The possibility that their success might be jeopardized by the resentment of people with whom they had no business dealings was not even considered. Likewise, the idea of government regulation by the acts of a distant legislature or Congress did not enter the mind of the nineteenth century businessman.

Growth of the Corporation

With the development of the corporation, the situation changed dramatically. The corporate person—that invisible being existing only in law who offers a channel for the wide expansion of business—was so small a factor that there was apparently no mention of it in all the debates leading up to the making of the United States Constitution. In 1800 there were probably less than 100 business corporations in the nation. According to Dean William Neilander of Case Institute of Technology there were less than 500 at the time of the Civil War.

But following the war came the "freedom" amendments to the Constitution—Thirteen, Fourteen, and Fifteen. The Fourteenth Amendment was originally designed to provide economic equality to the newly freed slaves through its famous "due process" clause, but within a few years lawyers had begun to plead that it meant the "corporate person" as well. At first the courts rejected this concept as being *ultra vires* of the amendment, but finally the corporate person was recognized in the famous Southern Pacific Railway Case in 1886 * as being protected under the due process clause.

* *Santa Clara Co. v. South. Pacific R. Co.,* 118 U.S. 394, 396.

This action was like opening Pandora's box. Immediately the corporate form of business began to grow as no business ever had before. Within a few years, the few struggling corporate entities had cousins by the thousands, and today there is hardly any form of business that is not incorporated.

The next natural step was the development of professional management, which grew out of necessity rather than planning. The stockholder wanted wider and wider markets, and the majority owner simply could not do the job.

Soon the mistakes of the new management teams brought about the passage of the Sherman Anti-Trust laws, designed to protect the general public from the new "Jack and the Bean Stalk" corporate creature. Eugene Debs, Samuel Gompers, and others came on the scene to meet the challenge of the problems created by this rapid corporate growth. Excesses were perpetuated by both management and its external "natural persons." Business began to find that its entire future depended more on external forces than on its immediate customers—or at least that the two factors were of equal importance.

A few men, notably John Wanamaker, saw the situation, though somewhat hazily. Then "Ford the First," in order to save the Model T from "the barons of Wall Street," went beyond his immediate employees and customers and began many adventures into mass communication: he deliberately provoked discussion of his car— always black; he paid $5.00 per day in a revolutionary decision well heralded by the press; he chartered a peace ship. The die was cast; each business was a part of the life of the whole nation.

Today, the great corporation superficially appears to be inviolate, both as a part of our national life and as a business organization secure in a framework of rights and privileges. But the courts remind us quite regularly that this security is more fancied than real. Corporate business only operates in interstate trade with "due process" because of the *interpretation* of this clause— not through any formally and permanently established position. For example:

In the case of *Wheeling Steel Corporation* v. *C. Emory Glander, Tax Commissioner of Ohio* * in 1948, the Tax Commissioner did not agree with the interpretation. A strong minority of the court brought in a sizzling dissent from the majority opinion, which had rejected Glander's thesis. If the majority of the court had agreed with the minority, the entire interstate corporate business in this country would have been in jeopardy. Here is a business structure on which we depend for more and more services, whose very existence hinges on the court's interpretation of a few words.

Keeping on Friendly Terms

I can see only two ways to guarantee the continued life of the private corporation in this country: a constitutional amendment making it a legal person, or the maintenance of a friendly public through good external public relations. Thus, the major concern of corporate business must be to assume its share of external responsibilities within the framework of our society so that the corporation will continue to be recognized as though it were "natural person," entitled to the full protection of the law.

But this problem does not vanish at the water's edge. Capitalism is under world-wide attack today, and the Communist crusade against our way of life is not directed at our government per se but against our business system—against capitalism. The external communications of our corporations must appreciate this situation, and business must assume its place as a defender of capitalism. Government cannot do the job, and the military can be only a holding operation in the war of ideas in which we are now engaged.

Unfortunately, business has largely failed to recognize that its very life is now at stake in world affairs, and it has left the interpretation of our system to government. So we are losing the battle for the minds of men to the Communists by default, and we will continue to lose until business accepts its full responsibilities within the framework of a responsible society. Freedom of oppor-

* Supreme Court of the United States, No. 447, October 1948.

tunity, ipso facto, demands a comprehension of and action in external communication within that society.

PRINCIPLES OF SUCCESSFUL COMMUNICATION*

All communication is selective. There are said to be more than 170 million people in the United States today, and I never have heard any public relations enthusiast claim that his program reached even half of them. The "Cinderella" TV show seems to have touched a new high for television audiences—it was estimated at around 72 million. Radio and television combined must have established somewhat higher figures at election times. But to say that even half our population ever received a simultaneous message would be an exaggeration.

The size of the audience therefore is narrowed by one of three factors, or a combination of them: the limitations of the medium of communication, the deliberate control of the communicator, or the unwillingness of the recipient to accept the message. I want to look at the third of these elements.

Attention, Belief, Understanding

Communications is a beguiling term, which only the naive will credit with magical and all-pervading powers. In every age men have sought some arcane phrase, some set incantation. Too often they have scorned the primary source of the blessings they sought, namely the meditations of their hearts.

The external communications of an industry must therefore be considered not entirely in the light of the media, the public to be reached, or the immediate purpose of the message to be imparted. The message also must be believed. In order for this to happen, the organization that sends out the message must have established a reputation for probity. Lies travel fast, it is true, and half-truths probably even faster. The message that really exerts the influence that the sender wishes, must have a substantial repute behind it.

* By Mr. Stephenson.

We never should become so engrossed in motivation research, in the business of trying to manipulate people and engineer their consent to our set of ideas or values, or so fascinated by techniques, that we overlook the plain obligation of the sender to the best interests of the individual people who receive the message. Too often we refer to this area of concern as "the public interest." But this term is all too vague, just as it is meaningless to talk about "molding public opinion." Actually we can only communicate to each man, woman, and child as a separate, individual person, and we have constantly to keep this rock-bottom fact in mind.

To inform people on any topic, an organization has to accomplish three goals:

- It must gain attention.
- It must win belief.
- It must impart understanding.

Public relations considered as advertising and publicity—two of its vital organs—has to do mainly with attracting attention. This we know how to do well. The refinement and development of ways to make the public sit up and take notice are endless and amazing. We also have at our command the mechanical devices we need for spreading the message across great distances.

But a lack of belief in the message presents a most difficult obstacle for public relations to overcome. At the point where information reaches the recipient there is a filter through which it must pass. If the recipient can believe the message, he can get to understand it. But if the recipient cannot believe the message, all the outside pressures, allurements, and devices in the world are useless. Here is the crux of the whole communications and public relations problem—to be believed is to be understood.

Reference to Reality

The development and refinement of the powerful new media— such as television—do not diminish the importance of this factor. As a matter of fact, we may be deceiving ourselves by putting so much faith in these means of communication, because they are, after all, only pictures and not the real article. Take such experiments as the educational TV programs in various school systems, for example. Personally, I cannot think that students *believe* as much when they watch a figure on a screen as they do when the living, breathing human being stands before them. By the same token, the American theater has been given many premature burials. It has changed but it has not died. The face-to-face, flesh-and-blood impact still is deeper than that of the transmitted image.

Consequently, some public relations people are developing another concept on a large scale: the reference to reality. They actually show people the products, devices, and processes of modern industry. American industry now has about 500 traveling shows on the road —displays and demonstrations of reality. These impart to audiences that are relatively small individually but quite sizable in the aggregate a firsthand view of what is going on in laboratory and factory.

The development of the plant tour and the open house—taken for granted now, but a novelty a dozen years ago—represents another aspect of this same need to see "in person." And in the past seven years industry has built up a reservoir of public speakers, operating through speakers' bureaus, who impart the industrial message face to face to possibly 50,000 audiences a year. This reference to reality is one of the most effective means of external communication.

I said we have to be selective, and this becomes doubly important when we recognize that quantity of audience is not enough. Quality, or specific characteristics, is often of even greater weight. Therefore, public relations practitioners are talking more and more of "key" people, "opinion leaders," and the like. This concept makes real sense, because it is built on the value of the personal, individual, human relationship. Alongside the development of impersonal media of communication, this extremely valuable factor—the reference to reality—is gaining marked headway.

Corporate Personality

One of the most worthwhile aims of present-day corporations is to establish an image of a corporate personality in the public mind.

By this term I do not mean the human individual, like the board chairman or some other chief executive officer, but a picture of the corporation itself. A favorite example of mine is The Hudson's Bay Company:

> Its corporate personality is described with rare felicity in its charter, granted by King Charles II in 1670, as "the Governor and Company of Gentlemen Adventurers, Trading into Hudson's Bay." If your company is known to the public as being made up of gentlemen, possessed of an adventurous spirit, and engaged in trade, you have made a good start!

Five Guideposts

A public relations program for a company interested in establishing a corporate personality can be a work of art—and indeed it should follow the classic pattern by having a beginning, a middle, and an end. I do not wish to imply that public relations ever really comes to an end, for it does not. But these elements can and should be structured into every program.

The beginning consists of research: finding and analyzing fact and opinion. The measurement of attitudes and opinions at the start can prevent many expensive and useless programs from getting off the ground.

The middle, or body, of the program is made up of three steps:

1. Pretest the program in miniature, when feasible.
2. Fit the program to the public needs and interests; do not expect the public to accommodate its attitude immediately to your wishes.
3. Set up listening posts, as you execute the program steps, to learn at every stage how things are going.

And the ending—the one phase of public relations programs most often neglected: evaluate. Bring in your best minds to review the results. Then adapt the lesson you have learned as part of future policy.

These five guideposts point the way to a structure for successful external communications in a mass economy.

INTERNATIONAL. COMMUNICATIONS*

I shall never forget the words of a 75-year-old veteran missionary in South Africa who met Mrs. Wickman and me when we first landed in Cape Town in 1938 to spend a few years in that country lecturing:

> There are just three things you must learn in order to get along out here. One is to go slow, two is to go slower, and three is to be able to come to a full stop!

I guessed what he meant at the time, but recently I have come to sense the value of that counsel for all of us, operating in a rapidly changing economy. Sometimes I wonder if it would not be well for the entire leadership of the world to stop for a day, think things over, and take a long, hard look! In my section of this chapter, I want to take just such a look at our public relations in the international sphere.

Twofold Function

Public relations is divided into two distinct functions:

1. Formulating clear and compatible policies within the framework of a corporation or organization in such areas as employee relations and, especially, fields that bear on external relations with Mr. and Mrs. General Public.
2. Establishing lines of communication between management and employees (a two-way street) and a similar two-lane "freeway" to the public—a business responsibility and a public service responsibility.

Such a program is a far cry from the concept of "engineering consent," to which many of us are succumbing today. It is not our job to be "molders of public opinion" as ghost writers would at times have us—and themselves—believe. Good communication is not to be confused with the "operators," "influence peddlers," and

* By Mr. Wickman.

"wanglers." A good, healthy economy demands an honest interpretation of the times—at all times.

Beyond our Boundaries

Today, this interpretation must go beyond our own borders. As Mr. Miller has said, the American businessman has to formulate his policies and establish lines of communication in terms of the world community, as well as his own state and nation. I have been especially conscious of this new responsibility imposed on executives because during the past 18 years I have traveled throughout the world in the field of international communications. I have worked with countless committees, with many kinds of leadership and all types of personalities in various language areas. My chief responsibility in the postwar period was to develop programs in cooperation with the people in many countries. These programs were varied: they included culture, education, home and health, inspiration and music. We established correspondence schools as a link between the program and the listener, and built studios in London, Paris, Beirut, Poona, Japan, Manila, and Australia. Programs were produced in 12 languages, and the correspondence schools carried on in over 50 languages. The weekly productions were also carried over two major radio networks in the United States.

Open Mind

The purpose of these programs in foreign territories was to fill the vacuum created by Nazi propaganda with a renewed hope and feeling of security. We found a ready response by resisting the temptation to impose our objectives on these countries, dealing with fundamental principles, and adapting ourselves to the thinking and ways of our audiences.

By the same token, in selling our business convictions both overseas and in this country we must start with the other fellows' point of view and not just our own. Such an adjustment is not easy to make; it was not until I lived in a foreign country for two years

that I saw the American tourist in the light that the people throughout the world see him. As a Hollander said to me once:

> There is a big difference between the Englishman and the Ameri-
> can. The Englishman travels all over the world and acts as if he
> owns the place. The American travels all over the world and acts
> as if he doesn't care who owns the place.

When traveling in the trains of India, it is not unusual to see
three or four strangers retire to their respective "bunk berths" in
the same compartment and perform their respective religious rites
before going to sleep. One might be a Moslem, another Hindu, and
the third Parsee. In this same way, the world must learn to travel
and work together, respecting the dignity of man as if traveling in
the same compartment. We in the United States have bartered our
way through the world too long, using the dollar as our communication link. This technique has proved to be poor public relations
for the American business system in the earth-shaking battle against
Communism which we are waging.

Open Purse

But not only is our approach wrong; we are niggardly to boot.
It is estimated that the Communist world spends some $3 billion
annually on its propaganda. What efforts do we put forth? Each
year the budget for the U.S. Information Agency is trimmed considerably. Our communication to foreign countries is grossly inadequate, and very few people in the country realize it. Possibly private
industry should tell the story—or maybe government agencies should
continue to furnish the information—but the point is that someone
had better start on the job!

As a guide to our efforts at external communication, both within
the country and abroad—and both public and private—I submit the
following quotation from a book by Dr. Charles W. Lowry:

> At the same time there is much that is great and lasting in the
> American tradition and the American accomplishment. We do not

need to be apologetic, inferior, defensive. We do need and should make now a fresh, informed, realistic evaluation of Americanism. We need to see what it is, where it has come from, where it is now, and where it is going. This can be made only if we desire to know the truth, only if we believe in seeing the things that are as they are.*

* Charles W. Lowry, *Communism and Christ* (New York, Morehouse-Gorham Co., 1952). Used with the permission of the publishers.

CREATIVITY AND IMAGINATION: THEIR MEANING TO MANAGEMENT

George Albert Smith, John E. Arnold,
Alexander T. Daignault, and William J. J. Gordon

IN THIS CHAPTER, the authors will discuss three key questions in the area of creativity and imagination:

(1) To what extent can we develop these qualities in ourselves at will?

(2) How can we develop them in others?

(3) How can we create an atmosphere in our businesses which will nurture these traits?

Note: Mr. Smith, who makes the introductory observations, is Professor of Business Administration, Harvard Business School; Mr. Arnold is with the Department of Mechanical Engineering, Massachusetts Institute of Technology; Mr. Daignault is Executive Vice President, W. R. Grace & Company; Mr. Gordon is Director, Design-Invention Group, Arthur D. Little, Incorporated.

282

A considerable amount of controversy is hidden away in these three questions. Some people, for example, say that either you are creative or you are not, and that is that. Others claim that the talent can be developed. But over and above such differences stands one fact on which we can all agree: business managers ought to seek out people with imagination and creativity in areas that are fundamentally necessary to the particular firm or the particular situation. Wise management does not leave such matters to chance; it deliberately and conscientiously sets out to see what kind of needs it has, or may have, and strives to attract the people into its organization who are most apt to produce ideas in these fields. For clearly the success of an organization depends on the ability of its people to produce ideas and carry those ideas out. Since these skills call for different kinds of characteristics, both kinds of people are needed and must be recruited.

THE CREATIVE PROCESS*

There are two facts about creativity which we must understand as background for our thinking. They may both seem obvious, but they are highly important nonetheless.

In the first place, imagination is a mental activity. It is something that actually takes place in the brain. It is true, of course, that the results are expressed orally, or in writing, or in models, but the process itself is a *thinking* one.

Secondly, it is the individual human brain that performs this creative activity—and only the individual human brain. It is synthesis that leads to new combinations, and this synthesis can take place only in the mind of some person.

No Creative Elite

This ability to create, happily, is not limited to just a few chosen souls. Everyone has the potential for creative activity, and the es-
* By Mr. Arnold.

sential factors are inherent in all of us to some degree. Obviously, there is a continuum of some kind; those of great genius are at one end of the curve, and a few who have very little potential for creative activity are at the other. Most of us are placed somewhere in between.

The difficulty is that we do not demonstrate the total capacity we have. If we were to plot a curve of realized creative ability, we would find the great majority at a much lower level than they ought to be. Consequently, it is possible to increase the realization of that potential by training, by exercise, and by understanding—as with any other natural gift.

Thus it follows that the creative process is universal; it applies to all kinds of activity that lead to creative results—art, poetry, science, engineering, business, homemaking. It is not a process reserved just for leaders. No matter who you are, if you are coming up with a really new innovation of some kind, you are going through a process that is common to everyone else who is developing something original. The tools vary from individual to individual, from class of operation to class of operation, but they are less important than the basic procedure which produces the tangible result.

Many Approaches

But this one process will not necessarily lead to just one right solution. Different people will produce an infinite variety of solutions, a whole spectrum of solutions. When a good answer is found, someone else will pick it up and develop a still better answer, and, unfortunately, vice versa. For every poor solution, you can find someone who will give you one that is even worse.

Within this framework of a general, universal process there are many variations of approach. The techniques will be different for different people. Furthermore, we are just beginning to feel our way around in this business. Therefore we cannot hand down any firm set of rules.

We can, however, spell out certain broad guides which should be of assistance to business managers who are seeking to harness and utilize this enormous human force.

The creative act is one which brings together past experiences, and modifies, distorts, and twists them around. It then adds to them in the hope that a person will create new patterns or configurations that produce a tangible result that will better satisfy one of man's needs. The combination arrived at is not just any old rearrangement but something which has increased value. You cannot predict the new total by simply adding up the sum of the individual parts.

Three Modes of Thinking

Creative activity ranges from the low level of recreative activity —the process a child goes through when he first endeavors to repair his own bicycle bell—up through major breakthroughs of great scientists and outstanding philosophers. It depends on three basic modes of thinking: analysis, synthesis, and evaluation. These three stages have each a certain loose counterpart in one of the three broad categories of management: preparation, production, and final decision making.

Preparation Preparation includes everything that goes on before one actually starts to produce ideas to solve a certain problem. It involves every experience from childhood on, elementary school, secondary school, college, social situations, industrial situations, and so on. All the work specifically carried out to prepare for a definite job is also included. There are certain features, important to the creative personality, that lend themselves to and are essential to effective preparation for creative problem solving.

First of all, the effective creative problem-solver seems to be more sensitive to problems, more acutely aware of what is going on around him, more open to total experience than the less creative individual. He somehow has the ability to see a relationship between his past experience and present experiences. He takes in all data indiscriminately from the outside world to get a true, relevant, adequate picture of what is going on. He is keenly aware of what is going on within himself and understands when he is becoming jealous or suspicious—in short, when he is setting up blocks to creative activity. He is open to the effects of culture and of society on him as an individual and as a problem-solver in a society, so that he is able to take in information, recognize important need areas, and very importantly, define problems distinctly, generically, and basically so that he has a clear but very broad path to traverse in his search for solutions.

The statement of the problem is highly important. If the problem is laid out too generally, it does not offer any clear goal at which to aim. If it is too narrowly defined, it is not challenging enough, and the alternative approaches are reduced.

The creative individual is highly goal-centered, and will take any kind of sensible approach necessary to reach his objective. He does not think in terms of designing better mouse *traps;* he figures out how to get rid of mice. He does not want to precondition his thinking by talking about "traps," but focuses his mind on the basic need.

Production. The second step is production. Here, the essential factors are fluency and flexibility. After defining a very broad and specific problem and inviting all alternative possible solutions, he needs a very fluent flow of ideas. This element seems to depend in large part on his ability to control evaluation. The goal, the conditions that must be met—the time limitations, amount of money, the help, the space—should be predetermined for use in final decision making. But they have to be forgotten for a moment in the effort to develop all the possible ways of solving the problem.

Thus the creative mind lays aside the possible obstacles, the limitations of the tools, the mechanics of implementing ideas, and searches out all the avenues of approach—however daring—that can be taken to the objective. In short, the creator loses himself in looking for new and always better paths.

At this stage, the creative person needs a great deal of drive to carry through the first flickerings of an idea to a final, tangible solution. He is daring, willing to take a chance, willing to gamble and lose, and start over.

Decision Making. The decision-making step rests on a base of a wide series of alternatives. At this point, some choice has to be made as to which of the alternatives uncovered is the best. In the decision-making process, he makes predictions, assigns some value or measure of desirability, and then brings his judgment to bear. At this point, criteria based on research, accumulated knowledge, and an understanding of the total situation are held up to the various alternatives, and one is chosen.

Turning Out Ideas

Of these three steps—preparation, production, and decision making—the first and the last are extremely important while the middle one is of lesser significance. This order of priority may seem strange, because most people are currently concerned with "How do you get ideas?" and "How do you get more ideas?" But the actual production of ideas comes quite mechanically if you have properly prepared yourself and are well organized to make proper decisions.

Before very long—I will make a prediction, to be provocative if nothing else—we will have machines to do our idea-generating for us. A good share of ideas are generated in our subconscious, over which we have no control, by a process which depends on proper preparation, thorough immersion in a problem, and soaking up all the details of the relevant facts and techniques. Then a trial-and-error chain reaction starts, until finally the answer comes out.

If this is what actually happens in our subconscious—and I am sure it does—I can program a machine to go through the same twistings and turnings if I take enough time, thought, and imagination in preparation. Here are three examples of how it can work:

⟨ Two or three years ago, Dow Chemical Company was looking for a new trade name. They decided, as a starter, to get all the possible four-letter combinations pronounceable in the English language, and they programed an IBM 650 to do just that. The machine turned out a great heap of "words," probably 30 or 40 thousand, and they went to work and picked out the best one—no mean task, I assure you! Ten or fifteen years ago, Dow might have had a contest and said, "Name this new product. If you win, we give you $5,000." Now they produce ideas mechanically.

⟨ About a year ago, some people on the West Coast decided to try their hand at writing popular tunes by machine. First they analyzed the important factors of a popular tune—a sort of systems analysis proposition. Then they fed the compiled data and some random numbers into a computer, and the computer went to work. If the final product worked out acceptably, it was printed up; if not, it was discarded. They started turning out popular music at a very high rate. Some of it was pretty poor, but some was good and went on the air. About six months ago they named one "Push-Button Bertha" in commemoration of the fact that the push button did generate Bertha!

❬ I have proposed to General Motors Corporation's design division that I build them a machine which will produce new styles for their cars. If we could get their best designers to pool their knowledge, feed the material into the machine, and program it properly, it would be possible to station several men in front of screens equipped with knobs which would make it possible for them to project all of the conceivable shapes of automobiles for scrutiny. They could have one dial for chrome, for instance, and have a fine time splashing the model on the screen with trimming!

Human Element

But fabulous as these examples may appear on the surface, they depend not on miracles but on painstaking preparation, rooted in imagination, thought, and creative ability. This is the important step.

Finally, they rest on wise decision making which brings sound value judgment and proper criteria into play. Thus the human factor will continue to be the key, and human creativity the wellspring—machines or no machines—of new products and of progress.

CREATIVITY: A MANAGEMENT SKILL *

In preparing to write my part of this chapter, I talked to a number of people who have demonstrated some high measure of creativity. It is of considerable significance that everyone with

* By Mr. Daignault.

whom I raised the question of creativity thought first of the quality in a technological sense. They considered it in terms of product design, new products, new fields, new ventures.

Yet, I think we all would admit that there are much broader areas of management in which creativity not only plays an important part, but also has a more lasting effect on the economy. All of us can list many examples of managerial creativity. We have seen new companies start from very modest beginnings and grow rapidly to substantial size. We have seen new managements radically change a company's attitude toward growth and innovation. We have seen managements take sick companies and restore them to health.

Creativity, as Mr. Arnold pointed out, ranges all the way from such broad applications down to far more mundane, day-to-day problems. From the standpoint of the executive, this kind of managerial creativity is the most significant variety, albeit the technological is highly important. Consequently, it is relevant to probe behind the scenes where companies and individuals have demonstrated this characteristic, to find out exactly what goes into it.

It would be satisfying indeed if we were to find in each case a magic ingredient behind each example of managerial creativity akin to the TCP in gasoline, and Irium in toothpaste. But any such quest is doomed to failure. Behind each record of success, our probing uncovers some combination of those characteristics which we have all been taught to recognize as the ingredients of leadership. If there is any difference, it is perhaps in emphasis, with strength of motivation, great energy, and sufficient faith in the ultimate outcome to stick to the program regardless of the inevitable setbacks and the adverse opinion of others among those characteristics which are most likely to predominate in the mix.

These qualities relate to an individual's desire to create. They determine whether or not he is likely to seek out new ideas himself, or equally important, accept them from others. They have an impact on his persistence, his willingness to stick with a job until the results have been realized.

If you will accept the rather plebeian definition of creativity I have given, then it seems to me that the measures which can be taken within an organization, large or small, to encourage creativity are about the same ones we are continuously discussing as being the foundation for good management.

The development of these talents is another matter. I doubt that the characteristics which make up this quality of creativity—energy, strong motivation, and persistence—can be taught to men who do not have them by the time they reach responsible positions in management. But a company certainly can find and hold and encourage people within it who have these requisite traits. It can either reduce or increase the number of such people who are working for it, through the climate it provides and through the encouragement which it gives to independent thinking and action. There is certainly some inverse relationship between creativity and a highly centralized, bureaucratic management, for example.

Various areas of business activity can be designed to stimulate the creative imagination of its personnel. Two specifically come to mind: organization and long-range planning.

Organization

In our company we have tried to break our operations down into clearly defined units, so that the effect of each manager's efforts can be measured as accurately as possible. The transition to a decentralized pattern has not been an easy one. As have most firms in the same situation, we found that men who previously appeared to be satisfactory managers were lost when asked to operate, plan, and make decisions on their own. As a result, we have re-examined and changed the criterion we use in selecting managers.

One of the criteria in a decentralized company is the imagination to recognize the creative people when you see them. Many managers do a relatively poor job in spotting and encouraging these individuals. Creativity may be developed; it may grow with age and experience; but it is recognizable in most people at a fairly early stage in their business careers. It is the responsibility of any progressive business organization to recognize that creativity early and make sure it is used to its fullest.

Long-range Planning

We have been working with our different divisions and subsidiaries to improve the quality of their long-range forward planning. In so doing, we have indicated that this process is not just forecasting but rather a considered evaluation of the various alternative courses of action, a measurement of risks and opportunities. We have asked them to focus on needs and problems, not just those processes that are going along smoothly. Such an approach, particularly when it is pushed down within the organization, improves the manager's understanding of his business as a whole and in our experience has awakened many to a new realization and interest in the opportunities available to them. It has presented them with problems in a format that stimulates their creativity, sparks their imagination, and encourages others in their organizations to think provocatively.

Thus, the current lively interest in creativity, healthy as it is, is in large measure a restatement of the broad principles of sound management which are designed to make the maximum use of the talents and energies of a company's personnel.

THE CREATIVE TEMPERAMENT AND THE GROUP *

First of all, I want to point out that just because creativity has been connected mainly with products does not mean it is serviceable in this area alone. Rather, it is because products constitute a pragmatic criterion by which the degree of creativity can be judged. This is tragic. It is too bad that we have to superimpose such a criterion on a process. This emphasis on products implies that it is the limit of creativity, whereas in actuality the creative nature of man involves all his activities.

* By Mr. Gordon.

Emotional Element

Be that as it may, I want to deal principally with the emotional content of the creative process. I become very short-tempered with Mr. Arnold when he tries to get pragmatic about the personality characteristics and the measurement thereof in a creative individual. This short-tempered attitude of mine on this topic—although characteristic of me generally—is based on an historical review of thousands of creative people.

There appears to be almost nothing common to all of them. We can, of course, superimpose some convictions of our own which simply stem from our subjective responses, but we are only fooling ourselves when we do so. Creative people are so different one from another that no generalities can be made.

Take this matter of stick-to-itiveness, for example. As Mr. Arnold pointed out, this capacity of persistence, this tremendous optimism and idealism, seems to be an indispensable attribute of the creative person. Yet, there have been some astonishingly creative people who were professional give-ups, constantly running from reality and using this escapism of implemented imagination to produce great works of art.

Creativity Means Conflict

Therefore, I find myself impressed with the emotional element in the creative process rather than any rational quality. For the last 15 years I have been attempting to clarify it, as the only alternative to giving up and saying, "This is an area we can never understand." But when it comes to utilizing the creative person, this very emotional quality on which his imagination depends gets in the way and creates problems. For example:

> A creative individual graduates from a university or a trade school and goes to a company that has been looking for just such a man. They hire him just as fast as they can. But they have no idea what

to do with him after they get him. They think they do, of course, but if he is a really creative person, the odds are that his personality will be inconsistent with the "proper" functioning of this company. There will be conflict because the man's feelings will be contrasted with and fought by the personality of the organization.

What can we do about that friction? How can we learn to use people who are creative? We usually take the easy way out and hand the problem down the line to somebody else—usually, somebody lower in the hierarchy than we are. But, of course, this dodge does not solve the matter, and the creative person becomes more and more lonely and more and more savage until he finally becomes a real drag on the firm.

Friendly Atmosphere

To meet this situation I have fought for the formation of creativity groups. Let me make myself clear: I agree with Mr. Arnold that creativity is an individual affair, not a group process. But the fact is that in a climate like ours, stamped by an extreme pragmatism and a Puritan self-consciousness, the creative person has to have friends. He has to be surrounded by people of whom he is not afraid.

This objective is best accomplished by establishing a group within which the people can begin to have confidence in one another.

The groups serve another purpose. Since the essential, initial process of creativity in group operation is verbal, the people participating can derive an insight into their process by reviewing their progress and the approaches they have taken. Thus, they can actually begin to increase their capacity to be constructively creative in a conscious manner.

Stimulus for Ideas

There is a further important aspect of this emotional factor. We all accept it in the creation of a painting or piece of sculpture, but we are apt to think that technical innovation requires some different kind of process which does not contain an emotional element. Actually, this is not so—the same factors operate, and the same irrationality is involved.

This segment of the creative process—this important element—is unfortunately the very portion which we spend money to have educated out of us. It is a tough job to put back what some poor young man has spent four or six years teaching himself to forget. It is much simpler to reinstate this needed irrationality if a man is part of a like-minded group than it is when he has to operate alone.

Collective Bargaining

There is still another reason for the group. If one man in a company has an idea in which he has great confidence, he will wait until he has a chance to speak to the person who must give him permission to implement this idea. But this important fellow is always busy with affairs that have to be handled at once. Basically, this idea fellow coming in to see him all the time annoys him.

If he has enormous confidence in his creative associate, or if the latter has great prestige with management, the boss may listen.

But the problems do not cease here, because the creative man may not describe his great idea very clearly. Perhaps it is meaningless when it is verbalized because it has not been refined, so the only sensible action is to defer judgment until after the project has been developed a bit—and there may be no funds available for this speculative phase.

But a group has more force when it wants to do something. When it shapes up a new viewpoint and wants the money to implement it, this group can stand up for its ideas and fight for them. Further, the members will have discussed the idea among themselves, and their articulation of it will be far sharper than the lone petitioner could have made it.

I should like to point out here that this group's scope is unlimited. They cannot work overnight, of course, but in a period of time they will come up with some radically new concepts which the specialist can help adjust and refine.

"Flash of Insight"

Finally, I would like to mention the expression, "flash of insight." I do not believe for a minute that it will ever be possible to hit the ball bearing with the spear, that it will ever be possible actually to identify and prophesy the actual moment of an instant of insight, but I do think we can hope to increase the probability of the creation of an insight by education and understanding. In attempting to do so, we must consider well the emotional factors in creativity and the organizational structure most appropriate to the release of creative energy.

QUESTIONS AND ANSWERS *

From the floor: How can you determine whether or not a man has more than average creativity?

Mr. Arnold: There are no really well defined techniques for measuring creative potential as yet. The approaches that do exist all need considerable refining. One of the best ways is to talk to a man and see how free he is with questioning. The questioning spirit, to me, is an essential, and a man who is ready with all kinds of answers, but cannot think of a single question, is probably pretty low on creative potential.

I know one professor at Harvard who was very daring in measuring and grading students. He was interested not in the answers they gave, but in the questions they asked.

From the floor: I read recently that the first 10% of the ideas in a brain-storming session were the ones that proved ultimately to be the most productive. What is your experience?

* Businessmen present at the panel session on which this chapter is based raised certain questions which brought about the interplay of ideas reported more or less verbatim in this section.

Mr. Gordon: I know nothing about brain-storming; I have no confidence in it.

Mr. Arnold: I do not have much confidence in it as a problem-solving technique. As a group technique for generating ideas, however, I believe it is quite effective. But I have challenged proponents of the device by saying that I can produce more ideas than one of their groups can in the same time, and no one has taken up the gauntlet yet. As I have mentioned, there are mechanical techniques that can produce a thousand ideas while six men produce one hundred—and the ideas are just as crazy and just as good.

In short, I look on brain-storming as a good exercise for freeing a man's imagination—a sort of therapy. I would recommend that groups sit down and think as wildly as they can, because even if they do not produce a solution, they open up their minds so that when they go back to their desks they are freer and abler to attack their problems from a different point of view. As a problem-solving technique, I do not know much about it, nor do I think much of it.

From the floor: How do you keep the unimaginative managers from firing or getting rid of those people who are creative?

Mr. Gordon: The first thing to do is to fire the guy who is firing such people!

There has to be somebody in management, preferably top management, who is really interested in this area and willing to set a creative group off, where they can work together. They should report to him.

Mr. Arnold: May I challenge Mr. Gordon? He has implied two or three times that there are two kinds of people: the thinkers and the doers. He says that you must get your thinkers and put them in a little group by themselves where they can damn the rest of the company who are there merely to carry out the ideas, or say "No" to the ideas. By getting together they can comfort each other, I suppose, with a mutual emotional understanding of the meanness and hostility of the outside world.

The difficulty, of course, is that there are not two kinds of people at all. The really effective person in industry and science and any-

where else not only can think up ideas individually or in groups
but also can carry them out.

Mr. Gordon: What do you mean by "carry them out"?

Mr. Arnold: Actually produce them; make them tangible.

Mr. Gordon: I assumed that.

Mr. Arnold: But I do not have to get myself off into a group and
therefore protect myself from the rest of society. If there are two
kinds of people, there are only these two: those who cannot do
what they are told, and those who can do nothing else but.

Mr. Gordon: I do not understand your point. But good luck
to you!

From the floor: Following up this argument, how do you increase
the creative side of creative people who are in line and staff management jobs without putting them in these special groups?

Mr. Gordon: Personally, I permit them to participate in this
creative group, so that they can begin to get a feeling of what happens when people think the way they do.

Mr. Daignault: We are overlooking the function of supervision
in all this debate. One of the responsibilities of good management is
to recognize and develop creative people and to provide a climate
within which everyone can be imaginative. To consider that the
development of creativity is inconsistent with good management is
a very definite error.

From the floor: We have been thinking principally about *stimulating* this creativity. How about the other side of the coin: the
reception of the ideas we have generated?

Mr. Daignault: The nature of the top people in a corporation
determines the way in which new ideas are received. In a small
company, one person can set the climate for the entire organization
fairly easily, so the quality of the man at the top affects everyone
all the way down the line. The problem is more complicated for
the large corporation, but the starting place is the same: the
chief executive.

From the floor: We have just faced this problem in our firm. A
group of rather rough sales managers up from the ranks were

virtually running the company, and they were entirely nonreceptive to new ideas.

In spite of Mr. Arnold's criticisms of brain-storming, it worked for us as a technique to loosen up these people. At every manager's meeting we had a session of brain-storming on some practical problem. Within a very short time their reception to new ideas from below as well as from above—salesmen are notoriously independent —increased rapidly and made a substantial difference in the management of that horribly spread-out operation.

From the floor: What do you do about a top-management group that is receptive enough to creative technological ideas which come up from below but very closed-minded to those in the area of general administration?

Mr. Arnold: The creative process is a universal one using universal tools. If you are a creative person in thinking up good ideas, then it behooves you to be a creative person in selling the ideas.

Nothing makes me so mad as the engineer who says, "I proposed the same thing ten times." It is about time he tried a different approach; and if he cannot, then I say he is not carrying through properly. It is up to him to be creative in selling as well as thinking.

From the floor: It seems to me that an atmosphere of receptivity simply means that a company provides some machinery which makes it possible for a new idea to be discussed and kicked around a bit. It isn't necessary to have formal, detailed consideration all up the line if someone or some group does take the time to talk it over and consider it.

Mr. Daignault: One of the real problems here was mentioned by Mr. Gordon—the time required for this activity. So many executives and managers have enmeshed themselves in the day-to-day paper work so that they just do not have the time to gain the understanding and feeling for a new idea that would give them some of the enthusiasm which its proponent exhibits.

Mr. Arnold: I am reminded of a director of research who told me how concerned he was about getting his group to feel there was an atmosphere of receptivity at the top-management level. I got his research assistants and project leaders together for him, and he started off: "I want some ideas. I want some wild thinking in this organization. I want ideas so wild they will knock me off my chair when you spout them out. Do not think you are wasting my time. You are not, as long as your idea is well-thought out to begin with and you know damn well it will work."

From the floor: What can you do with someone like that, aside from firing him?

Mr. Arnold: This is certainly one of the most trying management problems.

If the man is valuable over-all, you should try somehow to make him see that there is something lacking in his make-up. You might take this approach:

> "All right, Joe, you have a very good organization here. I do not blame you for defending it because we are making money in your branch. But can you estimate for the next two months and give me a survey showing me all the areas where this department might be improved? Can you relate what you are doing to other organizations of similar nature, and so forth? What techniques are they using? Are we so far ahead of them, or are they in some places ahead of us?

Thus you would endeavor to get him to analyze himself and his organization.

In most cases, he will see some ways of improving his area and he will certainly do some searching because he has to turn in some kind of report. Inevitably, he will seek help in preparing it.

From the floor: Suppose you have a company which cannot go off in all directions at once and do everything. How does top management, while trying to be receptive to creativity, avoid appearing hypocritical because it cannot accept more than a very small fraction of these ideas and really do something about them?

Mr. Daignault: You have to be very careful about what impression you give your people in this situation. One friend of mine compares creativity in an organization like that to the vermouth in the martini—you have to have it there for taste, but nowadays you almost just rinse out the glass with it.

I don't go along as far as that, but creativity has to be controlled somehow or you are going to find yourself with everyone sitting around being creative and no one doing the work.

Mr. Smith: Isn't part of the answer that you must be sure to tell your organization just what the facts are? Do not keep it a secret from them; explain that "we want ideas, but we cannot accept them all." Educate them as well as you can about the projects you have to keep going, but urge them to turn in their ideas anyway.

From the floor: Isn't that an advantage of the group? Frequently a group down in the organization will develop the idea into a practical one, or throw it out, so that top management is not blamed for rejecting it as "impractical."

Mr. Gordon: That is a very good point. Perhaps the most important discovery we have made in the last four and one-half years is the necessity for at least one person who is communication- or presentation-oriented in these groups. We have seen highly successful operation when such an individual has been present, because we can think in terms of shaping the idea for presentation up the line. He has a sense of how it will look to others. By the same token, we have observed real breakdowns at the acceptance level when no communicator is on hand.

From the floor: What about suggestion box schemes, which companies have had for a number of years?

Mr. Arnold: Some good suggestion systems exist, and so do some very poor ones. A suggestion system itself does not insure the proper permissive atmosphere; sometimes the procedure used simply stimulates the employee to say: "What is the point of handing in suggestions? I handed in five, and never heard from the committee. I do not know what they did with them; I never got any reward, I know that."

From the floor: Are there really any new ideas? Are we not simply uncovering or unfolding ideas that have always existed?

Mr. Arnold: There are two types of innovation. Certainly, discovery is one aspect; the kind of process any scientist follows, uncovering and perhaps recognizing for the first time certain combinations which have always existed. For instance, the atom and its parts were always there, but we are just learning about certain aspects of them today.

In contrast, there is such a thing as definite invention—bringing together old ideas and forming new patterns and new arrangements that never existed before. In that sense, everybody has new ideas.

Mr. Gordon: Where did they exist, if in fact they existed before they were discovered?

From the floor: You have to conceive of some overriding principle as governing this universe, and probably that principle is the source of the ideas basically. It becomes metaphysical at this point.

Mr. Gordon: But this is a pragmatic culture, and we are talking pragmatically. I question the value of assuming that new ideas existed before they were made useful. Making them useful is taking ideas, whether they exist metaphysically or not, implementing them, and reducing them to practice.

Mr. Arnold: On the contrary, talking pragmatically, as Mr. Gordon says, he devotes a large amount of time to the emotional component. I see no reason to think that there cannot be certain metaphysical aspects as well. There certainly is a great deal we do not know about the creative process.

Mr. Gordon: What you do not know about the creative process is not necessarily metaphysical.

Mr. Arnold: No, but it may be.

Part Three

PERSONAL PLANNING IN AN ERA OF CHANGE

CAREER PLANNING AND
SELF-DEVELOPMENT

IN THE STORIES of Bob Craig and Carl Lewis we see in very specific terms the impact of a rapidly changing, competitive, stressful economy on individuals and on their career plans. Both of these men faced tough decisions; both had to face important professional and personal choices against the kaleidoscopic background of new situations; both had to evaluate coolly the future of the opportunities and risks which were offered to them.

Craig, a man of 36, was doing extremely well in a staff position with a large company in Detroit; Lewis, ten years older, was a law-

Note: This chapter is a combined summary of two sessions on *Career Planning and Self-development*. James R. Surface, Dean of the School of Business, University of Kansas, led the discussion on the Bob Craig case, under the heading of "Graduates Out of School Fifteen Years or Less." Joseph C. Bailey, Professor of Human Relations, Harvard Business School, acted as discussion leader for the Carl Lewis case, bearing on "Graduates Out of School More Than Fifteen Years." The analysis of each case represents a synthesis of the views expressed by the participants in the discussion of that case.

yer who took on a line job that ended up by threatening his health and his family's well-being. Craig was offered the job of general manager of a housing construction firm in the Pacific Northwest. Lewis, on the other hand, after a three-months illness, was told by his company that he could either return to the private practice of law, rejoin the firm's legal department, or go back to his line post.

A careful analysis of all the pertinent factors was clearly demanded of these two men. In Craig's case, not the least of that study had to be devoted to the prospects for the firm that was bidding for his services. Given the facts on population growth, family formation, suburban expansion, and shifting centers of development, which are outlined elsewhere in this book, does the future for a company handling both the design and the mass production of contemporary homes look bright or gloomy? In what direction is the Pacific Northwest moving economically? By the same token, Lewis had to look ahead at the stresses of a line job in his industry over the next 20 years to see if it matched his own interests and talents.

But the probing and objective thought demanded of Lewis and Craig extended beyond the fast-moving economy into an examination of their own personal roles in that kind of world. What did they really want to do with their lives? What were their professional objectives? What scale of priorities did they set for themselves —where did their duty to their families, to themselves, to the community fit into their over-all plans? And, finally, what degree of responsibility did they feel toward their jobs, as such? Did they have a sense of obligation to take on significant management posts because the requirements of modern America are so great, even though they might rather do something else?

Before we actually turn to the cases themselves, a word about how to use them might be in order. As one of the participants in the discussions on which this chapter is based put it, "I think each one of us must ask himself what he would do in this situation, based on his own individual desires. By so doing—by putting ourselves in this man's place—we can get a lot of good out of this case."

THE CASE OF BOB CRAIG*

In November 1955, Bob Craig, then employed by Acme Motors, Detroit, Michigan, was offered a position as general manager of Pacific Homes, Inc., of Seattle, Washington. Upon receipt of the offer, Craig found himself in a quandary: on the one hand he was attracted by many features of the prospective job and, on the other, he was not unhappy in his current position.

At the time of the offer Craig was 36 years old, married, and the father of three children. Both Craig and his wife had been born and raised in the Pacific Northwest. They had been married while he was in the service during World War II. After his release from the Army in 1946, Craig had entered the University of Washington and upon graduation from there, he attended the Harvard Business School, receiving an MBA in 1951. He was employed by Acme Motors in June 1951, as a financial analyst. Since then he had had a number of different assignments in the company.

In Craig's opinion he had had a very satisfactory career thus far with Acme and he believed that he could reasonably expect to continue to progress in the organization. In November 1955, he held a responsible staff position which involved work that he found both challenging and rewarding. In this position he was making approximately $20,000 a year and his boss had already indicated that he could expect a raise in 1956 of about $1,000.

In considering his situation at Acme, Craig also valued highly his personal relationships in the organization. He had high respect and a personal liking for both his immediate superior, an assistant department head, and for the department head. His work frequently involved working with people from other departments, and Craig

---

* Copyright, 1957, by the President and Fellows of Harvard College. Case material of the Harvard Graduate School of Business Administration is prepared as a basis for class discussion. Cases are not designed to present illustrations of either correct or incorrect handling of administrative problems.

had found in most instances that these had been pleasant as well as productive associations.

Although the assistant department head to whom he reported was only 31 years old, Craig did not interpret this as meaning that he was blocked for promotion. On the one hand, he thought that his boss' great ability would probably mean that he would move rapidly upward in the company, and, on the other, he knew that the department head was considering setting up a new assistant department head office within the next two or three years and he felt that it was probable that he would be promoted to that post. In a discussion with his wife Craig summarized his future prospects with Acme in this way:

> I think we could be pretty certain of moving to the assistant department head level within the next three or four years, and I think the chances are good of moving on to be a department head within 10 years or so of that. Of course the pyramid sharpens to a point quickly from there on and whether or not we would ever make the next jump (to the vice president level) is much less certain. But the department head jobs are big jobs and staying there would probably mean making around $40,000 a year.

In appraising his present situation and future prospects, Craig was not as enthusiastic about some other features of his current career. Foremost among these was his regret at not being able to participate actively in community affairs. During his years in school Craig had always planned on having active interests outside of his job. He was particularly attracted to the thought of helping his community by working in service clubs, participating in school committees, etc. As he saw it, if he stayed with Acme, it would be many years before he could devote the time that he would like to devote to this kind of activity. For one thing he and his family resided in a suburb of Detroit, and Craig spent about 90 minutes a day commuting between office and home. He had also found that the challenge of his job meant that he often worked 10 to 12 hours a day and that he spent most Saturdays and some Sundays at the office. He felt that the two factors making it difficult for him to assume more community responsibility were, on the one hand, the press of his normal work load and, on the other, the unpredictability of certain "crash programs" which were instituted from time-to-time in the company and which absorbed even greater amounts of his time.

Another feature of staying with Acme which he viewed with some regret was his opinion that probably he would always be performing a staff function and that there was little likelihood that he could attain a position of general management responsibility. Although, as stated above, he enjoyed the kind of staff work that he had performed, he also had a desire to accept the challenge which he foresaw in the field of general management.

Although it did not figure as importantly in his thinking as the above features, the third reservation he held about a future with Acme was that as he saw it, success would mean staying in the Detroit area. Both he and his wife had made many good friends there, but they both had a preference for the Pacific Northwest. For one thing, they still had family and many friends in Washington and Oregon and, secondly, they preferred the climate of that area.

The attraction that the offer from Pacific Homes, Inc., held for Craig was that it seemed to promise an opportunity to do some of these things that he missed doing in his current career.

Pacific Homes, Inc., had been founded in the early 1950's by a group of architects and engineers in the Seattle area for the purpose of designing, building, and selling medium-priced contemporary houses. The founders of the company believed that through good design and some mass production economies they could build a house which was attractive and efficiently designed and which could be sold several thousand dollars below the price of a new house of comparable size and more traditional design.

The corporation had gotten under way with the proceeds from a public stock sale and had had good public acceptance from its initial advertising and promotional efforts. Its 1954 sales were approximately $700,000. The corporation was managed during this period by the president, an architect, and the treasurer, an engineer, who between them controlled a majority of the corporation's stock. The remainder of the stock was publicly held and no other owner took an active part in corporation affairs. The board of directors was composed of the president, treasurer, and the corporation's attorney.

Although the management had been pleased by the 1954 sales volume, they were disturbed to learn at the end of the year that they had not shown much profit from operations. Several bankers in the Seattle area with whom the president and treasurer had done business advised the two men in early 1955 that the corporation would not prosper unless it instituted some sounder business practices with respect to purchasing, extension of credit, and cost control. On several occasions the president and treasurer were told by respected businessmen of the community that the corporation was gaining the reputation for being a group of brilliant designers who had no business sense.

On two of these occasions, Bob Craig had been recommended to the president as a man who might be interested in joining the corporation. Following this lead, the president stopped in Detroit in April 1955, and discussed the situation with Craig. At that time the president was thinking of bringing in a man to be treasurer. After discussing the matter for several hours, Craig stated that he did not think he would be interested.

After returning to Seattle, the president became more and more convinced that Craig was the man the company needed. The two men then began corresponding, and as Craig thought more about the situation, he indicated to the president that the only basis that he would consider joining the company would be as general manager in charge of operations. As Craig explained later, "I didn't demand the general manager's job just to have a big title, but the more I saw of the situation the more it seemed to me that if the company was going to be successful, somebody had to have the authority to say, *no,* on occasion to the architects and engineers."

In the November 1955 offer Craig was to be the general manager and to have the authority that he had specified. As outlined, Craig was to be the manager of the firm. The president was to continue to hold that office but he would function more as a chairman of the board. The treasurer was to retain his position but report to the general manager. Craig was to be responsible for sales, purchasing, control, and financial transactions with banks. His salary was to be $15,000 a year and he was to get 2% of net profits before taxes beginning in 1956. The president estimated that net profits before taxes in 1956 would be between $200,000 and $300,000. The offer also included an option to buy 20,000 shares of stock during the next 10 years at $6 per share. The stock was then selling for about $5.50 a share.

As Craig considered the offer two other considerations appeared important to him. For one, he had seen a number of men leave Acme and join smaller organizations because they wanted to have a shot at a general management position. Frequently these men had returned to Acme in a year or so disenchanted with the glamor of being "top dog in a small show." In some cases these men had discovered that the actual job was significantly different from the one which had been described to them. In other instances the men found the job to be substantially what they had expected, but that they did not enjoy the work as much as they had thought they would. Therefore, before making a move, Craig wished so far as possible to feel convinced both that he wanted a general management position and that the one he accepted offered the maximum opportunity that he could expect. Secondly, he found that his wife believed that the decision had to be mostly his. In effect, she expressed the attitude, "Sure, if all things were equal, I would rather live in Seattle than Detroit, but having lived with you for 14 years I know that if you are not happy in your work, the rest of us can't be happy anywhere."

THE CASE OF CARL LEWIS*

Carl Lewis, two and one-half years after his appointment in April 1954, as Industrial Sales Manager of the Holman Co., was

* Copyright, 1957, by the President and Fellows of Harvard College. Case material of the Harvard Graduate School of Business Administration is

trying to decide whether to continue in that post or to return to his previous work as counsel for the company. The conflict was an especially sharp one because, as he pointed out, while relating the whole story to a case writer from the Harvard Business School, his first four years with the company while he had been general counsel and head of the legal department, had been "undoubtedly the four happiest years of my life."

"Whereas, today," Lewis continued as he tried to present the nub of his problem, "I have been of small use to the company during my illness of the past three months. Decisions in my office are not being made in my department where they would be made if I had given more attention to my staff and less to my salesforce. They are being made by outsiders, especially by one person who, to my people, appears to be 'moving in' on Industrial Sales—a goal he has long had in view. Whether or not the grapevine is correct the result soon will be a serious demoralization of my administrative personnel. My salesforce are not yet affected by all this, but they will be unless I make a prompt decision and set out vigorously to put matters right all along the line, even going back to correct a number of tasks I'm afraid I have neglected ever since I moved out of my legal sanctum and into the second most important—potentially, anyway—manager's job in this company.

"I wish there was a sort of clearing house for executives who are learning their trade. A place where you could go and tell them the mistakes you've made, along with the lessons learned from these mistakes, and then they could turn up another company needing a man who has just gotten the executive experience called for.

"I'm serious. While I've been idle from this 'silent' heart attack of mine I've had a chance to review where I've done well in this new job and where I've done poorly. Being as objective as possible, I think my shortcomings were as much from inexperience as anything else. It's true that I have shunned a number of the more dis-

prepared as a basis for class discussion. Cases are not designed to present illustrations of either correct or incorrect handling of administrative problems.

tasteful responsibilities of a good line man, but I think now that I see the picture more clearly I wouldn't ignore them a second time. The thing that is *really* hard to do is to go back and correct them inside the organization where your errors and omissions have already begun to yield their consequences. Maybe, taken all together, they have cast the die already and it's too late to fill out the opportunity I was given two years ago.

"I don't want to stay on as a figurehead for someone else who's 'taken over' my assignment. Nor do I wish to become a pensioner on the company thanks to the charitableness of the owner. That's why I'm serious about the idea of a clearing house for the executive trade: I think it could give a lot of men a fresh start, who could turn in a productive career in a new situation, but now are shunted aside into some dead end or who lose heart in the face of their initial blunders as a line manager."

Carl E. Lewis, who was 46 years old in the spring of 1956, had graduated with honors from the University of Chicago in 1933, and had taken a degree in law in 1936 at the Harvard Law School. With one partner he began the practice of law in a medium-sized city near Chicago immediately following graduation. In a short while he was widely known and well liked because of his participation in most of the civic and social activities of his community. Friendly, helpful, even-tempered, his practice was growing steadily when he accepted the offer in 1950 from the Holman Co. to head up their legal work. He accepted a salary of $15,000, which equalled the income from his law practice at that date, although he believed in time he would have earned substantially more from his practice than the company could ever afford to pay. By 1954 his salary and bonus totaled $25,000, and during his two years as industrial sales manager the totals had fluctuated between $30,000 and $40,000, depending on whether the year had been good, or only fair, saleswise.

Carl had married Lois Starbuck in 1940, also a graduate of the University of Chicago. They had two children, John, born in 1942 and Mary, born in 1944. John, who had shown signs when he was 10 years old of some obscure neurological damage, took a sharp turn for the worse during the winter of 1955–56, and had become a grave worry to his parents. Their anxieties were much increased by their inability to locate medical assistance able to make either a clear-cut diagnosis or to prescribe treatments that gave relief. John and his mother's worries were much on Carl's mind.

The Holman Co., founded in 1900, was the second in size in its industry. The industry, whose business was processing raw materials into a wide range of end-products consumed by food, drug, chemical and industrial users, had enjoyed a steady growth during the twentieth century. Each world war had required capacity production and brought financial stability and vigorously expanded markets. Holman sales in 1950 were just below $150 million and in 1956 were close to $225 million.

Within the industry, patents were few and of small importance. The manufacturing process was common to all of the dozen and a half major companies, and required high fixed assets, much space and was a heavy consumer of fuel, water and maintenance. The average break-even point was around 75%, placing a premium on continuous capacity production. Aside from an alert and technically competent purchasing department that operated through an assortment of commodity markets in the U.S.A. and abroad, the chief competitive stress in all the companies fell on the sales department. Holman Co., under its founder, had achieved an enviable record for aggressive salesmanship in its early days. The Industrial Sales Department, which originated 90% of all company revenues, was the spearhead of the company's effort to maintain and widen its share of the market. All other sales were thrown together under the catch-all title of the Retail Sales Department and were under the direction of Charles Lesure, a long-time vice president and member of the board, and who was the individual Carl Lewis believed to be reaching out for the Industrial Sales Department.

"I don't know how far back I need to go in order to give you a coherent picture of all this," Lewis resumed. "Although I can see involvements that reach back for years, and although it will sound complicated and muddled as I tell it, I believe that it is inherently a simple story: the mistakes and omissions of an inexperienced man learning to be a manager by trial-and-error, whose errors and oversights were capitalized on by a tireless, able rival bent on getting to the top at any cost.

"I'm bitter about this, but I suspect that I'm not bitter enough. Maybe I haven't got the right temperament for line work, because I can see what has happened too dispassionately. I can see, too, that no one is more responsible for what has happened than I am myself. I worked alongside Chuck Lesure for four years while I handled all the company's legal affairs. We got along fine. He is one of the most popular men in town and a fine host. He and his wife, who was his high school sweetheart, were married on their graduation at the time he started in the Holman Co. as a clerk. They are a happy, virtually an ideal, couple. Yet during that four-year period, I learned from many men in the company how single-mindedly Chuck reached out for all the power that he could acquire—fair means or foul. He is hated passionately by many men inside this company. In fact, the organization in all its upper ranks, could be separated into pro and anti-Lesure factions. The pros are those who are dependent on him, afraid of him, or are involved in some of the 'deals' he is forever launching. The antis are those who don't have to fear him, either because of connection with the family that still owns a majority of the company stock, or because they are out of his reach for other reasons: age, financial independence or unimportance. I guess I fell in the last category, until I accepted the Industrial Sales managership.

"Sooner or later I'll have to tell you how I came to take that job, after working in the law until I was well over 40. It surprised me, but it surprised most of my friends and the whole company a lot more!

"This is where the story tends to get tangled but I'll try to simplify it as best I can.

"The man who founded this company was an unmatched salesman. This was back in the days before advertising had gotten into such elementary activities as 'campaigns' let alone market analysis, sales forecasts and so on. In those days a good many companies got their growth from men like old Matt Adams whose hunches and gambles paid off more often than they didn't. He had about run out of hunches—as I suspect many of them had—when the First World War came along and built financial strength into his company. It was only a few years after that when Chuck Lesure went to work in the company as a clerk, about 1924 I think. The company was hardly a third its present size in terms of personnel (present size, approximately 3,000 workers at the main plant in Prairie Grove, Indiana) and it wasn't long before Chuck had become a protégé of the old man, who made a point of knowing personally all the men who worked for him.

"Chuck was bright, a tireless worker with unlimited ambition. He rose fast. In less than 10 years the old man made him Sales Manager. He was hailed as a wonder. He was written up. His words were quoted.

"Something happened then. I don't know what it was. Very few do know because a lot of the picture is hidden. There was a big family quarrel over several different issues. Chuck was only one of them. The old man had become distrustful of Chuck. More distrustful of his business judgment than he ever was of his character, but I suspect the latter was involved also, at least on part of the rest of the family and in-laws except for one member—Mike Adams.

"Mike, the second son, almost the same age as Chuck, had become fast friends with young Lesure during the summers that he worked in his father's plant while he was going through college in the East. Their friendship continued when Mike returned to work in the company full time about 1928. He rose fast, too, not merely because he was the old man's son, but because of great intelligence and a character that everyone in the company quickly came to admire and trust. Mike began as a laborer and in four years was plant superintendent in charge of 1,000 employees. Two years later he was made vice president and assistant to the president, and two years later he became president when his father retired.

"Mike came up through production and never had much interest in sales. Probably a matter of temperament, too. His older brother, who was an image of the old man, could sell anything to anyone. I sometimes think that merely his presence did it. People wanted to please Matt, Jr., they wanted his friendship and approval. He really never had to sell anything, he was your friend and glad to oblige you by taking your order! I've seen him do this time after time—sort of a magic. But, I'm getting off my story.

"When the old man wanted to fire Chuck, Mike said, 'No, if he goes, I go.' Mike already was nearly the most important person in the company, and was the steadiest and most respected member of their large family group. Anyway, he made that stick and the old man backed down for the first time in his life. A truce of some sort was arranged and the detail I'm getting around to is that Chuck was taken out of sales and put first into Accounting, then Control, and since then has accumulated other assignments. One of the brothers-in-law was given Industrial Sales, which is where the company derives 90% of its revenue, and he held it until his death about three years ago—which is where I come in.

"I've told you how surprised I was to wake up and find myself a sales manager—I guess I still am. Well, during the four years while I was counsel I had gotten into a lot of the company's business. For one thing, I reported directly to the president as my predecessor had done. For another, I was quickly taken in as a member of the luncheon group that ate together every day with Mike and Chuck and which functioned as an informal executive committee. When I first arrived as attorney I was the seventh member. The other four included the Industrial Sales Manager, the Vice President in charge of purchasing, the Treasurer, and the Vice President of Production. At that time Chuck was still a vice president and his principal title was Manager of Retail Sales. That luncheon group really ran the company, although the board of directors was not a rubber stamp, nor did we treat it so.

"Because of my wide acquaintance with all the company's problems, with most of its personnel, with all our big customers, and with our most important suppliers, I was *not* surprised when Mike called me in one morning and said he wanted my advice about filling the post of Industrial Sales Manager. After a bit of discussion I recommended our New England regional sales manager as the best available successor. Mike replied, 'I have offered it to him. He has declined, and recommends you.'

"Literally, I was speechless. I'd never thought along any line of heavy executive responsibility, and least of all as a sales vice president. Furthermore, I liked the law. I was having a better time in my legal work for the company than I had had in my private practice. My first articulate response was that I had never sold a thing in my life and doubted that I had any knack whatever for such work.

"Mike's reply was simple enough. He said he was not going to try to persuade me into something I didn't want. I was going to decide for myself, but the offer had been made for sound reasons: one, I had made more friends inside the company, in the community, among the company's connections, and made them faster than anyone in company memory. I was into more civic and social activities in the community than any member of top management. Furthermore, the essence of the job of sales manager was not to sell things myself, but help others to sell. Mike said that I could do that, and would like it.

"I said I had better remind him that during the whole period of my practice of the law I had never entertained a client socially, nor had used my home to promote or protect my business. Mike's reply, and I knew he meant it, was that my personal life was my own and that the way I behaved at work as sales manager was whatever I decided would do the job soundly.

"All this left me without much more to protest consciously, though I remained both startled and doubtful of the new idea of sales managership. The clincher came when Mike finished off the interview by pointing out that he himself was not as familiar with the sales operation as he should be; that he meant to work closely with the man who took that job because its importance was likely to become even greater in the future than it had been in the past; and, that as far as he was concerned, I was someone he had found easy and productive to work with.

"Well, as you know, I took it.

"I took it for more reasons than I was aware of at the time. I was pleased and flattered, of course, but stronger than I realized was the challenge of something I'd never done before, and a challenge which—if I could make good—might place me well up on the American executive ladder. I knew that probably a good many other men wanted it, that I would be envied as a winner even by accepting the job. Possibly I may have been overly conscious that Chuck Lesure and I would be seen as equals and as the only men in the organization second to the president. The consideration which, in the end, quieted all my qualms and sparked a readiness to learn an entirely new way of thinking and acting was the prospect of working closely with Mike. I had deep admiration for Mike as a man, very great respect for him as a fine executive, and a conviction that after five years' work with him I ought to be equipped to move into whatever posts might then be above me.

"I talked it over with three friends whose opinions I valued the most. They were helpful and encouraging. Only one said he thought I might discover I was better suited to the law, though he added that I would enjoy sales management. As I was later to recollect, every one of the three had some comment to make on my relations with Chuck. The first one mentioned as an asset the fact that my relations with Chuck had been excellent. The second man made almost the same point but added that I would have to work to keep them that way. The last man was careful with his language saying that I would manage to get along with Chuck better than others had because I was not as ambitious as Chuck was. Chuck himself never spoke of the issue while it was pending, though he was informed of it, and only once afterwards when—without congratulations or good wishes—he merely remarked, 'Well it'll be a new life for you.'

"It was.

* * * * *

"To keep this story as clear as possible I'll try to stick as close to the chronology of events as I can.

"One week after I took over my new job in June 1954, as Manager of Industrial Sales there was a simultaneous announcement, inside the company by Mike and outside by a White House press release, that Mike had accepted membership on an important presidential commission to survey America's trade relations with the free nations and recommend broader and more consistent policies. Three months later he left and was gone one year.

"He was drafted, I expect, because his name is widely known on the commodity markets of the world because of his father and the company's activities.

"Naturally I speculate on how things might have worked out differently for me if he and I had been in continuous contact during those first twelve months as we originally planned. But he wasn't, and I end up half the time thinking I would find myself roughly in the same spot I'm in now whether he'd been here or not.

"It took me unpleasantly by surprise, but I was so busy learning the ropes in my new job that I hardly missed him, at least no more, it seemed to me, than any of us did.

"He arranged for his job to be carried on by three men, all vice presidents and members of the board. Chuck operated as an acting president but without the title; the other two, who were older, were there to approve or disapprove while Chuck did the work. He was very careful not to antagonize either of them, which was just as well because they detested him cordially anyway. Still it worked well enough.

"I made my first job getting to know my regional sales managers and their salesmen. I was acquainted with most of them, of course, but not the way I went at it this time. I spent enough time at each regional office to make sure I found out what they thought their worst problems were, to find out what kind of help they expected of me, and then tried to find out if they were holding out on me and whether I could get them to let their hair down—at least a little, for a starter. All in all that went pretty well.

"I had some problems with my salesforce. At least three of them had wanted my job and were sore that they'd been passed over. In time I got all three of these relationships cleared up and all of them working well and on a friendly basis with me. I had a couple of tough problems I inherited—one man who had become a real drunkard and had very cleverly bluffed the home office into a hands-off policy for years. The other was a double-crosser who played every kind of crooked deal available to buyers and sellers, yet had contrived to stay just beyond the reach of the law.

"I handled those all right too. It took time, but usually all sides ultimately accepted the solutions we worked out.

"I'm not going to spend time in detailing whatever successes I made. I think I know how I did it and that I can do it again. It was my oversights and errors that got me into trouble and that is what I want to come to—for my own sake, and for any of your people who study a case like mine. Before I leave off on the sales side, though, let me add this: company sales as a total rose higher proportionately during the 30 months I had hold of things than it had under either of my two immediate predecessors, and the company's share of the industry's total business increased likewise. Mike told me later, after my heart attack, that he had never seen better relations between a manager and his sales force. 'Your troubles arise almost entirely from your administrative necessities here in the home office,' he said, 'and with your staff. You don't like that kind of work and tend to be soft in those situations.' I think he was right, but I'd better go back to my chronology.

"My first run-in with Chuck—if you can call it that—came about three months after Mike had left the country. It arose over the division of the ending year's bonus allocation within the executive incentive formula we used. I recommended eight or nine of my men for the total of twenty-five to be rewarded and I submitted a memo showing why I believed they were entitled to a larger cut than before. Chuck opposed this and we had an argument about it before I left that day for New York. I was pretty adamant about it so we didn't settle anything then. When I reached my hotel I found a message from Chuck asking me to phone him whenever I arrived. I did. He apologized and said he had been wrong and wanted me to know it before either of us went to bed that evening.

"Well, I was pretty surprised. I thanked him and said I would remember how decent he'd been to call me up and tell me of his change of mind. It was a long time before I realized what an unheard of thing he'd done. Chuck is very proud, as well as able, and probably that was his first apology in his whole business life. I accepted it much too matter-of-factly, for one thing. For another, it took me still longer to realize the true motive behind his gesture: I was only six months in my new job, results were beginning to appear, I was—like Mike had said—on friendlier terms with more people in the company than anyone else. It must have occurred to Chuck, after I left for New York, that I was mad enough to resign and *that* he did not want to be responsible for, while acting in Mike's absence.

"I spent a great deal of my time on the road during all of 1954–1955 helping my sales force find new ways to get new business, helping them explore their problems, trying to see things the way they saw them so that I could help where they thought they needed it before I made any suggestions of my own. Probably I got myself too much immersed in their problems. I think I was unwise to spend the bulk of my time away from my office when I was still new to them too. Not only did they appear to others to be neglected, but some of them felt that way, I later discovered. I think my long and frequent absences from home were more upsetting to John than any of us realized at the time. He was about twelve then and soon began to show new and more alarming symptoms. When I was at home I was working so long and so late I saw very little of him, or Mary, or Lois either. When I was at the house I fell asleep at once and was most irritable when anything or anyone woke me up—which John invariably did. It's little wonder I had a heart attack. I had been asking for it.

"Mike returned in the fall of 1955. By that time I was beginning to feel thoroughly acquainted with my sales force, their problems, the personnel I had in the field, where we were weak, and the goals I wanted to shoot for—those close by, as well as those three to five years away. I began to spend the bulk of my time in the office, picking up threads with Mike and reorganizing all office routines to key in better with my sales force. I also brought in some marketing consultants to help me come up to date on all postwar developments in my area, for the previous incumbents had hardly introduced an innovation since before the war fifteen years earlier. Before the winter was over it was clear enough to me what I needed in the way of new headquarters arrangements, facilities, specialists and so on, to recapture the sales drive the company had once had under old Matt Adams. I was beginning to feel that, if all went along as I was planning for, that I would be able to turn in a really good record by the third year, and better from then on.

"I don't know why it never occurred to me to think how all this might strike Chuck. For one thing I was busy; as busy as he always was, so I must have assumed we were both working hard at our jobs. For another, Lois and I were both beginning to worry in earnest about John. We cut down sharply on our social life. I had resigned from, or reduced my activities in the community organizations I belonged to—at least until I got my new job over the hump. So I tended to see only a few people outside the office. Finally, there was a conference Mike held with me soon after his return.

"After a bit of chat about some of his foreign experiences, Mike turned to the subject of Chuck Lesure. 'What did I think about making him president?'

"Mike had been president and chairman of the board ever since his father's retirement nearly 20 years earlier and I expect he was hoping to lighten his own load. Moreover it was pretty clear that the president's job was what Chuck had been aiming at all his life, so I wasn't surprised. It is true that company talk was that Chuck never made worthwhile profits for the company from any of the openings that he'd been given or had taken. He was always shading prices to insure capacity operations. I think that, from a business standpoint, his meager profit showing is his only serious disqualification. That was ground, however, that Mike and I never touched.

"I considered a bit and said, 'He ought to have it. He's earned it. Whether this is just the moment for it, I can't tell. Several of the old feuds he's had seem to me to have ended through deaths or retirements, or else are abating in their animosity. I'll keep my ear to the ground, if you like, and report back later if I find more opposition than I am supposing.' Mike thanked me and asked me to come back if I found truly serious opposition existed.

"That's the last time we talked about it. I know he talked with some of the older men in the management group, but I don't know what he heard. In any event, no action has been taken up to now and none is in sight over the next six months.

"I mention this for two reasons. First to indicate how oblivious I was to any effect my activities were having on Chuck. Although I may have begun to appear to him as a threat to his ambitions, I was not aware of it, nor did I consider him any threat to mine. The other reason bears on the relations between himself and Mike. I'll come back to those later on.

"After the winter 1955–1956 when I first began to feel I was getting my house in shape at last, I encountered some new kinds of problems. Some of these seemed odd or petty aggravations among the office staff. Others arose out of some of the new business we were just getting into. Still others came in the wake of some efforts I was making to work together with Chuck on matters properly concerning both of us. It didn't occur to me then that there was any significant connection between all these. Even now I'm not sure, but I believe there could have been and, whatever the truth is, I am pretty certain that I've got to decide whether I want to cope with warfare that could be like that.

"As examples of some of the trouble that grew up in my office there was an older woman there who had been private secretary to both my predecessors. She had been pretty close to the last one who had sided, years before, with Matt Adams, Sr. when he sought to get rid of Chuck. That feud ran on until his death, and longer— it now begins to look like. Alice is an excellent worker and I can rely on her to straighten me out on how things used to be done, why certain practices were once adopted—things like that—whenever I need to know. She seems to run into trouble from time to time, like having her vacation schedule changed upstairs a month or two after it had been cleared down here. Or finding she had been assigned to a new parking space six or seven minutes walk away from this office.

"I called this petty stuff, but when I found her pretty unhappy one day and tried to find out why, she wouldn't tell me. Finally, in my office, she broke into tears and I heard quite a long tale about what she regarded as calculated persecutions. It took me still longer to get her explanation of all this, but she finally charged it to Chuck's enmity against her old boss and against herself. 'He never forgives or forgets anyone,' she said. She was opposed to my trying to do anything about it, 'It will only get you into the same kind of trouble, and I've seen too much of that in my time.'

"I selected two of the most recent complaints on which it seemed to me she had a good case and tracked them down. Officially, everything was in order; there was an understandable reason for upsetting her vacation dates and for altering her parking space. But both actions had emanated from Chuck's office, where most of the unspecified powers in the organization had gravitated over the years.

"It was something like that with another older employee, an assistant to one of my key subordinates, who had been given most of an office manager's duties. He had quit his job with the company some three or four years ago, but came to see me about going back to work again. I looked up his record and finding that he had worked in one of Chuck's departments for years, I asked Chuck about him and whether I should take him back. Chuck said he had never been better than mediocre, but if I was willing to use him for that kind of job he wouldn't want to object. I hired him and found he was a good worker. I was glad to have him. Yet he, too, began to have problems. We had to persist a long time with the salary office to get his classification solidly fixed where I intended it to be. Then we got into endless red tape over his pension status. One day, trying to get to the bottom of this last problem with him I said, 'We'd all be better off if you never had quit, Gene. Next time take a leave of absence!' I was joking, but his reply was, 'That's what I tried to do last time and then found out I'd been fired.'

"Well the story I finally got was that some ten years earlier he had transferred out of Chuck's department and into my predecessor's Industrial Sales. After his new boss died three years earlier, Gene had been doubled up with some infection in his knee and had put in a request for leave of absence. It had been granted without a word or question. Later on he had asked for an extension. No answer came to that, but when he wrote again he received a reply delayed 'til one day past the expiration of his leave and was simply a notification of a separation for failure to comply with clearly understood rules.

"Gene blamed this on Chuck. He said, 'He never forgave my transferring over to Mr. Olsen's department. He's like that.'

"I discounted these occurrences. Even more because I was beginning to really lose sleep over John and the effect that his incomprehensible moods and strange lapses in behavior were having on all of us at home. We were all losing sleep and I knew I was getting jumpy. I really tended to write them off—probably too much—as at least 50% imaginings descended from the days when the big battle to oust Chuck had failed and everyone since then found it easy to see ghosts. Let me go on to more substantial issues.

"While I was out with my salesforce it grew on me week by week that we were getting into a new era of some sort. We have several low profit by-products that I discovered could be transformed into two or three different synthetics with an enormous potential outlet. I began talking with all the chemists I could find in the company and found they were all agreed that such a possibility was feasible. I began by hiring a good chemist or two and formulating plans in my mind to start shifting significant research and preliminary sales effort in a direction entirely new for our company and for our industry. I think I can foresee the day when we must require a rather high qualification in chemistry for our sales force.

Not a Ph.D. necessarily but nearly that good—at least for our head-quarters people.

"I discussed this with Mike and he encouraged me to follow up until I was sure what I had. I brought it up at our luncheon meetings after that, during this past winter. No one was too enthusiastic, because these ideas were as unfamiliar as I suppose missile weapons are to an old artillery man. No one opposed me though they were apt to ask cautious, even anxious, questions. Still I went ahead with my preparations and, in planning ahead, began to include items in my next budget. Usually I presented this to the luncheon group informally and tried to thresh things out there. If there was no trouble I sent it into Mike's office to go, with others, before the board. These estimates now began to show modifications and reductions, not large, but from my point of view, often crucial. My forecasts of capital expenditures were more widely revised. When I inquired of Chuck about this—for his office handled the preparation of budgets for formal presentation to the board, as a delegation from Mike's office—he said that he didn't think they were very serious. And, in any case, it was about all he thought the old-timers on the board would risk. Mike confirmed this, more or less repeating what Chuck had said.

"Well, there is another sample of a variety of stumbling blocks I've stubbed over more and more frequently. Why, I don't know. Evidently Chuck did not himself make the initial moves in the board room, but the people who did are ones who either work with or never oppose him.

"How much of all this is Mike cognizant of? I don't know. The longer I know both of them the more I come to think they are indispensable to one another. One is all action, the other all thought. One is an extrovert and enjoys incessant action, schemes, improvisation—and is totally unperturbed at any means he uses. The other is an introvert, who is almost unable to talk with more than one or two persons at a time, judicial, far-seeing, scrupulous, painfully fair. He has scarcely one warm personal friend. The other has enemies by the score, yet outside the plant he is popular and hail-fellow-well-met. One does all the dirty work that I suppose someone has to do, the other can give his word on anything and the union, for example, accepts it as binding as their contract.

"What I think I'm turning over in my mind is, Is this the way most organizations are? Is there always a Chuck around somewhere to make you pay for your mistakes? Is this the rat race? I used to think it was mostly too much work and trying to push jobs through. Does it also mean an incessant, covert warfare? And aside from whether I approve or not, now that I've had my taste of it I think I can deal with that too, but do I want to? What more price is there to pay? Can I charge my family with its cost too?

* * * * *

"Let's see if I can't wind this story up for you.

"Late in 1956 while I was working in the office late one evening I passed out. The night watchman must have found me pretty quickly because I was in the hospital before midnight.

"That was a little over three months ago. Right now no one seems to know whether I had a heart attack or not. They thought so at the hospital and handled my case that way. At Mike's insistence I went to a famous clinic in the East and, because they were unable to locate any evidence of damage, I've gone back two more times. Same result. No evidence of damage.

"Everyone connected with my case agreed on the situation, overwork for 30 months—or longer, increasing strain at home and decreasing rest and recreation. The remedies were virtually those required for a heart attack, so we have let it stand that way.

"After I returned from my first trip to the clinic, Mike and I had a talk. We could easily see three alternatives. I could return to private practice if my tastes really ran that way, and the company could and would do a great deal to rebuild a remunerative practice for me. I could return to the Legal Department, probably as its head again in a short while if I desired. Or I could continue in Industrial Sales, though it was clear I would have to find a really able assistant and lean on him heavily for the next year or two.

Mike said not to make a choice until I felt my health and spirits were approaching a state of dependability so that I could be sure that it was I, and not my ill health, that was making the decision.

"That's easier said than done, you know. Every day that passes is probably settling the issue without me. I must be feeling a lot better, though, because my mind keeps going back over things I should have done and I'd like a chance to get in there and show I can do them now. I think also of the plans I've made ahead and I'd like to see them get a fair test because, if they work out, they would make a big difference to this company. Still I would have to rely heavily on a capable man for the next one to two years, and if he is as capable as I think he ought to be it looks as though I'd be making myself a figurehead in my own department.

"I never imagined I could get myself into such a complex dilemma. If you were in my shoes what do you think you would do?"

Discussion of Cases

Both of these men need to do some thinking, for they face turning points in their professional lives. Although there are obvious similarities, there are also important differences in these two cases, which become clear when we take a detailed look at each of them.

Should Craig Take the Job?

In breaking down the analysis process, several sharp questions emerge for Craig to answer:

- What do I really want to do with my life, professional and personal?
- What am I capable of doing?
- What kind of company is Pacific Homes?
- What really is my present situation?
- What, specifically, can I do about finding replies to these queries?

What Do I Want? There are, apparently, several goals in Craig's mind. He wants to live in the Pacific Northwest; he wants to make money; he wants to participate in community activities. He is interested in trying his hand at general management instead of staff. Furthermore—and these considerations may not be so obvious at first glance—he may be more intrigued by a small than by a large firm, and he could be looking more for prestige than security, for conflict and competition in place of harmony.

His rapid rise at Acme, as evidenced by his responsible position and his high salary, have made it unnecessary for him to do any real soul-searching about his basic objectives. Thus, he has been trapped by his own success. Life was full and good; there were no decisive career choices to be made. Perhaps he was unlucky in being so lucky. Maybe it would have been better if he had been forced to make some moves somewhat earlier in his career which would have established a priority for his objectives.

In setting these priorities, the governing consideration is *how much* does he want these various things. He says he wants to be in a line job, but in his conversation with his wife he seemed to be contented with the prospect of a department head position. By the same token, he appears perfectly happy with his current salary. How hungry—how anxious—is he to forge ahead? How urgent is this objective of general management?

The same paradox appears in the matter of community participation. He is working 10 to 12 hours a day in his staff job—and is happy with it. Does he, in fact, feel very strongly about joining in the affairs of his home town? Would not he make some arrangement for assistants if this was truly an important goal?

Even granting that he is aiming at all these apparently conflicting targets, he would be well advised to recognize that the achievement of some is going to mean a sacrifice of others, or, at best, a delay in reaching them. The first step—and most important—then, is for Craig to make up his own mind about what is most important to him.

It should be pointed out here that making up one's mind is far more easily said than done, and that no clear-cut, completely satisfactory final answers can be expected. Objections and desires collide;

they are muddied by emotional reactions of the moment and by inhibitions. Anyone who has gone through the process knows how complex it can be. Bob Craig's dilemma is not unique to him!

Furthermore, there is no way he can be sure he would like being general manager of Pacific Homes except by taking the job. He may be able to cover himself against the unpleasant aspects, to *estimate* his reactions once he takes over, but he can never be sure.

What Can I Do? The prospecting president of Pacific Homes has been very persistent in tracking down this young man. He must have made many flattering comments; he may well have a somewhat unreal picture in his mind about what Craig can do for him and his company. It is far from unusual for prospective employers to glamorize a man in whom they are really interested.

Consequently, Craig has to recognize and compensate for the ego-inflating effect of suddenly finding himself a fair-haired boy and think out his own capabilities and limitations. Pacific Homes depends largely on production for its business position—can he handle a production job? What experience—service or otherwise— can he point to that will indicate that he has the ability to exact performance from subordinates? Being a boss with the reins in his hand is a very different proposition from being a staff officer with a head full of suggestions.

Furthermore, a small company presents many hazards which are not characteristic of a large business. Working closely with a corps of men whose training and functions are dissimilar is unlike participation in a joint staff operation with people who are homogeneous and oriented in the same direction. Furthermore, smaller enterprises often exist on a life-or-death basis where every mistake counts, while large firms can absorb some bad errors. There are many other differences, too—and what does Craig know about them? Does he think he would function well in a small firm—and why?

He is considering a number of changes for himself all at once. From motors to houses, from line to staff, from big business to small, from fiscal to production, from straight salary to salary-and-bonus, from a field with which he is conversant to one where he is unacquainted, from security to risk, from one part of the country to another—all these fundamental moves are being made at the same time. Clearly, he should ask himself how much he can handle simultaneously. It is true that only major change is accompanied by a whole series of new experiences, but this move seems to involve an unusual number.

Further, one cannot help but wonder why he is working so many hours a day and so many days a week. Possibly, he is so entranced by his responsibilities that he cannot tear himself away, or maybe the company is involved in a crash program which demands heavy concentration on the part of most of its executives. On the other hand, it could be that Bob Craig has not yet learned how to delegate or organize his work properly. If this is true, he is likely to find himself working 20 hours a day in a management job. A thoughtful study of his present work habits would seem to be a part of an analysis of his capabilities.

In short, what is he sure that he can do—or, at least, reasonably sure —and what does he honestly think he can learn to do within the fairly short period of grace he will probably find waiting for him in Seattle?

What Kind of a Company? There are some clear indications in the case that all is not entirely healthy at Pacific Homes. We have comments from some local businessmen; we have the president scurrying around the country desperately trying to find an assistant; we have a mediocre earning record.

On the other hand, certain facts about the economy would seem to give promise of a sparkling future for such a concern, if its personnel and organization are sound.

Starting at the top, what kind of man is the president? He says he will "step down" and let Bob run the operation, but this is his baby. Can he actually abandon it to a nonarchitect, a professional manager who can never have the emotional ties to the concern which its founders have? Craig could, conceivably, find himself the third man in a three-man company, behind the architect-president and the engineer-treasurer who own the bulk of the stock.

Craig is going to have to find out how the stockholders feel about bringing in a new man, and, especially, what the treasurer's reaction is. He will have to get his lines of authority very clear indeed, and be scrupulously careful about his evaluation of the two key people with whom he will be working. What have they done in the past—what is their reputation in the community?

As a fiscal specialist, it is natural to assume that Craig will look at the financial underpinnings of the firm. They may have a solid line of credit—or they may not. They may be able to grow fast enough to pay him substantial bonuses—or they may be incapable of sufficiently rapid expansion. How popular are their houses? Are the banks willing to take mortgages on them? Is this a shoestring operation, or a well-planned and intelligent financial structure?

Suppose that in his survey Craig discovers that Pacific Homes is in even worse shape than he had imagined. Common sense might decree that he should stay away—but actually this very fact might be a real challenge to him and attract him to the coast. "Here is a *real* tough one," he might well say, "and I am the guy who can do it!"

Where Am I Now? In talking the situation over with his wife, Bob seems to have a pretty clear picture of the possibilities of his current job. But he has not, apparently, looked around the company as a whole. It might be that Acme has faced this sort of problem before—a staff man who wants to try his hand at line work for a change. Certainly, they would be wise to make such rotation possible, in their own interest. There may be some management development program, either in-company or outside, which could help prepare Craig for the transition.

Even if there are no opportunities at Acme, there may well be other openings available if he looks around. Here, of course, he runs into the problems inherent in job hunting when already employed. Aside from the time involved, the reaction of one's present employer has to be considered. But the point is that he does not have to take this particular offer—it is not all or nothing.

Finally, what is Acme's policy on men who leave them? The

case explains that this is not an unusual occurrence. Possibly they welcome these people back, once they have some line experience under their belts—or maybe they greet them with a distinctly cold shoulder. There are plenty of positions in which a returnee could rejoin a company—including on his knees! In short, is Craig running a risk that he will find himself in a beautiful location, but without a job—or can he look on this whole venture as a try-out period, with confidence that he can always go back to ACME with dignity, however his fling turns out?

What Steps Can I Take? Craig certainly needs more information than he has now, and most of it can be garnered only by talking with people. One office he might well visit is that of his boss. He seems to have a very friendly relationship with his superior; if anyone could advise him, this man can. Furthermore, he could make clear the company's policy in such situations.

Of course, there might be a snag here. Some businessmen have a pretty clear-cut response to men who talk to them about leaving a job or about "wonderful opportunities" that they have been offered elsewhere: they say, "Fine, I think we should be of all the help we can to you. From this moment on you can spend your full time looking over this 'wonderful opportunity,' instead of only part-time. In brief, you're fired!"

But Craig should be able to work out an approach which would not put him out on the end of a breaking limb. After all, he knows his superior pretty well by this time and would be unlikely to handle him in the wrong way.

A trip to Seattle would seem to be necessary. He might want to talk to local bankers and suppliers, to those with whom he will be working, to builders, and to economists in the area. In so doing, he would be well advised to keep his lines clear with the president; the latter might not take too kindly to Craig's "snooping," if he heard about it secondhand from business friends instead of directly from Craig himself.

Finally, some conversations with Detroit companies in the housing field and research on similar firms in other parts of the country would be helpful to Craig. He would benefit from some yardsticks by which to measure his prospective employer, and his experiences with Acme would probably not be particularly helpful to him.

So Craig has plenty to do before he can make a definite move one way or another, starting with his own self-examination. Happily for him, he is under no great pressure; his job at Acme is secure, and he has no reason to think that the Pacific Homes offer is the last one he will receive or can uncover.

How Can Lewis Resolve His Dilemma?

Carl Lewis, gradually recovering from what he calls a "silent" heart attack, has several alternatives before him. He can leave the Holman Company and take either a line or a staff job elsewhere; he can return to its legal department, with reasonable assurance that he will rise to be its head once again; he can go back into private practice; or he can return to the rough-and-tumble of his old job, possibly with a strong assistant on whom he could lean for a few years.

But unlike Bob Craig, Lewis does not have the luxury of time in which to make his choice. Nor is he deciding this important question under a minimum of emotional pressure. Each day that he stays away from the office, each hour that he delays his decision, he feels that the choice is, in fact, being made for him. Carl's old job is being steadily whittled away by Chuck Lesure's apparent aggression and hostility. Furthermore, he is still tired and over-wrought from his illness and the months of overwork and family tension which preceded it. In short, he is forced to make his choice under the most trying of circumstances.

A Bad Tangle. What are the ramifications of the choices which present themselves? If he returns to his job as Industrial Sales Manager, he will be forced to live with his old errors, as he points out. Furthermore, he will have to continue to do battle with Chuck, an enterprise for which he has little taste. And in an economy which is developing and changing rapidly, there is little reason to hope for much long-range improvement in the travel and tension inherent in his sales job. Thus his family situation might well continue to deteriorate under the impact of his preoccupation with his professional responsibilities.

He could "retire" into the company's legal department, where he started, and return to the situation which gave him "the four happiest years of my life," as he put it. But he seems to be very firm about not wanting to be a "pensioner" of the company. He is young, able, and has a promising future. He does not like the thought of being inactive, or a "figurehead" in any job. Furthermore, he has some responsibility to society which falls on him by virtue of his unusual talents. There is a real shortage of top executive manpower, and many tough problems ahead because of the competition with the Soviet Union and the demands of a growing nation. Could he live with himself if he took the "easy way out"? Could he reconcile himself to moving onto the sidelines?

Mike has suggested that Carl could go back to the private practice of law, with clear indications that the company would take good care of him. Though Carl is fond of the law, he has already made this decision once, when he originally joined the Holman Company. In the meantime, he has acquired a taste for business; he has some plans under way he would like to complete; he thinks he has learned many lessons about the functions of a line executive which would stand him in good stead. Then there is the unpleasant sense of failure—and a return to the office he left six years before would certainly carry implications of defeat.

The move to another company offers some good possibilities, but these moves cannot always be accomplished as easily as one might wish, especially under circumstances like Carl's. Furthermore, that would not really solve the problem of line versus staff. Finally, is one company so much unlike another? Will he not find counterparts of Chuck Lesure anywhere he goes? Are not his difficulties really just the facts of organizational life, a part of the executive landscape in any company? If he cannot handle the situation at Holman, what reasons does he have for thinking he can take care of it anywhere else?

Guidelines for Decision Making. In selecting one from the several alternative courses of action which lie before him, Carl Lewis has to settle several important questions in his own mind.

For one thing, he has to make certain that his decision is not springing from his illness and the residue of months of overwork. It is not unusual to search for a haven after an experience like Carl's; it may well be that he wants to return to private practice, and should indeed do so, but that choice—or any other—ought to be a sincere decision and not a path of escape.

Secondly, he would be wise to look ahead at the shape of the various jobs as they may be five or ten years from today. What kinds of functions will an Industrial Sales Manager for a firm like the Holman Company have to perform in the future? Is he going to be a research and development man, a specialist in marketing or merchandising, an administrator and teacher of a sales force, the top dog in a kennel of bright but individualistic scientists? In an economy like this one, no executive can safely assume that his job will be the same a decade hence as it is now.

Still a third issue is the matter of his duty Is his first responsibility to his family or to his job? Which is the important one—which comes first? If a man wins professional success at the price of an uncorrected home situation, has his life been a success or a failure? Carl's son has been stricken with an obscure disease—does this make his situation unusual?

Most important of all, like Bob Craig in the earlier case, Carl Lewis has to make a reasonable guess at what he wants to do and what he can, in fact, do. He can, perhaps, be strongly criticized on this score, because he seems to have missed the larger picture of the company and the relationships within it by concentrating his thoughts so sharply on the problem of Chuck Lesure. For example, he has not, apparently, wondered why he was named Industrial Sales Manager. He expresses no real curiosity as to why Chuck has not long since been made president to succeed the overloaded Mike Adams. The possibility that Mike was hoping to bring him—Carl—along quickly enough to make him president does not seem to figure in his thinking. He seems, in short, to have had real difficulty in putting himself into Chuck's shoes or Mike's shoes and making some judgments on what is really going on inside the Holman Company.

Thus, he may be looking at only a part of the story, and a small part at that. Maybe he should have been grooming himself for the presidency, learning about the art of line management, instead of spending so much time out in the field.

Certainly he had shown some weaknesses as a manager, along with very real strengths. His failure to develop his office people is probably his greatest failure in this area. He does not seem to have grasped firmly the concept of teamwork, for, apparently, he let his all-important lines of communication with Chuck deteriorate over a period of years. He does not seem to have worked closely enough with Mike after his return; at least, he has only the haziest idea of Mike's personnel plans for the firm. He seems to have been more of a doer, and not enough of a planner and policy-maker—and his reference to his fears of bringing in a strong, capable assistant lest the second man take over his role provides a hint that he still does not really grasp the role of an executive.

Is Mike at Fault? Aside from Carl's problem, this case can be studied from Mike's situation. Has he fallen down? He has apparently let Chuck go along for years without knowing whether he was in line for the presidency or not. If he was not suitable material, should he have been told honestly much earlier? Or would this have foreclosed his possible future development, which might come along lines no one could foresee? How should a top executive handle such appraisals of his subordinates? If he is honest with them, he may discourage them from forging ahead; if he does not tell them where they stand, they turn into Chuck Lesures. Maybe the answer lies in between, in a combination of frankness about weaknesses and strengths with skillful guidance toward those areas in the company where a given man can be most productive.

Then, again, Mike does not seem to have done much of a coaching job with Carl. Granted, he left early in Lewis' tenure for

Washington, but he has been back for some time and there is no evidence of any continuing relationship as Mike himself had pictured it when offering Carl the post.

Where, then, does the individual's responsibility in career decisions end and the company's begin? Though obviously the basic job is in the hands of the man himself, his superiors play such a significant role in the decision that they must bear some of the credit—or blame—for it.

Craig and Lewis at a Crossroad

The stories of Bob Craig and Carl Lewis are by no means atypical. In the life of one executive after another, basic professional and personal objectives do not get clearly set until the man finds himself forced to make some kind of decision. Those who, like Craig, can make the choice under circumstances which are not charged with emotion, conflicts, and time pressures are fortunate. Craig may find that, whether he takes the job or not, the decision-making process has been of real value to him. But for those who have to make a choice under pressure, like Carl Lewis, the beneficial nature of the outcome is not so certain and a sound and forthright decision far less likely.